New Testament Survey

William A. Simmons
B.A., M.A., M.Div., Ph.D.

CONTENTS

OVERVIEW

New Testament Survey is to provide a panoramic view of all the books of the New Testament. It is generally understood that to truly understand a part one must first see the whole. For example, to really understand the function of a carburetor one must first realize that it is simply a part of much more complicated mechanism. In the same way, to fully understand an individual book of the New Testament one must perceive its relationship to the entire revelation of the Bible. That is, one must come to understand that each book of the New Testament is an intricate part of the 27 books of the entire New Testament canon. This type of understanding demonstrates the continuity that exists in God's word and brings into focus the entire stream of revelation from the Gospel of Matthew continuing through to the Book of Revelation. The purpose of this course, then, is to present the student with an overall view of the New Testament so that he/she might better understand the individual parts contained therein.

A cardinal principle of the Christian religion is that God has not spoken in a vacuum. That is, Christians believe that God has revealed Himself in history. God has spoken and acted in time. He has communicated to real people living in real-life circumstances. For this reason, it is imperative for the student of the New Testament to understand the context in which each book of the Bible was written. This involves studying the historical context, cultural context, political factors, and social/economic contexts of each New Testament writer. Additionally, it is important to know the immediate context of the church or persons to whom each book was addressed. For example, Paul's epistle to the Romans addresses a church that differs widely from the church to which James wrote his epistle. Similarly, the circumstances under which John wrote the Book of Revelation differ greatly from the situation in which Paul wrote his epistle to the Philippians. To understand the meaning of an individual book of the New Testament one must first perceive the overall context in which that book was written.

Finally, it is not enough to understand the meaning of a particular New Testament work. One must make a contemporary application. In many respects the complexity of our world demands competence in every field and that includes biblical studies as well. Therefore, the student of the New Testament must be familiar with certain technical aspects of the field. Also today's environment is in some respects a hostile environment, especially to evangelical faith. So, a conscientious study of the New Testament aids apologetics, that is, a defense of the Christian faith. Finally, and perhaps most important, the church is in dire need of good biblical exegesis and interpretation. The sheep need to be counseled, the sheep need to be fed, the sheep need to be healed. Such ministry can only result from a thorough and responsible understanding of God's word.

In conclusion, this study seeks to demonstrate the unity that exists in the midst of the diversity of New Testament writers. It also seeks to contextualize each New Testament work. And finally, the course seeks to equip the student of the New Testament to deal with some of the technical issues addressed to the Word of God today. It is vitally important that well-trained defenders of the faith promote Christianity and edify the Church of God.

LESSONS

Each segment of the course is called a lesson. It must be understood at the outset, however, that one lesson cannot be completed at one setting. The lessons might well be thought of as *units*. It normally will require several hours of study to perform the reading and complete the exercises associated with each lesson. Because the study and learning pace varies considerably from one person to another, you are advised to carefully keep track of the time required for completion of the first lesson, then schedule study time accordingly for the remaining lessons.

KEY WORDS

Mastery of a subject area requires knowledge of that subject's vocabulary. Just as a mechanic does not really understand the functioning of an automobile engine unless he/she knows what a spark plug is, or a person canon successfully follow a recipe unless one understands what is meant by *teaspoon*, a minister will be unable to fully grasp the content of these lessons without being able to define key words.

Key words are listed at the beginning of each lesson. Most of the time, the words will be defined within the lesson. On occasions when I have taken for granted that you already know the meanings and do not define them, you may have to look up the words in a dictionary. Do not overlook this vital aspect of learning. Take time to find word meanings and write them down.

NOTEBOOK

You should use a notebook of your choice as a part of your study materials.

The best use of a notebook will be made in connection with lesson objectives. At the beginning of each chapter and spaced throughout the study guide are numbered statements.

Self-tests will be related directly to the lesson objectives. As an absolute necessity for preparing for the tests, you should write each lesson objective in your notebook as you come to it in the study process and write the answer. Writing the information is an aid to learning it. Then, when you are ready to prepare for the self-tests, review the lesson objective notes you have written.

SELF TESTS

Self-tests are at the conclusion of each lesson. Each test will be made up of a number of questions. These questions may be, but are not limited to: multiple choice, true/false, listing, or matching. Each test is final over the material covered in the lessons preceding it; that is, after you have been tested over one series of lessons you should not expect questions on future tests to be related to these lessons. There is not a comprehensive examination at the end of the course.

A FINAL WORD

The call to ministry in God's kingdom provides you with one of the greatest opportunities a person can ever experience. It also carries with it the responsibility of preparation. At times this study requires considerable discipline. Do not become discouraged. Keep at it! God will honor diligent attempts to prepare for His service.

> Throughout the entire study, concentrate on two aspects:
> 1. What do I need to learn?
> 2. How can I use what I learn?

May the Lord bless you as you continue to serve Him and further your abilities for ministry.

SECTION 1:

BACKGROUND INFORMATION ON THE NEW TESTAMENT

Lesson 1	The World of the New Testament
Lesson 2	The Canon

SECTION OVERVIEW

In the parable of the wise and foolish builders, Jesus stated,

> *Therefore everyone who hears these words of mine and puts them into practice is like a wise man who built his house on the rock. The rain came down, the streams rose and the winds blew and beat against that house. Yet it did not fall because it had its foundation on the rock, but everyone who hears these words of mine and does not put them into practice is like a foolish man who built his house on sand. The rain came down, the streams rose and the winds blew and beat against that house and it fell with a great crash* (Matthew 7:24-27).

By these words Jesus emphasized the importance of laying a firm and stable foundation for spiritual growth. The same holds true when beginning our study of the New Testament. One could immediately proceed to the Gospel of Matthew, yet without preparation, the effort would be like building a castle in the air. So, it's important to lay a firm foundation before we proceed into the documents themselves.

The intent of this section is to provide that firm foundation. This foundation will consist of an overview of the world of the New Testament. In this lesson we will speak of the political world, the social/cultural world, and the religious world of the New Testament. The next lesson will be concerned with the canon of the New Testament. This lesson will define the canon, address the process of canonization, and briefly review the content of the New Testament.

BLANK PAGE

LESSON 1—THE WORLD OF THE NEW TESTAMENT

Part 1	The Political World
Part 2	The Social/Cultural World
Part 3	The Religious World

OVERVIEW

In a very real sense, even at the time of Jesus, Christianity was not a "new" religion. The roots of Christian belief and practice ran deep in the soil of historic Judaism. The historic and religious continuity that exists between Christianity and Judaism was even realized by such pagan rulers as Gallio of Corinth (cf. Acts 18:12 ff). It is clear that this Roman governor understood that Christianity was not a new religion. Rather he perceived that Christianity was essentially related to the history, religion and law of the Jews. So, to properly understand the New Testament, one must understand its relationship to the Old Testament. This is *contextualization.* By understanding the political, social, cultural and religious factors at the time of the New Testament, one comes to better understand the content and meaning of its message.

OBJECTIVES

- Outline the major political factors at the time of Jesus.
- Relate how the Babylonian captivity influenced the Jews' understanding of the law.
- Describe how the Persians were used by God in the restoration of historic Judaism.
- Explain how Greek domination evidently lead to the production of the Septuagint.
- Discuss how Syrian domination sparked a militant religious rebellion among the Jews.
- Discuss how the Maccabeans successfully re-established historic Judaism in Jerusalem.
- Explain how Roman domination affected the life and ministry of Jesus.
- Explain the major social and cultural factors that existed at the time of Jesus.
- Define "Hellenization" and describe the Jewish response to increasing hellenization.
- Discuss the important characteristics of the religious world at the time of Jesus.
- Identify the Pharisees and list the major characteristics of their theology.
- Identify the Sadducees and describe how they relate to the ministry of Jesus.
- Discuss the origin and program of the Zealots.
- Explain the theological significance of the tax collectors in the Gospels.
- Identify "the people of the land" and how they relate to the ministry of the historical Jesus.
- Identify the sinners and discuss their theological significance in the Gospels.

HELPS FOR LEARNING AND REMEMBERING

1. Carefully review the study guidelines and hints which are given in the introduction of this study guide. They will enable you to get a firm grasp on this first lesson.

2. Regularly refer to the lesson outline. It will enable you to see both the progress of your study and the direction it is leading.

3. Familiarize yourself with the key word list. A dictionary will assist you as well as the study text.

KEY WORDS

Puppet king	synagogue	lingua franca
Diaspora	Septuagint	*LXX*
Pharisees	Perush	Perushim
Sadducees	Zealots	hellenization
Essenes	Qumran	Am Ha-aretz
Halaka	Haburah	Haberim
Inter-cultural	intra-cultural	quisling
Zelotism	Pentateuch	contexualization
Hellenize	Hannukah	Hasidim

PART 1—THE POLITICAL WORLD

With this lesson, we will begin the process of contextualizing the life and ministry of Jesus. This will be accomplished by examining six major periods in the history of Israel.

I. BABYLONIAN PERIOD

In 597 BC, Nebuchadnezzar overran Judea and captured the city of Jerusalem. As part of his program to undermine the Jewish people, he deported the leaders and skilled persons of Israel and took them to Babylon. Nebuchadnezzar also robbed the temple of its sacred vessels (cf. Jeremiah 28:1-6). In order to gain control over those who were left in Judea, Nebuchadnezzar appointed the *puppet king* Zedekiah. *Puppet king* refers to a person who is willing to sell out his people for the purpose of personal advancement and power. He was a *quisling*, that is, one who betrays his own people for personal benefit. Yet Zedekiah made a secret alliance with Egypt in an attempt to overthrow the domination of Babylon. Nebuchadnezzar took drastic measures to undermine this new Israeli/Egyptian coalition. In 587 BC, Nebuchadnezzar retook Jerusalem, burned the temple and pulled down the walls of the holy city. This captivity lasted for 70 years.

The Jews organized prayer cells in order to continue the worship of God and to intensify their identity as a distinct people of God. These prayer groups came to be known as *synagogues*. The word "synagogue" comes from the Greek word *sunagoge* meaning "to lead together." So, in effect, the synagogues became alternative sanctuaries which took the place of the temple. On the other hand, the study of the law became a substitute for the animal sacrifices and ceremonies of the temple.

As a result of the Babylonian captivity we have the development of the synagogue and an extraordinary emphasis on the written word as compared to a dynamic relationship with the living God. The Jews became a people of the book rather than a people of the living God. A major aspect of the ministry of Jesus was to refocus the life of Israel on the God of Abraham, Isaac, and Jacob, rather than on a slavish, obsession with the letter of the law.

What is a synagogue? How did this religious institution develop during the Babylonian captivity?

II. PERSIAN PERIOD

In 538 BC, Cyrus, the king of Persia, conquered the Babylonians by diverting the waters of the Euphrates River around the city. Since the river had previously run through Babylon, the dried river channel allowed Cyrus' armies to march directly under the walls. Historical records show that the Babylonians fell to the Persians without a fight.

Cyrus was a benevolent ruler and allowed the Jews to return to Palestine. He ordered the temple be rebuilt and that all the sacred vessels taken be returned (Ezra 6:1-5). Additionally, he decreed that all expenses for building the temple be financed out of his royal treasury. One might expect that every single Jew who was held in captivity would be anxious to return to their Palestinian homeland. But only about 42,000 Jews returned to Palestine. In effect, the Babylonian captivity destroyed the geographical and political significance of the 12 tribes of Israel. Nevertheless, individual families were able to trace their lineage to particular tribes. For example, Luke tells us that Joseph was from the lineage of David, that is, the tribe of Judah, and Paul knows that he is from the tribe of Benjamin (Luke 2:4; Philippians 3:5).

Three important personalities were used of God to reestablish the Jews in the Holy Land after the Babylonian captivity. They are:

<u>Zerubbabel</u>	- noted for rebuilding the temple
<u>Ezra</u>	- reestablished the priority of the law of Moses in the minds of the people
<u>Nehemiah</u>	- refortified Jerusalem by rebuilding the walls of Jerusalem

Those Jews who were left behind in Palestine were deprived of the leadership and institutions which identified them as a distinct people of God. As a result, many began to intermarry with Gentiles. Their offspring were of mixed blood being half-breeds; half-Jewish, half-Gentile. Yet the returning Jews from Babylon were very intent on accentuating the purity of their Jewish heritage. So they would have nothing to do with this mixed multitude. In fact, the concern for the ethnic and national purity of Israel forbade them from allowing those of mixed blood to work on the rebuilding of the temple (Ezra 4:1-5). A rift developed between the ethnically pure Jews returning from the Babylonian captivity and the Jews of mixed lineage who were left behind in Palestine. These half-Jews came to be known as the *Samaritans*. Even in the day of Jesus, the Samaritans were a despised class. Because of the great tension that existed between them and the orthodox Jews, the Samaritans built their own temple on Mt. Gerazim and developed their own peculiar interpretation of Judaism (John 4:1-19). The Gospels make it clear that Jesus sought to break down the division that existed between the Jews and the Samaritans (Luke 10:25-37).

Discuss briefly how the Samaritans came into being.

III. ALEXANDRIAN OR THE GREEK PERIOD (332-301 BC)

The Greeks, led by Alexander the Great, successfully challenged the Persian Empire and greatly expanded their influence and power in the ancient world. Alexander the Great was the son of the great military genius, Philip of Macedon. Philip desired his son to take a more philosophical and less militaristic approach to life. Therefore, he employed the great Greek philosopher, Aristotle, as the personal tutor for Alexander. Nevertheless, Alexander was more interested in waging war than contemplating ancient philosophy.

Perhaps the greatest contribution of Alexander was his tendency to *Hellenize* all the lands he conquered. "Hellenize" means the spread of the Greek culture, philosophy, and language throughout the Mediterranean world. Within a relatively short period of time the Greek language became the *lingua franca* of the known world. That is, the Greek language quickly became the second language of the peoples of the Mediterranean. This held true for the *Diaspora* Jews as well. *Diaspora* literally means "spread throughout." So, the Diaspora refers to those Jews living outside of the Holy Land, literally scattered throughout the Mediterranean world.

A problem arose when the children of the Diaspora could no longer speak Hebrew, but in fact spoke Greek as their mother tongue. They could no longer read the scriptures in Hebrew. A Greek translation of the Hebrew Old Testament was needed. Six Jewish scholars from each of the 12 tribes was commissioned to render the Hebrew Bible (called the *Massoretic Text*) into the Greek language. The new Greek translation was called the *Septuagint*, which means "The Seventy" (because of the number of translators involved). The Roman numeral for 70, i.e., *LXX*, is frequently used to refer to this Greek translation. The *LXX* was extremely important for evangelism in the early church, for it permitted cross-cultural ministry in the Greek language.

Briefly identify the following terms:

1. Hellenize—_____

_____

2. *lingua franca*—_____

_____

3. Diaspora—_____

_____

4. *LXX*—_____

_____

IV. THE SYRIAN PERIOD (198 BC—167 BC)

The Syrians ultimately gained control of Palestine under the leadership of Antiochus IV, who continued the process of hellenization. He proved to be an oppressive dictator who brought the people of God much pain. His egocentricity knew no bounds. He referred to himself as Antiochus Epiphanes which literally means *the manifest god*. Rather than calling him Epiphanes the Jews called him *Epimanes*, which literally means "the madman" or "the moron."

Incredibly there were *pro-hellenistic Jews* who viewed the victory of Antiochus as an opportunity to advance their own cause. They welcomed the Greek culture and mindset as a means of broadening the influence of Israel throughout the world. So, they encouraged Antiochus to undermine the power of orthodox Jews by robbing the temple and dedicating it to Zeus, the chief god of the Greek pantheon. The *apocryphal* (meaning "hidden," hence non-authoritative) Book of 2 Maccabees 6:12 clearly states that on December 15, 168 BC, Antiochus placed a large image of Zeus on the altar in the temple. He also forbade the practice of Judaism, suspending the sacrifices, prohibited the observance of the Sabbath and canceled the traditional feasts (cf. 1 Maccabees 1:41-64; 2 Maccabees 6:1-31). The situation under Antiochus became intolerable when he sacrificed a sow on the altar of Zeus within the Holy of Holies. Orthodox Judaism was pushed to the breaking point.

V. MACCABEAN PERIOD (167 BC—141 BC)

Antiochus sent forth an embassy whose mission was to force the Jews to sacrifice to heathen gods. When they sought to coerce an old priest by the name of *Mattathias* to offer up sacrifice, he refused. A less orthodox Jew stepped in and offered up a sacrifice on his behalf. Mattathias killed him and all the king's agents. He and his son fled to the mountains and started a resistance movement. They carried on guerrilla warfare against their oppressors.

When Mattathias died, his son, *Maccabeus* (literally "the hammer"), took over the resistance movement. He hammered away at the Syrians until they recaptured Jerusalem and cleansed the temple in 164 BC. This rededication of the temple is referred to as the *Feast of Dedication* or the *Feast of Lights* (John 10:22-23), and is presently celebrated by the Jews as *Hanukkah*. Although Maccabeus captured Jerusalem in 164 BC, the guerrilla movement continued until the establishment of an independent Jewish state in 141 BC. It was during this period that the *Zealots* and *Pharisees* came into existence.

VI. ROMAN PERIOD (63 BC ONWARD)

This particular period brings us up to the time of Jesus, the apostles, and the period of the early Christian church. For two centuries before Christ, the Romans continued to gain power throughout the Mediterranean world. In 63 BC, the Roman general, *Pompey*, conquered Syria and annexed all of Israel. Pompey crushed Jewish resistance and brutally killed thousands of Jews. This created intense hatred for Rome.

By 49 BC, *Julius Caesar* had succeeded Pompey and established *Herod* as the "puppet king" over Judea. The fact that Herod was also a half-Jew only intensified the Jewish hatred of him. Nonetheless, from 37 BC onward, this quisling was placed over Galilee and the rest of Judea. This is "Herod the Great," the one in power at the time of Jesus' birth. In an effort to win the favor of the people, he restored and expanded the temple. This is why it's commonly known as Herod's Temple. Herod's oppression of the people was only matched by his paranoia. Fearing a "new king," he ordered the slaughter of the infants in Bethlehem (Matthew 2:1-18). It was rumored that his wife Mariamne was plotting his overthrow, so he had her assassinated. After his death, his kingdom was divided among his three sons. His son Archelaus was to rule over Judea and Samaria (Matthew 2:22). Philip the Tetrarch was given jurisdiction over the territory northeast of Galilee (Luke 3:1). Herod Antipas (which literally means "after the father") was given jurisdiction over Galilee. Antipas is the Herod most prominent in the Gospels whom Jesus calls "that fox" (Luke 13:32). He had John the Baptist beheaded (Matthew 14:1-12) and mocked Jesus just before his crucifixion (Luke 23:11-15).

In summary, the significance of the Roman period is as follows. This is a time of brutal, foreign oppression of the Jewish people, who are longing for a promised deliverer from God. Zelotic sentiment is high. Questions of one's obligation to Rome are crucial. For example, should one pay taxes to Caesar or not (Mark 12:14; Luke 20:22, 23:2)? Should one submit to the dictates of an ungodly emperor (Matthew 5:39-48; Luke 6:27-36)? Such an environment characterized the life and times of Jesus and the early church.

Identify the following persons:

1. Antiochus Epiphanes _____

_____

2. Judas Maccabeus _____

_____

3. Herod the Great _____

_____

SELF TEST:

A. Babylonian Exile (587 BC)
B. Persian Period (538 BC)
C. Alexandrian Period (332-301 BC)
D. Syrian Period (198-167 BC)
E. Maccabean Period (167-141 BC)
F. Roman Period (63 BC onward)
G. Apocryphal

1. _____   Zerubbabel built the temple, Ezra reestablished the law, and Nehemiah rebuilt the walls of Jerusalem.

2. _____   The *lingua franca* of this period led to the production of the *LXX*.

3. _____   "The Madman" oppressed the Jews and sacrificed a sow in the temple.

4. _____   The Samaritans came into existence during this period.

5. _____   Nebuchadnezzar conquers Jerusalem and takes many Jewish captives.

6. _____   "hidden"

7. _____   Herod the Great came into power during this period.

8. _____   The synagogue developed during this period.

9. _____   The spread of Greek culture, thought, and language (hellenization).

10. _____   Mattathias killed the representatives of Antiochus Epiphanes and starts a resistance movement.

PART 2—THE SOCIAL/CULTURAL WORLD

INCREASING HELLENIZATION AND THE JEWISH STRUGGLE TO SURVIVE

In addition to understanding the political experience of the Jews one must come to understand the social/cultural factors as well. The years of foreign domination began to effect the social and cultural make-up of the Jewish people. One of the most significant cultural factors at the time of Jesus was increasing *hellenization*.

Briefly stated *hellenization* describes the imposition of the Greco-Roman culture and language over the peoples of the Roman Empire. I say "Greco-Roman" because in conquering the Greeks, the Romans basically adopted their philosophy, religion and culture. The Roman domination of Israel continued the process of hellenization which began with Alexander the Great. The continued expansion of Roman influence in the life of Israel meant that important institutions and offices became dominated by Rome. The land and the government offices of Israel became subject to Roman control and taxation. This foreign cultural and political influence affected the organization of Israel's governing constitution, determined the law of the land, molded the education of the Jews, and even influenced contemporary fashion and dress. In short, the Israeli culture was being taken over by the philosophy, thought and the cultural values of the Romans. Many Jews felt that Jewish distinctives, language, dress, philosophy, and religion were being undermined by pagan influences. So they resisted the influence of foreign powers in their life and experience.[1]

The following discussion will examine the various ways the Jews tried to stem the tide of hellenization.

THE JEWISH RESPONSE TO INCREASING HELLENIZATION

Jews found themselves in a desperate struggle to preserve the identity of their people and their ways. They resisted hellenization in two primary ways.

I. ACCEPTANCE AND ACCOMMODATION

Even in our day, those most willing to cooperate with conquering powers are those who have the most to lose. They are motivated to cooperate by the threat of losing their own power, influence, and possessions. The same held true at the time of Jesus.[2] The upper class, the Jewish nobility, sought to accommodate Roman domination in order to maintain their place in life. There were some Jews, as we saw previously, who sought to capitalize on the political and economic advantages of becoming part of the Roman Empire. By and large this was the route that the Sadducees took. The Sadducees were the ruling aristocracy in Israel and had the most to lose as a result of Roman occupation. They sought to cooperate with the Romans as much as possible so that they might hold on to their power and position in Jewish society.

---

1. Schuerer, *The History of the Jewish People*, 52.
2. Riches, *Jesus and the Transformation of Judaism*, 65.

II. REJECTION AND REBELLION

This type of resistance movement took two major forms.

A. Zealotism

Zealotism took extremely violent measures to overthrow Roman domination. The Zealots believed that the true Jew was subject to God alone, not Caesar. That Caesar Augustus was being worshiped as a god was especially disturbing to the Zealots. Even paying taxes to Caesar was viewed as renouncing one's Jewishness and collaborating with the enemy (Matthew 22:17 ff). To the Zealots, the only good Roman was a dead Roman. From about 35 BC to 135 AD there was continual rebellion and terrorism throughout the Palestinian region.[3]

A particularly vicious sect of the Jews was the *Sicarii*. The word *Sicarii* describes the long-curved knife that these Jewish Zealots used to cut the throats of the Romans and then disappear into the crowds. At the time of Jesus, political tension was high, and the threat of terrorism was on every hand.

B. The Pharisees

On the other hand, the Pharisees generally practiced a non-violent religious resistance to increasing hellenization. The word *Pharisee* comes from the Hebrew root *perush* which means "to be separated." The Pharisees were the *perushim*, or "the separated ones." The Pharisees sought to resist increasing hellenization through a stricter observance of the law and the teachings of the fathers.

Phariseeism was not an official organization, but rather it was a religious way of life. So in this respect, Phariseeism was a lay movement. It was a religious movement which began among the people and was for the people. In the eyes of the Pharisees the official priesthood of the temple had compromised the law of God. The priests had forfeited their right to interpret the Torah (the Jewish law). The "Separatists" viewed themselves as the true interpreters of God's word for the masses. They sought to insulate Israel from foreign contamination by a very rigorous obedience to the law and a meticulous observance of the teachings of the fathers. Exodus 19:5-6 forms the basis for their religious program. It reads, "Now if you obey me fully and keep my covenant, then out of all nations you will be my treasured possession. Although the whole earth is mine, you will be for me a kingdom of priests and a holy nation. These are the words you are to speak to the Israelites."

The Pharisees viewed themselves as a kingdom of priests who must keep all the purity regulations that the priests practiced <u>in the temple</u>. They demanded that these regulations were to be practiced by everyone, every day and in every place. They sought to protect Israel from foreign contamination by means of *Halaka*, or "the teachings." "Purity" has nothing to do with personal hygiene or being dirty. Rather purity refers to the religious requirements which preserve one's relationship with God. The Pharisees viewed religious or ceremonial purity <u>as a prerequisite to God's grace</u>. One can readily see that ceremonial purity for the

---

3. Sigal, *The Emergence of Contemporary Judaism*, 378.

Pharisees was not academic or simply a peripheral matter. Purity was at the heart of Israel's struggle to preserve its identity and achieve liberation from foreign domination.[4]

This understanding of the religious life had far-reaching consequences for Israel. First, the Pharisees" understanding of purity meant that doing the law became interpreted as <u>not doing as the Gentiles do</u>. Obedience to the law was no longer framed in terms of being like God. Rather, obedience to the law came to mean not being like a Gentile. Secondly, since God separated Israel from all other nations, Israel is obligated to be separate from everything that is unclean. A true Israelite is only to eat that which is clean and come into contact with only that which is ceremonially clean. The most extreme form of this religious mentality can be seen in the *Essenes* or the *Qumran* community. The people of Qumran completely separated themselves from Jewish society. Not only did they view Gentiles as unclean, but they also viewed <u>all Jews</u> who lived in everyday life as ceremonially unclean. The people of Qumran viewed the priesthood of Israel as corrupt, they viewed the temple as unclean, and they viewed the everyday warp and woof of Jewish life as an abomination in the sight of God. They considered themselves to be the Sons of Light who will overthrow the Sons of Darkness (i.e., everyone apart from their community).

The critical reader will already have drawn some conclusions about how the Jewish response to hellenization affected their society. Indeed, <u>social polarization</u> or <u>social fragmentation</u> quickly developed in Israel. Large sectors of society became alienated from one another. For example, one sector welcomed hellenization (i.e., Sadducees) while another sector violently rejected it (i.e., the Zealots). On the other hand, the Pharisees rejected everyone who was not ceremonially pure. And finally, the Qumran community believed that anyone who attempted to live in society was condemned of God.

To sum up the matter, *inter-cultural* segregation quickly developed into *intra-cultural* segregation. Israel's intense desire to be separated from the Gentiles degenerated into a desire to be separated from one's non-observant Jewish brother. There existed unofficial divisions between "the true Israel" and "the fallen or lax Israel."[5] Thus "holy fraternities" came into existence throughout Israel. So, Jesus lived and ministered in a society that was alienated from itself. The question of who a true Jew was vital at the time of Jesus. Acceptance by God was not simply a theological question, but it was also a question of national identity. Such issues introduce us to the next major topic: the religious world of Jesus.

Discuss the two major ways in which the Jews responded to increasing hellenization.

1.

---

4. Riches, *Jesus and the Transformation of Judaism*, 117.
5. Theissen, *The First Followers*, 84.

2.

PART 3—THE RELIGIOUS WORLD

In this part we will further examine the religious environment at the time of Jesus. Our approach will involve a more in-depth study of the various people groups. They are:

I. THE PHARISEES

The exact origin of the Pharisees cannot be determined. Earliest references to the Pharisees are found in Josephus, a Jewish historian roughly contemporary with Jesus. In *Antiquities* 13:288-300, Josephus speaks of the *Hasidim*, who came into existence at about 135 BC. This would be during the period of the Maccabean revolt (cf. 1 Maccabeus 2:42, 7:12). During the political turmoil of the Maccabean Period a religious movement arose which may be the roots of Phariseeism. Josephus states that the Pharisees believed they possessed an unbroken train of tradition which began with Moses.[6] Additionally, Josephus indicates that the primary motivation of the Pharisees was to expand to all of Israel the possibility of meeting God's demand for a holy people (Exodus 19:6; Leviticus 11:44ff, 19:2, 20:7). In this sense, Josephus rightly describes the Pharisees as "the peoples party."[7]

The Pharisees formed an informal fraternity known as the *Haberim*. This Hebrew word means "the companions" or "the brotherhood" indicating the Pharisees formed a "holy fraternity" within Israel.

They were characterized by three central religious practices:

A. Absolute purity was required for table fellowship

Pharisees could only eat with other Pharisees. They could only eat ritually clean foods as prescribed by the Levitical purity regulations. These regulations required a continual cleansing of the hands prior to eating (Mark 7:1-23). In fact, 67% of all the legal passages of the Pharisees are concerned with the proper way to eat food. They have been described as a table fellowship sect. This point will become increasingly important when we observe the theological significance of Jesus' table fellowship with publicans and sinners.

B. A careful observance of tithing

Absolutely everything had to be tithed. They even tithed the herb gardens that hung outside their windows (Luke 11:42 ff).

C. A very careful observance of the Sabbath day

The fellowship meal of the Pharisees was called the *Haburah*. This meal was not simply for physical nourishment but represented mutual acceptance on a religious basis. It represented communion in the presence of God. Consequently, Jesus' table fellowship with the outcasts and sinners of his day was particularly disturbing to the Pharisees.

---

6. Neusner, *From Politics to Piety*, 11.
7. Meyer, *The Aims of Jesus*, 232.

II. SADDUCEES

The Sadducees also originated in obscurity. It is possible that the Sadducees originated from the priesthood of Zaddoq during the time of David in ca. 1,000 BC.[8] In his *Wars* 16:2, Josephus substantiates that the Sadducees formed the ruling aristocracy in Israel and that they were the major mediators between the Jews and Rome.[9] From the time of Herod the Great until the Jewish revolt against Rome in AD 64, the Sadducees held the high priesthood.

Since the Sadducees only accepted the Pentateuch (the first five books of Moses) as the authoritative word of God, they were the theological conservatives of the day. They did not accept any religious teachings which were not explicitly taught in the five books of Moses.

On the other hand, the Pharisees embraced the entire Old Testament, from Genesis to Malachi. Additionally, the Pharisees accepted relatively new theological developments which arose during the intertestamental period. For example, apart from Job 19:25-27 and Ezekiel 37:1-10, the doctrine of the resurrection was not well developed in the Old Testament. However, by the time of Jesus, belief in the physical resurrection was well-established. Like Jesus, the Pharisees believed in the resurrection (John 11:23-25; Acts 23:6-8). Similarly, the existence and the role of angels is not a prominent theme in the Old Testament. But Jesus speaks of legions of angels (Matthew 26:53). Again, the Pharisees accepted the active role of angels and their dynamic intervention into the affairs of everyday life (Mark 12:18-27; Acts 23:8-10).

Although Jesus rejected the legalism and insensitivity of the Pharisees (cf. Matthew 12:1-14, 23:13-36; Mark 2:18, 7:1-13), in some ways he was much closer to their "theological liberalism" than to the extreme conservatism of the Sadducees.[10] This is true because both Jesus and the Pharisees accepted the entire Old Testament, believed in angels and the resurrection, and believed it entirely possible to live holy within society.

III. THE ZEALOTS

The word "zealot" comes from *zealos*, meaning "to boil." No doubt this militant resistance movement against foreign domination arose during the Maccabean revolt studied earlier.[11] The Zealot movement was not a highly organized or structured military campaign. Anyone who refused to accept foreign domination and sought guerrilla warfare as a solution to their problems, could be classified as a Zealot.

The exact relationship of Jesus to the Zealots is debated. The Gospels indicate that the Zealots were active at the time of Jesus. For example, the question of paying taxes to Caesar was a burning issue among the Zealots (Mark 12:14-17; Matthew 22:15-22; Luke 20:20-26). Barabbas more than likely was a revolutionary Zealot (Mark 15:6-15; Matthew 27:15-26; Luke 23:13-25). Jesus' teaching about non-retaliation in the face of oppression is to be understood in the context of zealotism (Matthew 5:38-48; Luke 6:29-30). One of Jesus' own disciples was "Simon the Zealot" (Luke 6:15). Yet Jesus' answer concerning paying tribute to Caesar demonstrates him to

---

8. Neusner, *First Century Judaism in Crisis*, 36-37.
9. Meyer, *The Aims of Jesus*, 238.
10. Neusner, *From Politics to Piety*, 74.
11. Meyer, *The Aims of Jesus*, 236.

be apolitical and non-Zealotic.[12]   While Jesus did conduct a holy war against evil, his weapons were not the spear or the sword; rather he fought with love and prayer.

IV. THE TAX COLLECTORS

The Romans did not collect taxes directly but sold <u>tax collecting franchises</u> to the highest bidder (a chief tax collector). He, in turn, would sell portions of his franchise to lesser tax collectors. It appears that Zacchaeus was a chief tax collector and therefore an extremely influential and wealthy person (Luke 19:1-10). The tax collectors were hated for three major reasons:

1. Their very occupation accepted Roman domination and thus, were viewed as collaborators with the enemy of Israel.

2. They were continually coming in contact with Gentiles and were ritually impure.

3. They were viewed as thieves and extortionists. The Romans required a set amount of revenue, and any revenue above this quota was kept by the tax collector. The tax collector was motivated to collect more than was required.[13]   In general, the Jews made no distinction between a tax collector and a Gentile sinner. Yet in the name of God, Jesus ate with tax collectors.[14]

V. "AM HA-ARETZ

The Hebrew word *am ha-aertz* literally means "the people of the land" and refers to the common people of Israel. They did not reject the Torah, but they lightened the burden of the Torah when it became too impractical to bear. For example, the Roman imperial tax, customs taxes and the temple tax could comprise up to 40% of a poor person's yearly income. Many common people of the land chose not to pay the temple tax or to pay tithes. Also, these *am ha-aertz* could not purchase the sacrifices to maintain ritual purity. As such, the Pharisees considered them to be *fathers of impurity*. Any contact, carrying, shaking or even pressure against anything that belonged to a common person would render one ritually impure.[15]   There were even two separate routes to the temple; a "high road" for the pure and a "low road" for the *am ha-aertz*. During the national feasts, once in the temple, the *am ha-aertz* were considered as clean. But once the celebration was over, the Pharisees began elaborate cleansing procedures.

The intense desire of the Zealots, the Pharisees and the Essenes of Qumran to preserve the identity of Israel ultimately led to the destruction of Israel.[16]   A large portion of Israeli society felt alienated from God. Once again, the sense of being a "second-class citizen" within the commonwealth of Israel must have been overwhelming to many during the time of Jesus. The tremendous following that Jesus received from the masses of people represented a religious and social revolution of major proportions. And again, Jesus was communicating the message that God receives all persons, just as they are, regardless of their state of purity or impurity.

---

12. Sigal, *Emergence of Contemporary Judaism*, 380.
13. Neusner, *First Century Judaism and Crisis*, 28.
14. Harvey, *Jesus and the Constraints of History*, 50.
15. Oppenheimer, *"Am ha-aretz*, 85.
16. Theissen, *The First Followers of Jesus*, 85.

VI. THE SINNERS

The scriptures continually speak of Jesus as a friend of tax collectors and sinners (Mark 2:15-17; Luke 5:30-32, 7:34, 15:1-2). The sinners consisted of apostate Jews who either viewed their religious heritage as irrelevant, or deliberately chose to reject it altogether. They were sinners not because they simply disregarded the purity regulations of the Pharisees, but because they were morally corrupt and spiritually bankrupt. They were not sinners just in the eyes of the Pharisees, but were regarded as apostate Jews by the general populace of Israel. They were *the most despised* group in all of Israel, even more despised than tax collectors and Gentiles. They were hated because they had knowledge of God, and the temple and the priesthood were continually at their service, yet *they deliberately rejected* all of these things. The tax collectors may have betrayed Israel as a people, but the sinners had betrayed the God of Israel.

One can imagine how rejected and isolated such persons felt in light of the intensive religious program of the Pharisees.[17] Yet Jesus sought them out and had table fellowship with them. E.P. Sanders has some interesting yet controversial views concerning Jesus' relationship to the sinners. He says that the controversy here was not so much that Jesus accepted the sinner, but rather that he actively sought out notorious sinners and offered them a place in the kingdom of God. Sanders further maintains that Jesus did not require such persons to repent in accordance with the norms and standards of Judaism.[18] He claims that if Jesus required repentance, then the Pharisees would have rejoiced at his success. No, Sanders says the offense of the ministry of Jesus was that he promised prostitutes and sinners a place in the kingdom if they followed him. His habit of eating with sinners was symbolic of their participation in the Messianic banquet. This acceptance in the name of God was offered completely apart from the temple, the sacrifices, and the authority of the priests. In other words, wholehearted identification with the person of Jesus assured one a place in the kingdom.

In conclusion, the Jewish struggle to survive had devastating effects on their society. They became socially fragmented and divided in their understanding of how to serve God. The Pharisees sought an intensive obedience to the law and the traditions of the fathers. The Sadducees took an accommodating position and sought to cope and perhaps even prosper under Roman domination. The Zealots interpreted service to God in terms of terrorism. The tax collectors sought personal gain from their oppressors. The vast majority of people, the "am ha-aretz, were seeking to cope in the best way they knew, which often meant lightening the burden of the Torah. Finally, the sinners lived apostate lives in total rebellion against God and the morals of Jewish society. In the midst of such a troubled and volatile environment, Jesus came preaching the kingdom of God.

---

17. Borg, *Conflict, Holiness and Politics*, 70.
18. Sanders, *Jesus and Judaism*, 25, 45, 206-208.

List the three central religious practices of the Pharisees:

1. _____

2. _____

3. _____

SELF TEST:

A. hellenization
B. *perush*
C. *halaka*
D. purity
E. inter-cultural
F. intra-cultural

1. _____   The ceremonies, rituals and cleansings associated with being right with God.

2. _____   "to be separate"

3. _____   A segregation or separation between different cultures.

4. _____   "the teachings"

5. _____   The stamp of Greco-Roman culture on all of existence.

6. _____   A segregation within groups of the same culture.

----
1. The Pharisees:
      a. followed a violent approach to Hellenization.
      b. accommodated Roman domination.
      c. were a lay religious movement which sought to protect Israel from the contamination of Gentiles.

2. The Sadducees:
      a. were the aristocracy at the time of Jesus.
      b. resisted Roman domination.
      c. accommodated Roman domination.
      d. A & C
      e. B & C

3. The Zealots:
      a. believed in the sole rule of God.
      b. sought a militaristic solution to Israel's problems.
      c. all of these
      d. none of these

A. Pharisees
B. Sadducees
C. Zealots
D. tax collectors
E. "am ha-aretz
F. sinners

1. _____   Perhaps from the ancient priesthood of Zaddoq

2. _____   Thoroughly rejected the religious heritage of Israel

3. _____   "The people of the land"

4. _____   Sought a violent military solution to Israel's problems

5. _____   Sought to financially profit from Roman domination

6. _____   The most despised group in Israel

7. _____   Haberim who could only participate in the haburah

8. _____   The ruling aristocracy of Israel

9. _____   From *zelos* meaning "to boil"

10. _____   Part of the tax farming system of the Roman Empire

----

1. List the three areas that Jesus has in common with the Pharisees:

    a. _____

    b. _____

    c. _____

2. List three reasons why the tax collectors were despised in Israel:

    a. _____

    b. _____

    c. _____

LESSON 2—THE CANON

Part 1	Definition and Tests for Canonicity
Part 2	The Necessity of the Canon
Part 3	The Process of Canonization
Part 4	The Content of the Canon

OVERVIEW

The New Testament is the inerrant, inspired word of God. This is especially true for the Church of God. This is true because the Minutes of the Church of God state:

> The Church of God stands now, as it has always stood, for the whole Bible rightly divided, *and for the New Testament as the only rule for government and discipline.*[19]

But why these 27 books of the New Testament? How did the church come to recognize the inherent authority of these books? Were all of the books accepted by the church, or did some of the writings have difficulty in getting into the canon? Is the canon closed, or can the church expect new authoritative revelations in the future? These are some of the questions that will be addressed in this lesson.

2 Timothy 2:15 states, "Do your best to present yourself to God as one approved, a workman who does not need to be ashamed and who correctly handles the word of truth." Understanding the origin and content of the New Testament is basic to rightly dividing the word of truth. This panoramic view of the whole promotes a genuine understanding of the parts. The purpose of this chapter is to present the student with a comprehensive view of the New Testament and its content in order to prepare for a more particular analysis of its parts.

OBJECTIVES

- Define the word "canon"; describe the process of canonization and relate its necessity.
- List the 27 books of the New Testament and give a one-sentence description of each book.

HELPS FOR LEARNING AND REMEMBERING

1. Avoid the 'snowball" effect by mastering the material in each lesson before proceeding to the next.

2. Develop note cards as you study. This will allow you to divide the lesson into smaller units.

3. Complete all the self-test materials. Write the answers to each question and recite your answer to the question. This involves the principle of *synergism* (i.e., combining several

---

19. *Minutes of the 63rd General Assembly of the Church of God* (Cleveland, TN: Pathway, 1990) 101.

processes such as sight, touch, and sound). This process greatly helps in retention of the material.

4.   Learn the meaning and definition of all the words in the key words list. A dictionary of New Testament terms may prove helpful in this regard. Once again, make flash cards of each word in the key words list and review often.

KEY WORDS

Canon	synoptic	inspiration
Christological	codex	Judaizers
Parchment	parousia	velum
Apocalyptic	papyrus	biblos
Homolegoumena	dokeô	antilegoumena
Logos	Gnostic	pseudopigraphal

PART 1—DEFINITION AND TESTS FOR CANONICITY

Words change their meaning over time and depend upon the particular context in which they are used. For example, *canon* originally meant "a straight rod" or a "measuring stick."[20] However, in time the word came to mean a standard by which things are measured. Further still, the word canon came to be associated with the concepts of authority and validity. And finally, the word canon became equivalent to the authoritative books of the Bible. So when we speak of the canon of the New Testament we are referring to the 27 authoritative books that comprise the New Testament.

The following are four critical tests for determining the canonicity of the New Testament:[21]

1. Authorship

A book had to be written by an apostle or a close associate of an apostle. For example, Mark was not an apostle, but he was a close associate of the Apostle Peter.

2. The nature of the book

Does the message of the book agree with the content and spirit of divine revelation in the Old Testament? Does the book reflect the character of the person and work of Jesus Christ and agree with the existing apostolic writings?

3. Universality

Is the book being read and practiced in the churches throughout the body of Christ? This criterion addresses the degree to which the people of God recognize and accept the authority of the book under consideration.

4. Inspiration

The word *inspiration* literally means "God-breathed." Does the book have a spiritual character that agrees with the Holy Spirit who indwells all believers?

With regard to the canon, it is believed that all of the New Testament documents were written down between AD 45-100. It is fairly certain that the original books of the New Testament were written on scrolls which may have measured up to 35 feet in length (cf. Luke 4:17). It was not until around AD 200 that the New Testament writings were put into *codex* or book form. They were written on the following materials:

1. **Papyrus**—This was a very crude writing material made from the papyrus or *biblos* reed which grows in the Nile Delta of Egypt. These reeds were beaten flat and then woven together in a solid sheet to form a very primitive paper. Interestingly "Bible" is derived from "biblos" which in turn yields "book."

---

20. Tenney, *New Testament*, 401.
21. Ralph P. Martin, *New Testament Foundations: A Guide for Christian Students*, vol. 2 (Grand Rapids: Eerdmans, 1978) 289-95.

2. **Parchment**—This material is also called vellum and refers to very fine leather or treated animal membrane.

List the four critical tests for determining New Testament canonicity:

1. _____

2. _____

3. _____

4. _____

Define:

1. canon—_____

_____

2. papyrus—_____

_____

3. parchment—_____

_____

PART 2—THE NECESSITY OF THE CANON

Three major factors led to the official recognition of the canon:

I. THE SPREAD OF FALSE DOCTRINE

The very existence of the church was seriously threatened by *Gnosticism*.[22] Gnosticism was a Greek philosophical system which sought salvation through *secret* or *hidden knowledge*. A central premise of Gnosticism is that matter is evil and spirit is good. The thought that God, who is Spirit, would create the material world became totally unacceptable to some teachers in the early church. Also, the doctrine of the Incarnation was completely antithetical to Gnostic thought, and the belief in the physical resurrection of the dead had no place in Gnosticism.

Marcion, the son of a Christian preacher, spread Gnostic beliefs throughout the second century church.[23] He claimed that the God of the Jews was a primitive, lesser god who created a material world. Hence, he excluded the vast majority of Old Testament books and completely revised the New Testament. Any book that contained Jewish elements was rejected as uninspired. The Epistle to the Hebrews, the Epistle of James, the Epistle of Jude, and the Book of Revelation were excluded from his canon. He revised the epistles of Paul and rewrote the Gospel of Luke to conform to his Gnostic beliefs.

The orthodox leadership of the church needed to formulate an authoritative response to the influence of such persons as Marcion. That is, the threat of Marcion forced the church to clearly establish what is the authoritative word of God.

II. DEVELOPMENT OF FALSE WRITINGS

A major motivation for the production of false writings or *pseudepigrapha*, was the desire to know more about the childhood of Jesus, and to have more information about such New Testament personalities as Thomas, James, and other apostles.[24] Very soon false writings began to appear which gave fantastic stories about the lives and ministries of such major Christian figures.

Another motivation for the production of pseudepigrapha was to provide a vehicle for the spread of heretical doctrines. Heretics wrote false documents containing their peculiar beliefs and circulated them in the name of the apostles. For example, the false Gospel of James (ca. AD 400) deals with the childhood of Mary. Here Mary is defended against the accusation of the Jews. The false Gospel of Matthew records the story of Joseph and Mary's flight into Egypt with the baby Jesus. It says that lions and leopards bowed down and honored Joseph and Mary as they went along their journey. When the baby Jesus is brought into pagan temples all of the Egyptian idols fall down and crash to the floor. The Gnostic Gospel of

22. Harris, *New Testament*, 8.

23. Brooke Westcott, *A General Survey of the History of the Canon of the New Testament* (Grand Rapids: Baker Book House, 1980) 312-14.

24. Donald Guthrie, *New Testament Introduction*, (Downers Grove, IL: Inter-Varsity Press, 1970) 33, 37, 152, 123, 251, 263.

Thomas represents the boy Jesus as a miracle worker, yet Christian ethics go by the wayside. When the child Jesus wants to impress his friends with some clay pigeons he has made, he simply makes them come to life. When a child bumps into Jesus and knocks him down, the boy Jesus strikes him dead. And finally, the Gospel of Peter is a document produced by the *Docetists*. The word Docetists comes from the Greek word *dokeo*,[25] which means "to seem." The Docetists claimed that Jesus only seemed to have a real body. So, when Jesus and his disciples walk along the seashore, Jesus leaves no footprints because he is a phantom.

In addition to false gospels, there are the Acts of Paul, the Acts of John, the Acts of Andrew, the Acts of Peter and even an Acts of Thomas. There are also false epistles.

III. PERSECUTION

In AD 303, the *Edict of Diocletion* declared that all Christian books must be destroyed. This forced the church to determine which books were of real value and which books could be cast into the fire. The leadership of the church had to draw up a list of canonical works.

In summary, the word "canon" refers to the authoritative books of the Bible. The emergence of heresies, false writings (pseudepigrapha) and official Roman persecution forced the church to determine the parameters of the word of God. We now begin our discussion on the *process* of canonization.

Define:

1. Gnosticism—_____

_____

2. pseudepigrapha—_____

_____

List the three major reasons for the necessity of the canon:

1. _____

2. _____

3. _____

---

25. Price, *New Testament*, 452 ff.

PART 3—THE PROCESS OF CANONIZATION

The central question here is, "By what means did the church come to recognize and endorse the authoritative books of the New Testament?" A primary means was through general church councils. The major church councils were:

1. The Council of Laodicea (AD 363)

This particular council accepted all of the books of the New Testament except the Book of Revelation.[26] The council's difficulty with the Book of Revelation will be discussed later.

2. The Council of Carthage (AD 397)

This council was chaired by the preeminent early church father and theologian, Augustine. The Council of Carthage accepted all 27 New Testament books.[27]

3. The Council of Hippo (AD 419)

This council simply reaffirmed the decision of the Council of Carthage.

It must be noted that these three great councils did not actually grant authority to these books, but rather simply recognized the divine authority already present in the books. The Holy Spirit, resident in the church, testifies to the divinely inspired authority resident in the books of the Bible. This subtle, yet important distinction is one of the major differences between the Roman Catholic Church and the Protestant churches. The Catholics view the church as producing the Word of God, elevating the church over the Word of God. This explains why the Catholic Church believes that its traditions are equal in authority to the written Word of God. On the contrary, Martin Luther, the great 16th century German reformer, claimed that the Word produced the church. This means that the church is subordinate to the Word.

The process of canonization was a difficult process because there was no unanimous consent on what books should be included in the canon. The deliberations of the councils fell into two categories:

1. Homolegoumena

Those works which were unanimously accepted by the councils were called *homolegoumena*. The Greek prefix *homo* means "the same." The root word *logo* means "to say." So, the word homolegoumena means to say the same things or to agree.

2. Antilegoumena

The disputed works were called *antilegoumena*. The prefix *anti* means "against" and so the antilegoumena were those works which were 'spoken against" by the councils.[28]

---

26. Tenney, *New Testament*, 409 ff.
27. Ibid.
28. Ibid., 406-07.

The disputed works of the New Testament were:

a. Philemon—The early church fathers argued that Philemon was simply a letter addressed to an individual concerning a very secular, non-religious subject. It had nothing to do with the person and work of Christ, the nature of the gospel and the edification of the church.

b. Hebrews—In that Hebrews is an anonymous (i.e., the author is not named in the work) it could not be proved that it was written by an apostle or close associate of an apostle.

c. The Epistles of John—These letters are also anonymous, very brief, of unknown destination, and had a limited circulation in the church.

d. 2 Peter—Its author appears to have borrowed much material from the Epistle of Jude.

e. Jude—This work frequently quotes from apocryphal works, particularly the Books of Enoch and the Assumption of Moses.

f. Revelation—It was the most disputed work of all the New Testament, because by AD 400 few understood its message. The apocalyptic imagery (end time visions and symbols) of Revelation proved to be confusing to the saints but also served as fertile ground for the Christian Gnostic heretics.

In summary, the process of canonization was a very long and difficult process which continued through the 4th century. Yet by the 5th century, the church affirmed all 27 books of the New Testament.

Define:

1. homolegoumena—_____

_____

2. antilegoumena—_____

_____

List the three great councils of the church that helped to establish the New Testament canon:

1. _____

2. _____

3. _____

PART 4—THE CONTENT OF THE CANON

Here we will give a brief synopsis of each of the books of the New Testament. This section will serve as a blueprint for the rest of the course. By presenting a thumbnail sketch of the New Testament canon, the student should be able to recite the books of the New Testament and give a brief description of the content of each book.

I. THE GOSPELS

The Gospels fall into two categories. They are:

A. The Synoptic Gospels

The term *Synoptic Gospels* refers to the first three Gospels (Matthew, Mark, and Luke). *Synoptic* is a Greek word consisting of a prefix *syn* meaning "together" and *optic* meaning "eye." The term means "to see with the same eye." This means that Matthew, Mark and Luke were written from the same perspective or view point. They generally follow the same structure and rehearse the same biographical material of the life of Christ.[29]

The Synoptic Gospels are:

1. The Gospel of Matthew

The Gospel of Matthew was clearly written to Jews. One of the central themes of this gospel is that Jesus is the royal Messiah from the family of David, the tribe of Judah. The fulfillment of prophecy is very important for Matthew, because Jesus fulfilled all the messianic prophecies delivered to Israel.

2. The Gospel of Mark

Mark, the shortest in length, is considered to be the first written gospel. It appears to provide the basic framework and content for both Matthew and Luke. Mark was addressed to the Romans, and thus explains many Jewish practices, and translates particular Jewish words and phrases. Since the Romans were fascinated with authority, power, and sensationalism, Mark emphasizes such themes.

3. The Gospel of Luke

Luke addresses the entire Gentile world, and is thus universal in scope. God loves all persons. He particularly loves the outcasts, the poor, and the weak. Luke places special emphasis on women, children, and those who do not have power and influence in the world. Such persons have a special place in the heart of God. Unlike Matthew, he does not often quote the Old Testament nor emphasize the fulfillment of prophecy.

---

29. Harris, *New Testament*, 50-54.

B. The Gospel of John

The Gospel of John is not included in the Synoptic Gospels. His structure is completely different, and John does not follow the biographical approach of the Synoptics. He is vitally concerned with demonstrating the divine nature of Jesus by emphasizing the "I am's" of Christ and the powerful miracles of the Lord.

John was written to Greeks and employs the *logos doctrine*. The Greeks believed that the order and beauty of the universe was attributable to a "divine reason." This divine principle was called "the Logos" or "the Word." John employs the logos doctrine of the Greeks, but modifies it to communicate the distinctively Christian message of his gospel.

II. THE ACTS OF THE APOSTLES

Also authored by Luke, Acts is the only book which attempts to give a history of the early Christian church, serving as a link between the gospel material and the epistles. Luke's history, then, is theologically informed. He records only those events which contain a theological message. The central theme of Acts can be found in Acts 1:8 (the spread of the gospel from Jerusalem to Rome).

III. THE PAULINE EPISTLES

The study of the Pauline epistles is important for an understanding of the New Testament. Paul's 13 epistles comprise almost 50% of the entire New Testament. What's even more remarkable is that Paul was not a disciple of the historical Jesus, nor one of the original 12 apostles. Yet apart from the Lord Jesus Christ, Paul has done more to determine the form, content, and practice of Christianity than any other person. His works include:

A. Romans

Paul addressed this epistle to a thriving church in Rome, a church which he did not found, nor had he yet visited. Here Paul outlines the central principles of his theology. The major question addressed in this letter is: "How can a person be saved?" The answer to this question forms the central theme of the entire epistle (justification by faith).

B. 1 Corinthians

The Corinthians had corresponded with Paul concerning the many problems that were plaguing their church. 1 Corinthians is actually an answer to their letter. In 1 Corinthians, Paul deals with such problems as divisions in the church, sexual immorality, idolatry, false wisdom, the abuse of the gifts of the Spirit, and the denial of the resurrection of the dead. In dealing with these problems, Paul presents the central doctrines of the Christian faith.

C. 2 Corinthians

One of the major differences between 1 Corinthians and 2 Corinthians is the tone of 2 Corinthians. Paul is more personal and less doctrinal in 2 Corinthians. Yet there are still pockets of resistance in the church. So, Paul continues to respond to his opponents and clearly exposes their errors.

D. Galatians

Galatians is perhaps one of the most passionate epistles Paul wrote. The central issue relates to *Judaizers* who have infiltrated the churches of Galatia. The Judaizers were Jewish "Christians" who taught that Gentiles had to be circumcised and keep the law of Moses in order to be saved. This heresy completely undermined Paul's doctrine of grace and being justified by faith. So, the very existence of the gospel is being threatened in Galatia.

E. Ephesians

Ephesians has been described as "the royal epistle." Its central theme is the preeminence of Christ over the church and over all powers which oppose his kingdom (Ephesians 1:18-23). Another major theme is the nature of the church as it relates to the Lord Jesus Christ. The church is described as the building of God, the bride of Christ, and the body of Christ.

F. Philippians

Philippi proved to be Paul's most trouble-free church. The Philippians continually supported Paul in his ministry. The major theme of the Epistle to the Philippians is true Christian joy. It is a letter of encouragement which beautifully outlines the proper Christian state of mind. A recurring Pauline exhortation in this epistle is "Rejoice in the Lord!"

G. Colossians

Colossians is very similar to Ephesians. Heresy has entered the church and has threatened the preeminence of Christ. Again, it appears that some type of Judaizing heresy has come into the church. Paul is defending the divine nature of Christ in the face of the worship of angels, the observance of special feast days, and seasons, and a general spirit of works righteousness.

H. 1 Thessalonians

Paul's Thessalonian correspondence may be some of his earliest writings. A central concern in 1 Thessalonians is the Second Coming of Christ. In the earliest decades of the church, Christians believed Jesus would return within their own lifetime. When the Lord delayed his coming, some were genuinely puzzled about the fate of those who died prior to the *parousia* (the "coming" or "presence" of the Lord). This led Paul to outline significant events which must occur before the coming of the Lord and to assure the Thessalonians that the Lord will indeed come a second time.

I. 2 Thessalonians

Once again, a major concern of 2 Thessalonians is the nature and timing of the Second Coming. However, it appears that the Thessalonians have overreacted to Paul's first epistle. Some are teaching that the Lord had come already. Apparently, such persons interpreted the Second Coming in purely spiritual terms rather than a literal physical Second Coming of Jesus. Paul now must argue that the Lord is coming, yet his coming still lies in the future.

J. 1 and 2 Timothy and Titus

These three epistles comprise the "Pastoral Epistles." They seem to have been written in the latter stages of Paul's career. One senses that a great transition is at hand. The church is rapidly approaching the end of the apostolic era and preparing to enter the period of the early church fathers. For this reason, Paul clearly outlines the requirements for church leadership and the process for selecting the future leaders. The pastorals are letters of encouragement and exhortation to young pastors, instructing them to take heart and be faithful during the difficult times ahead.

K. Philemon

Philemon was a Christian slave owner who was converted under Paul's ministry. One of his slaves, Onesimus, has escaped and through various circumstances has come to be with Paul in prison. Paul pleads for a reconciliation between Philemon and Onesimus. This brief epistle is extremely rich in Christian symbolism reflecting the salvation of Jesus in the life of every believer.

IV. THE GENERAL EPISTLES

A. Hebrews

Hebrews is the first non-Pauline epistle that we encounter in the canon. It is anonymous, and as the title indicates, it is addressed to Jewish Christians. They are being pressured by non-Christian Jews to abandon Christianity and return to the synagogue. So, the major theme of Hebrews is "Christ is better." The author of Hebrews demonstrates the superiority of Jesus Christ and Christianity over historic Judaism. He also sternly warns that returning to Judaism will cause them to forfeit their salvation.

B. James

James is clearly addressed to the Jewish sector of the church. However, the problem at hand is not an excessive legalism or works-righteousness. On the contrary, James confronts an abuse of grace which undermines the integrity of faith. Therefore, James argues for a living faith that is evidenced in every aspect of our lives. The central theme of James is faith without works is dead.

C. 1 Peter

This epistle also appears to be addressed to Jewish Christians. The Jewish Christian church is increasingly coming under persecution. So, a central theme of 1 Peter is the role of suffering in the life of a Christian. Peter points to the life and experiences of the historical Jesus to substantiate that suffering is an essential part of the Christian life.

D. 2 Peter

Heretics have entered the church and are denying the literal return of the Lord Jesus Christ. Much of 2 Peter is concerned with exposing the motives of the false teachers, explaining their destiny and arguing for the validity of the Second Coming.

E. I, 2 and 3 John

1 & 2 John are primarily concerned with defending the Johannine community against heretics and false doctrine. The heretics and heresies are of a *Gnostic* variety. They were denying the Incarnation, the atoning blood of Christ, and the physical resurrection of the dead. John sternly warns that such persons are manifesting the spirit of the antichrist. With regard to the community itself, 1 & 2 John are epistles of comfort and reassurance. John confidently explains that their salvation is not threatened and that each and every believer is a secure member in the family of God.

3 John is not so much concerned with doctrinal matters as it is with administrative matters. Responsible church leadership is affirmed but irresponsible and self-centered church leaders are exposed and condemned.

F. Jude

Jude is also addressed to the Jewish sector of the church. He too is dealing with false teachers and so Jude contains many stern warnings against teachers of false doctrine and vividly describes their terrible destiny.

G. Revelation

Revelation is the only New Testament book totally dedicated to prophecy and thoroughly characterized by Jewish apocalyptic. Although its meaning remains obscure, its structure is very organized. In a sequential manner, Revelation speaks of future events and the ultimate consummation of the ages.

This brief synopsis of the content of the New Testament reveals the variety and richness of God's revelation. The Synoptic Gospels present a similar picture of the life and ministry of Christ, while the Gospel of John delivers a strikingly different portrait of the Lord. The Book of Acts supplies us with that link joining the gospel material with the epistles of Paul. The Pauline Epistles provide a body of literature which practically touches every major Christian doctrine. The epistles of Hebrews, James, and Jude give insight into early Jewish Christianity. The epistles of Peter reveal some of the thoughts and burdens of this great apostle. Finally, the

Book of Revelation provides that note of consummation and victory needed to give closure to the entire Word of God.

Briefly describe the differences that exist between the Synoptic Gospels and the Gospel of John.

Define:

1. synoptic—_____

_____

2. Judaizers—_____

_____

1. Which epistle is the "royal epistle"?

2. List the Pastoral Epistles:

SELF TEST:

A. canon   B. Gnosticism   C. inspiration
D. papyrus   E. biblos   F. parchment
G. pseudepigrapha H. codex

1. _____   The word "Bible" is derived from this word

2. _____   A Greek philosophy emphasizing knowledge

3. _____   A 'straight rod" or "measuring stick"

4. _____   "God-breathed"

5. _____   False writings

6. _____   A crude form of paper

7. _____   In book form, not on a scroll

8. _____   Treated animal skins for writing

----

1. List the four major criteria for canonicity:

        a. _____

        b. _____

        c. _____

        d. _____

2. List three of the antilegomena and state why they had difficulty getting into the canon:

        a. _____

        b. _____

        c. _____

A. church council   B. canonization   C. homolegomena
D. antilegomena   E. apocalyptic

1. _____   The ecclesiastical process of recognizing the divine authority resident in a book of the Bible.

2. _____   An ecclesiastical meeting convened for the purpose of determining the canon.

3. _____   A type of religious literature which employs symbols, bizarre images, and visions.

4. _____   "disputed works"

5. _____   "unanimously accepted works"

A. Matthew	M. 1 Thessalonians
B. Mark	N. 2 Thessalonians
C. Luke	O. 1 & 2 Timothy and Titus
D. John	P. Philemon
E. Acts	Q. Hebrews
F. Romans	R. James
G. 1 Corinthians	S. 1 Peter
H. 2 Corinthians	T. 2 Peter
I. Galatians	U. 1 & 2 John
J. Ephesians	V. Jude
K. Philippians	W. Revelation
L. Colossians	X. 3 John

1. _____   Seeks the reconciliation of a runaway slave and his owner.

2. _____   Addresses the abuse of the Lord's Supper and the gifts of the Spirit.

3. _____   Warns that a return to Judaism is to lose one's salvation.

4. _____   This gospel is written to Gentiles.

5. _____   Speaks of the church as the body, building, and bride of Christ.

6. _____   The major theme is "joy."

7. _____   Only book dedicated to prophecy and totally characterized by Jewish apocalyptic.

8. _____   The Judaizers are undermining justification by faith and salvation by grace.

9. _____   Emphasizes the family of God and the security of believers.

10. _____   This gospel was written to Jews.

11. _____   Confronts tendencies which show the abuse of grace by Jewish Christians.

12. _____   The recipients have overreacted to his first letter and believe that the Lord has come already.

13. _____   Angel worship is a problem addressed in this epistle.

14. _____ Written to young pastors to encourage and strengthen them.

15. _____ Its central theme is justification by faith.

16. _____ This gospel was written to Greeks and emphasizes the *logos*.

17. _____ Some believers were concerned about the dead in Christ and what would happen to them at the Second Coming.

18. _____ "Christ is better"

19. _____ The "universal" gospel

20. _____ Quotes from the apocryphal works of 1 Enoch and the Assumption of Moses.

SECTION 2:

THE GOSPELS

Lesson 3	The Gospel of Matthew
Lesson 4	The Gospel of Mark
Lesson 5	The Gospel of Luke
Lesson 6	The Gospel of John

SECTION OVERVIEW

The Gospels serve as the foundation for the entire biblical revelation. All of the law, the prophets, and the message of the New Testament rest upon the person and work of Jesus Christ. The Gospels serve as the focal point of the Old and the New Testaments.

In relatively few words, the Gospels speak of the pre-existence of Christ, the Virgin Birth, the Incarnation, the atonement, the resurrection, and the Second Coming. They are the "doctrinal storehouse" for the faith and practice of the church.

The Gospels also serve as the gateway to Christendom. They are the *euaggelion* (the "proclamation of good news"). The message of the Gospels is confined to the geographical area of Israel during the first century and is limited to the lifetime of one central person, Jesus Christ.

One can see how critical a thorough understanding of the Gospels really is. So, the purpose of this section is to present the student with a thorough treatment of each Gospel. Background material will be given on each, as well as the unique contributions and theological content. In this way, the student will have established a solid basis for understanding the rest of the New Testament.

BLANK PAGE

LESSON 3—THE GOSPEL OF MATTHEW

Part 1	Background Information
Part 2	Outline and Content
Part 3	Special Emphases and Characteristics

OVERVIEW

Matthew is the first of the Synoptic Gospels to be studied. Therefore, it will serve as the pattern for our study. We will be concerned with background information such as authorship, date and destination. The central themes of Matthew as well as its organizational principles will also be studied. Finally, special emphases and unique characteristics will be brought to light.

OBJECTIVES

- Discuss the authorship and date of the Gospel of Matthew.
- Outline the general content of the Gospel of Matthew.
- List the geographic divisions set forth in Matthew.
- List the five narrative sections and the five discourse sections in Matthew.
- Give two special emphases of the Gospel of Matthew.
- List two unique characteristics of the Gospel of Matthew.

HELPS FOR LEARNING AND REMEMBERING

1. Review the self-tests of Section 1. Ask yourself the question, "Do I really have a handle on this material?" Restudy those areas of which you are not sure.

2. Focus on the central issue of each section of the lesson. For example, under authorship write down the important points in favor of Matthean authorship and those points which are against Matthean authorship.

3. Completely read the Gospel of Matthew. As we address various topics in Matthew, read the corresponding sections in the Gospel of Matthew. This will help you contextualize your study on Matthew.

4. It is suggested that the student have a map of Israel. This map will reflect the geographic divisions of the life and times of Jesus.

KEY WORDS

Internal evidence	Papias	eschatological
External evidence	Irenaeus	passion
Logia	discourse	catechetical ecclesia
Eusebius	Narrative	ecclesiastical genre

PART 1—BACKGROUND INFORMATION

I. AUTHORSHIP

The very earliest evidence ascribes authorship of this gospel to Matthew. Although the name "Matthew" is not mentioned as the author, by AD 125 it became consistently associated with this gospel.[30] Yet there is considerable debate whether Matthew actually wrote this gospel or not.

A. Internal Evidence Supporting Matthean Authorship

"Internal evidence" refers to that information that can be obtained from the Gospel itself and includes:

1. When listing the apostles, the Gospels and Acts speak of "Matthew" (cf. Mark 3:13-19; Luke 6:13-16; and Acts 1:13), but the Gospel of Matthew has "Matthew *the tax collector*" (9:9). The descriptive words, "the tax collector," may be a personal note made by the author himself.

2. At times, Mark and Luke use the formal "Levi" (Mark 2:13-17; Luke 5:27-32), yet in Matthew, the more familiar "Matthew" is used.[31] Similarly, both Mark and Luke note that *a great feast* took place in Matthew's house, yet Matthew simply states that a feast took place in "the house." It appears that Matthew is playing down his role in giving the feast.

3. The writer of Matthew is clearly interested in genealogies and in parables which involve money. A tax collector would be interested in both.

In conclusion, all of these personal touches seem to point to Matthew as the author.

B. External Evidence Supporting Matthean Authorship:

"External evidence" refers to information obtained from sources outside of the Gospel and includes:

1. The authorship of Matthew was never an issue in the early church. Matthew, the tax collector, was assumed to be the author of this gospel.

2. Eusebius (AD 325), considered to be the first church historian, quotes the early church father Papias (AD 100) as stating that Matthew wrote down the *logia* (words) of Jesus in the Hebrew dialect.[32]

3. Irenaeus (AD 130-202) in his *Against Heresies* also says that Matthew wrote a gospel to the Hebrews in their own dialect, while Peter and Paul preached in Rome. This would

---

30. Guthrie, *New Testament,* 33.
31. Tenney, *New Testament,* 149.
32. R.V.G. Tasker, *The Gospel According to Matthew,* (Grand Rapids: William B. Eerdmans, 1983) 11.

be during the early 60's AD. Origen (AD 185-254) repeats Irenaeus" statements concerning authorship.[33]

C. Objections to Matthean Authorship:

1. Matthew lacks the vivid lifelike touches of an eyewitness and seems to be a second-hand account.

2. Since much of the Gospel of Mark is found in the Gospel of Matthew, wouldn't borrowing from a non-apostolic source have lowered Matthew's apostolic authority?

3. An analysis of the Greek text of Matthew does not indicate that it was translated from a Hebrew original (as Papias and Origen indicate).

Finally, why would a forger write in the name of an obscure apostle like Matthew? Would he not have chosen a more authoritative and popular figure like Peter or John?

II. DATE

The exact date of the writing of Matthew is unknown. Two general theories prevail:[34]

A. Late Date

Matthew is the only gospel which mentions the word *ekklesia* or "church." It is argued that this indicates a well-developed stage in the history of the church, possibly as late as AD 125.

In response, the word *ekklesia* was used in the LXX long before the writing of Matthew. Also, Paul's term for "church" is ekklesia and some of Paul's letters predate Matthew.[35]

B. Early Date

Both Irenaeus and Origen stated that Matthew wrote his gospel while Peter and Paul were in Rome. This would indicate that his gospel was written in the early 60's AD. Also, since the apostles were in Jerusalem and could have preached, taught and given answers to the questions of the Jerusalem church, there would have been no need for a written gospel prior to the persecution of the Jerusalem Christians. But, once the persecution of the church began, the need for a written gospel would have become acute.

Secular history indicates that the temple was razed in AD 70. Since there is nothing in Matthew which indicates that the temple has been destroyed, (cf. Matthew 24:1-25), then

---

33. R.C.H. Lenski, *The Interpretation of Matthew's Gospel,* (Minneapolis: Augsburg, 1961) 10.

34. W.D. Davies and Dale C. Allison, *A Critical and Exegetical Commentary on the Gospel According to Saint Matthew,* (Edinburgh: T & T Clark, 1988) 127-28.

35. Guthrie, *New Testament,* 45-46.

Matthew's gospel was probably written during the time of Nero (in about AD 62-64, as Irenaeus and Origen indicate).

Discuss the internal and external evidence for the authorship of Matthew.

PART 2—OUTLINE AND CONTENT

I. BIOGRAPHICAL DIVISION

Matthew has clearly defined purposes and organizes his gospel accordingly. A major purpose is to prove that all messianic prophecies, beginning with Abraham and continuing through David, are ultimately fulfilled in Christ (1:1). This helps Matthew in structuring his gospel.

The Gospel or "good news" is largely biographical in nature. That is, the literary *genre* or type of writing, forces Matthew to pay attention to chronology (the ordering of events). He clearly divides his gospel into two major parts by using the phrase "at that time."[36] Matthew 4:17 states that *at that time* Jesus began to preach, speak repentance, and to proclaim the kingdom of God. This marks the beginning and future development of Jesus' public ministry. The second "at that time" is in Matthew 16:21. Here we read that *at that time* Jesus tells his disciples of his impending death and resurrection. This division marks the decline of Jesus' popularity which ultimately leads to the cross.

These two divisions demonstrate that Christ fulfilled the two major aspects of his calling:

1. To preach and minister to the people.
2. To provide an atoning sacrifice for our sins so that we might be saved.

II. GEOGRAPHIC DIVISION

The geographical divisions in Matthew are:

1. **Galilee** (4:12–13:58)—this records Jesus' ministry in the northern most part of Palestine, in the region of Galilee.

2. **Judea** (16:1–20:36)—this records Jesus' life and ministry as he began to move southward throughout the entire region of Israel in route to his final destiny in Jerusalem.

3. **Jerusalem** (21:1–27:66)—Matthew records Jesus' final days in the holy city of Jerusalem.

III. SPECIFIC INTERNAL STRUCTURE

Matthew is a highly structured gospel, divided into six narrative sections, each followed by discourse sections.[37] "Narrative" refers to *Matthew's own words* about the historical Jesus. "Discourse" refers to *Jesus' own words*. This alternating of narrative and discourse creates a highly structured literary framework as seen in the following outline:

A. Background Narrative (1:1–4:25)

Important themes include:

---

36. Tenney, *New Testament,* 151.
37. Guthrie, *New Testament,* 48-50.

1. The Virgin Birth and related events.
2. Jesus' preparation for public ministry (his baptism and temptation in the wilderness).
3. The beginning of the Galilean ministry and the call of his disciples.

B. The Sermon on the Mount Discourse (5:1–7:29)

Here Jesus explains the spiritual principles of the kingdom of God. He demonstrates his ability to fulfill and transcend the law of Moses, thus in Matthew's eyes, Jesus is the "new Moses."

C. The Miracle Narrative (8:1–9:34)

This narrative records Jesus' power over disease, demons, the forces of nature, and even death. Its purpose is to substantiate his teaching in the Sermon on the Mount.

D. The Mission Discourse (9:35–10:42)

In this discourse the miracle working power of the Lord is delegated to his disciples. Jesus sends forth the disciples and empowers them to evidence the kingdom of God on earth.

E. The Testimony Narrative (11:1–12:50)

Matthew uses "testimony" in a legal sense (testifying against someone in court). Jesus testifies concerning John the Baptist, his own generation, the cities of Galilee, the Pharisees, and the nature of his true family.

F. The Parable Discourse (13:1-52)

Matthew includes eight parables about the kingdom of Heaven. Matthew's preference for the phrase "kingdom of Heaven" no doubt relates to the Jewish sensitivity to pronouncing the name of God. Rather than risk blaspheming God by improperly using his name, orthodox Jews simply substituted other words for "God." As a result, there is no substantial difference between the phrases "kingdom of God" and "kingdom of Heaven."

The most noted parables in this section are "the parable of the sower," "the parable of the wheat and the tares," and "the pearl of great price." These parables have a discriminating effect (they differentiate between those who are ready to receive the word of the Lord and those who are rebellious and reject the word of the Lord).

G. Conflict, Confession and Crisis Narrative (13:53–17:27)

This particular narrative marks the end of Jesus' popularity. With regard to *conflict*, Jesus is rejected at Nazareth, John the Baptist is killed, and the Lord is continually confronted by the Pharisees and the Scribes. In relation to *confession*, Peter confesses that Jesus is the Christ. Peter's confession forms a pivotal point in Matthew's narrative. From henceforth Jesus repeatedly teaches concerning his impending death and crucifixion. Finally, with regard to *crisis*, Jesus predicts his suffering and also the suffering of his disciples.

H. The True Spirituality Discourse (18:1-35)

In his own words, Jesus describes spiritual greatness in terms of serving, not doing anything to cause another to stumble and extending mercy and forgiveness.

I. The Judean Narrative (19:1–22:46)

Matthew records Jesus' journey from Galilee throughout the land of Judea and his ultimate arrival in Jerusalem. In this section, Jesus speaks about marriage and divorce, one's relationship to riches and the source of his authority. He again predicts his crucifixion, experiences the triumphal entry and cleanses the temple.

J. The Eschatological Discourse (23:1–25:46)

The hostility towards Jesus has reached a crisis point and Jesus blasts the Pharisees, weeps over Jerusalem, and foretells of the last days and his Second Coming.

K. The Passion and Resurrection Narrative (26:1–28:20)

Matthew describes the events of the Last Supper, Jesus' arrest in Gethsemane, his trial, the crucifixion, burial, resurrection, and the Great Commission.

PART 3—SPECIAL EMPHASES AND CHARACTERISTICS

Matthew is a Jew, writing to Jews, to demonstrate that Jesus is the Messiah.[38] The following special emphases and characteristics demonstrate the thorough-going Jewishness of Matthew.

I. SPECIAL EMPHASES

A. Catechetical Emphasis

The word "catechetical" is derived from the Greek word *katecho* meaning "to grasp." It means to grasp the teachings of the church (hence "catechism"). Matthew might have been the first catechism of the church used to disciple new converts. As noted above, its clearly defined structure would have aided in memorization. The extensive discourse sections present more of the sayings of Jesus than any other gospel, making it a very popular gospel in the early church.

B. Eschatological Emphasis

All of chapters 24 and 25 are devoted to the last days. Matthew includes more of Jesus' own words concerning the end time than any other gospel. Additionally, many of Matthew's parables have an eschatological emphasis as well.

C. Ecclesiastical Emphasis

As noted earlier, Matthew's gospel is the only gospel that mentions the church by name (16:18, 18:17).

D. Royal Emphasis

Much emphasis is placed on the kingdom of Heaven and on Christ as King.[39] The genealogy of Jesus proves that he is of the royal line of Judah and that he is God's chosen Messiah. Herod is enraged that Jesus is called the "King of the Jews." The Triumphal Entry (21:5, 7) also reflects the royalty of Christ. Matthew 25:31 speaks of Jesus sitting upon his throne in glory.

E. Fulfilled Prophecy

All events in the life of Jesus have prophetic significance. The place of his birth, his flight into Egypt, and the slaughter of the infants in Bethlehem are fulfilled prophecies. This would have been very important to a Jewish audience.[40]

---

38. Tenney, *New Testament,* 156.
39. Ibid., 158-59.
40. Harris, *New Testament,* 87.

II. UNIQUE CHARACTERISTICS

The following are unique to Matthew:

A. Peculiar Incidents

1. The vision of Joseph to wed Mary (1:20-26). Recorded from Joseph's perspective, Jewish males would have needed an explanation of the Virgin Birth.

2. The visit of the Magi (2:1-12).

3. The flight of Joseph and Mary into Egypt (2:13-15).

4. The bribery of the guards at the tomb (28:12-15).

5. The Trinitarian baptismal formula (28:19, 20). Matthew alone records Jesus exhorting his disciples to baptize in the name of the Father, the Son, and the Holy Spirit.

B. Unique Parables

1. Parables concerning money: the pearl of great price (13:45-46), the parable of the talents (25:14-30).

2. Parables concerning the end time: the marriage of the king's son (22:1-13).

C. Unique Miracles

Matthew contains only one unique miracle, yet it also involves money. Matthew alone records the miracle of finding the gold coin in the fish's mouth (17:24-27).

List the three major geographical divisions found in Matthew:

1. _____

2. _____

3. _____

SELF TEST:

1. T or F   Matthew never refers to himself as the "tax collector."

2. T or F   Matthew is fond of parables which concern money.

3. T or F   Matthew is the least structured gospel.

4. T or F   Matthew records the Virgin Birth from Joseph's perspective.

5. T or F   Matthew is very concerned with eschatology.

6. T or F   Having been written to Gentiles, Matthew is not concerned with the fulfillment of prophecy.

7. T or F   Matthew may have served as an early Christian catechism.

8. T or F   As with the other Gospels, Matthew does not mention the church.

9. T or F   There is a royal emphasis in Matthew.

10. T or F   Matthew alone records the visit of the Magi.

LESSON 4—THE GOSPEL OF MARK

Part 1	Background Information
Part 2	Central Themes
Part 3	Special Emphases
Part 4	Unique Markan Characteristics
Part 5	Unique Contributions of Mark

OVERVIEW

Mark probably was the first to record the story of Jesus in "pen and ink."[41] Therefore, he represents an important transition in the church; oral tradition is coming to an end and the teachings of Jesus are rendered into a fixed literary form (a gospel). So the collective beliefs of the church are being expressed with increasing clarity and authority.

This process of codifying the words of Jesus had the following implications:

1. It means that the church would be in the world for a while. The Lord did not return immediately, and the apostles are passing from the scene. The need to secure the message of Jesus for future generations became urgent.

2. The form of Mark's gospel set the pattern or literary framework for writing Matthew and Luke.

3. The precise expression of Christian doctrine automatically defined the limits of the church. Only those who accept the gospel are Christians.

OBJECTIVES

- Explain the background information for the Gospel of Mark.
- Articulate the central themes of the Gospel of Mark.
- List the special emphases for the Gospel of Mark.
- Present unique Markan characteristics.
- Discuss unique Markan contributions.

HELPS FOR LEARNING AND REMEMBERING

1. Beware of the principle of "interference." "Interference" means the tendency to confuse two or more subjects which have a similar content. There will be a tendency to confuse the information learned under the Gospel of Matthew with the information of Mark's gospel.

2. Use the *loci* method to master the material. "Loci" meaning "the place" involves picturing a particular object or place and then associating each part of the lesson with that particular object

---

41. William Hendriksen, *Exposition of the Gospel According to Mark,* (Grand Rapids: Baker, 1975) 15.

or place. You might imagine a house where the door represents the "introduction" and the living room is the outline, etc.

3. Every time a question arises with regard to the lesson, write out that question in the margin of the text. At the end of the lesson, collect all the questions you have written in the margins and then answer them. This can serve as a good study guide.

KEY WORDS

Christology	messianic secret	*euthus*
Kai	*parataxis*	

PART 1—BACKGROUND INFORMATION

I. AUTHORSHIP

The author's name does not appear anywhere in the text of Mark. Also, there is very little information within the text which helps us to identify Mark as the author. Observe the following:

A. Internal Evidence

1. Mark alone records the story of a young man fleeing naked at the time of the arrest of Jesus (14:51-52). Could this have been a "personal touch" of Mark?

2. Mark was not one of the 12 apostles, yet he knew some of the apostles personally, and may have been a disciple of Peter (cf. Philemon 24; 1 Peter 5:13; Colossians 4:10).[42] We can learn much about his nuclear and extended families from the Scriptures (cf. Acts 4:37; 11:30; 12:12,13,35). He played an active role in early Christian ministry (Acts 13:3).[43]

B. External Evidence

1. The early church fathers, Papias, Irenaeus, Clement of Alexandria, and Jerome all claim that Mark is the author of this gospel.[44] Additionally all of these sources associate Mark with the Apostle Peter as far as the production and organization of this gospel is concerned.

2. Eusebius in his *History of the Church* quotes Papias (AD 100) who claims that Mark did not hear Jesus personally. Rather, he states that Mark wrote down the sayings of Peter accurately, but not necessarily in order.

II. DATE

A. Internal Evidence

Our study of the internal evidence has revealed that Mark most certainly knew the Apostle Paul and the Apostle Peter.[45]

B. Early Church Fathers

Clement of Alexandria (AD 180) and Origen (AD 225) state that Mark wrote his gospel *while Peter was still alive*. The Roman emperor Nero burned Rome in AD 64, blamed it on the Christians and may have killed Paul and Peter shortly after. So, Mark probably wrote his gospel prior to AD 64.

---

42. R. Alan Cole, *Mark,* (Grand Rapids: Eerdmans, 1983) 28-30.
43. R.C.H. Lenski, *The Interpretation of St. Mark's Gospel,* (Minneapolis: Augsburg, 1961) 6.
44. Tenney, *New Testament,* 161-62.
45. Guthrie, *New Testament,* 72-76.

C. The Temple

The fact there is no mention of the destruction of the temple seems to indicate that the Gospel was written prior to AD 70. Mark must have been written somewhere between the early 50's to the early 60's AD.

PART 2—CENTRAL THEMES

Mark 1:1 sets forth the central theme: "The beginning of the Gospel of Jesus Christ, the Son of God." Mark is vitally concerned with demonstrating that Jesus is the authoritative representative of the Father on earth. Jesus is the "God-man" who evidences the principles and powers of the kingdom in this world. Unlike Matthew and Luke, Mark is not interested in the birth narratives. Rather the man Jesus is portrayed as the miracle working Son of God. If Matthew could be described as a teaching gospel, Mark would most certainly be classified as an action gospel.[46] Thus Mark lays less emphasis upon the words of Jesus and focuses upon His actions. Jesus crushes the power of Satan, casts out demons in the name of God and alleviates suffering and oppression through spectacular healing and deliverance.[47] Yet those in this warfare must be prepared to suffer, even unto death.[48] In fact, in Mark, suffering becomes a sign of true discipleship.

Even though the name of the author does not appear in the text of the Gospel of Mark, what internal and external evidences support Markan authorship?

---

46. Ibid., 53.
47. Harris, *New Testament,* 68-70.
48. Ibid., 75.

PART 3—SPECIAL EMPHASES

A study of the Gospel of Mark reveals four major emphases: 1) Christology, 2) the Messianic secret, 3) the special interest in Roman Christianity, and 4) the Passion (the cross of Christ). We will now discuss the significance of each emphasis.

I. CHRISTOLOGY

The Gospel of Mark has a very high *Christology*.[49] The word "Christology" is a compound word consisting of the two Greek words *christos* meaning "the anointed" and *logos* meaning "a word, or message." So, the word Christology means "words or messages concerning Christ." The Father testifies in an audible voice that Jesus is the true Son of God (1:11, 9:7). Ironically, even the demons audibly proclaim that Jesus is the true Son of God (3:11, 5:7). Jesus himself testifies that his Father is God (13:32, 14:61). Finally, a Roman centurion claims that truly Jesus is the Son of God (15:39).

II. THE MESSIANIC SECRET

The phrase "Messianic secret" refers to Jesus' insistence that those whom he healed and delivered keep his identity a secret (7:36, 8:22-26, 27:30).[50] But why? Many Jews desired a militant Messiah who would overthrow the oppressive yoke of Roman domination (cf. John 6:16; Acts 5:36-38). No doubt Jesus was wanting to suppress any premature evaluations of his life and ministry. It was important for him to live out and accomplish the entire plan of God which included the cross and the resurrection.

III. GOSPEL FOR THE ROMANS

In our discussion of the content of Mark in the lesson on "The Canon," we noted that Mark addressed his gospel primarily to the Romans.[51] He is careful to explain Jewish practices and customs, such as the washing of hands, which might not have been familiar to Romans (7:3-4). For example, in the eschatological prophecies of Matthew, Jesus warns that their flight not be in winter or on the Sabbath. In the Gospel of Mark, Jesus simply says that their flight not be in winter (13:18). It appears that Mark has deliberately eliminated the word "Sabbath" because the travel restrictions of the Jews on the Sabbath would have been incomprehensible to his Roman readers. Similarly, Mark is careful to explain the Jewish custom of washing hands and various vessels (7:3-4). All Aramaic expressions are translated (15:34). As noted previously, even a Roman centurion confesses that Jesus is the Son of God (15:39).

All of these factors seem to indicate that Mark has especially designed his gospel for a Roman audience.

---

49. Harris, *New Testament,* 75.
50. Price, *New Testament,* 116.
51. Guthrie, *New Testament,* 54.

IV. THE PASSION

The word "passion" comes from the Greek word *pascho*, meaning "to suffer" and refers to the suffering of Christ. Less than halfway through Mark's gospel, Jesus is already predicting his death and crucifixion (8:31-38).[52] Fully 1/3 of Mark is devoted to the cross. Proportionally, this is greater than any other gospel. Theologically this means that Mark is very concerned with the atoning sacrifice of Christ. Mark 10:45 states that Jesus came to serve and be a *ransom* for many.

What is the "Messianic secret"?

---

52. Ibid., 57.

PART 4—UNIQUE MARKAN CHARACTERISTICS

The three major characteristics of Mark are:[53]

I. VIVID DETAIL

The Romans were impressed with power, action and authority. Mark seeks to communicate in vivid detail, conveying a sense of excitement and action. For example, in the healing of the deaf and dumb man (7:32-35), Mark does not say that the man could not talk at all, but that he had "a speech impediment." Jesus put his fingers into the man's ears, he spit and touched his tongue, and sighed "Ephphatha" ("be opened"). Mark literally says that the 'string of his tongue was loosed." All of this adds a dramatic effect to the healing (cf. also Mark 2:1-12, 8:23-25). Also, Mark 6:39 notes that Jesus made the people sit down on *green grass*. The grass in Israel is only green for a few short weeks in early spring. Thus, the feeding of the 5,000 must have taken place during the early spring, and this in turn allows us to further calculate that Jesus' public ministry lasted approximately three and one-half years.

II. A GOSPEL OF ACTION

It is clear that Mark was vitally concerned with presenting a very vivid and graphic impression of the life of Jesus. It is almost as if a motion picture is unfolding before one's eyes. The very writing style of Mark continues this sense of movement and activity. As an example, Mark uses the Greek adverb *euthus*, "immediately" or "straight away" 42 times. This is more than the rest of the entire New Testament combined. He also employs the stylistic device of *parataxis*, meaning "to carry along." He writes in a way which "carries the story along" by joining one story after another with the Greek conjunction *kai*, meaning "and." Just as an excited child will string several events along by using the word "and," so too Mark strings along the life of Jesus. This interjects an element of speed and activity. For all of these reasons, Mark gives more space to miracles than any other gospel.

III. A GOSPEL OF PERSONAL REACTION

Not only is Mark vivid and a gospel of action, it is also a gospel of personal reaction. The writer is concerned with communicating the subjective emotional states of Jesus, the people and the enemies of our Lord. In Mark, Jesus shows love, anger, and sorrow (1:41, 3:5, 8:12, 10:14,16,21). The people are "amazed" (1:27). The awesome power of the Lord even instills fear in the people (4:21). The chief priest and scribes are hostile to the Lord (14:1). In the Gospel of Mark, there are 23 such references to the emotional states of persons.

---

53. Tenney, *New Testament,* 170.

1. The Gospel of Mark can best be described as a gospel of:
    a. power
    b. the Spirit
    c. the law

2. The Gospel of Mark was written to the:
    a. Romans
    b. Jews
    c. Gentiles

3. List four special emphases of the Gospel of Mark:
    a. _____

    b. _____

    c. _____

    d. _____

PART 5—UNIQUE CONTRIBUTIONS OF MARK

Mark contains some aspects of the life of Jesus which are not recorded in the other Gospels. For example, the confusion of the disciples concerning the resurrection of the dead is only found here (9:10). When the disciples sought to prevent the children from coming to the Lord, Mark records that Jesus sharply rebuked them for this (10:13-14). In this instance, Mark adds that Jesus was *much* displeased. The natural qualities of salt are recorded by Mark as well (9:49, 50). Finally, the confession of the Roman centurion is unique to the Gospel of Mark (15:39).

1. Define the word "passion" in the context of Mark's gospel.

2. Define "Christology" by describing the two distinct parts of this word:

a. _____

_____

b. _____

_____

SELF TEST:

1. Mark is:
   a. the longest gospel
   b. the shortest gospel
   c. the earliest gospel
   d. A & B
   e. B & C

2. Mark, the author,
   a. was one of the original 12 apostles
   b. was a disciple of Peter
   c. provided the 'synoptic framework" for Matthew and Luke
   d. A & C
   e. B & C

3. The Gospel of Mark:
   a. was written to Romans
   b. is concerned with the atonement
   c. is a gospel of action
   d. all of these
   e. none of these

4. Mark was written:
   a. after the temple was destroyed
   b. while Peter was still alive
   c. about the middle of the 1st century
   d. B & C
   e. A & C

5. Mark:
   a. contains a very high Christology
   b. presents the "Messianic secret"
   c. emphasizes the "passion" of Christ
   d. all of these
   e. none of these

LESSON 5—THE GOSPEL OF LUKE

Part 1	Background Information
Part 2	Central Themes
Part 3	Structure and Content
Part 4	General Characteristics
Part 5	Special Lukan Characteristics

OVERVIEW

The Gospel of Luke makes a unique contribution to the canon in the following ways:

A. *By volume*, the Gospel of Luke is the longest gospel (although Matthew has more chapters).

B. Luke was written as a "companion volume" to the Book of Acts.

C. Both Luke and Acts contain some of the most sophisticated Greek of the New Testament. [54]

Most of the New Testament was written in what is called *koine* Greek. *Koine* literally means "common" (the Greek spoken by the common man). The Greek of both Luke and Acts is, however, very similar to the classical Greek of the *Iliad* and the *Odyssey* of Homer (ca. 600 BC). This testifies to the intellectual prowess of Luke and also to the intelligence of Theophilus.

D. The Gospel of Luke is the most "universal" Gospel we have. [55]

If Matthew was addressed to the Jews, and Mark was addressed to the Romans, Luke was most certainly addressed to the entire Gentile world. God wills peace on earth and goodwill *to all people*. The temple is not simply an exclusive sanctuary of the Jews, but it is to be a house of prayer *for all the nations*.

E. The Gospel of Luke contains a very powerful social and political message.

Luke consistently demonstrates that God is on the side of the poor, the weak and the socially disenfranchised. [56] In Luke, God deliberately takes the initiative to identify with women, children, and those who have been rejected by society.

OBJECTIVES

- Discuss the background and the central themes of Luke.
- Outline the structure and content of Luke.
- List the general and special Lukan characteristics.

---

54. Leon Morris, *Luke,* (Grand Rapids: Eerdmans, 1983) 26.
55. Harris, *New Testament,* 120.
56. Morris, *Luke,* 40-41.

HELPS FOR LEARNING AND REMEMBERING

1. The principle of "compare and contrast" may be helpful here. Study how Luke compares and contrasts with Matthew and Mark.

2. Use "mind mapping." "Mind mapping" simply means making a visual representation of the content of the lesson. For example, write the central theme of Luke in the center of a piece of paper, and then draw arrows outward to lesser themes, and from these, draw additional arrows outward to subtopics. Often a visual representation of abstract concepts helps one get a handle on the subject.

3. Keep in mind the interrelationship between the Gospel of Luke and the Book of Acts.

4. As you read through Luke, jot down any theological themes that might come to your mind. When you read the parable of the Good Samaritan, you might want to write down some thoughts on God's care for everyone. Or when you read the parable of the Prodigal Son, you may want to write down some thoughts concerning the unconditional love of God. If you follow this procedure throughout the Gospel of Luke, you will have obtained a collection of theological reflections by the time you get to the last chapter.

KEY WORDS

Treatise	Theophilus	koine
Pneumatology	"We Sections"	Tertullian
Milieu	prologue	

PART 1—BACKGROUND INFORMATION

I. AUTHORSHIP

Since the Gospel of Luke and the Book of Acts are essentially interrelated, the authorship of both works will be addressed here.

A. Internal Evidence

1. Written to Theophilus—It is clear from both Luke and Acts that they were addressed to the same person, Theophilus (Luke 1:3; Acts 1:1).[57] The name "Theophilus" consists of two Greek words, *theos*, meaning "God" and *philos*, meaning "love." Theophilus literally means "one who loves God," or "one who is beloved by God." The identity of this person has been open to much debate.[58] In fact, it has been argued that the name Theophilus does not refer to a single individual, but rather it is a code word for an entire Christian community. The basis for this theory is that Luke and Acts were written during a time when the church was experiencing severe persecution. Therefore, it would have been dangerous to identify the addressee in the Gospel itself. This would have immediately identified the recipient as a Christian and therefore could have resulted in that person's death.

Of course, this theory is based on the assumption that both Luke and Acts were written during a time when the church was being persecuted by the Roman Empire. If this be true, then both Luke and Acts would definitely be dated 2nd century rather than the traditional dating of 1st century. More than likely Theophilus does refer to a single individual. But the question remains as to the identity of this individual. As will be noted below, it does appear that Theophilus was a very powerful and influential person. He may well have been part of the Roman governmental hierarchy. Is he a believer, or is he just a seeker? In any case, the Gospel states that Theophilus is in need of more accurate information concerning the early Christian movement.

2. The "former treatise—Acts 1:1 refers to the "former treatise," meaning that Luke and Acts are essentially and thematically linked together. The word "treatise" denotes an extremely important and lengthy proclamation, frequently used to describe official statements by Roman emperors. Luke indicates that he is writing an extremely important document, indeed a proclamation from the King.

3. Universalism—Both Luke and Acts focus on the Gentiles and this reflects the theme of universalism.

4. Prominence of women and children—Both Luke and Acts give special prominence to women and children.

5. Jerusalem—Since Theophilus would have known about the religious and political center of Judaism, the resurrection appearances are restricted to the area of Judea, particularly Jerusalem.

---

57. Tenney, *New Testament,* 176.
58. I. Howard Marshall, *The Gospel of Luke,* (Grand Rapids: Eerdmans, 1978) 34-35.

6. <u>Writing style</u>—The vocabulary and the writing style of both Luke and Acts are very similar.

7. <u>The "We Sections"</u>—The extraordinary similarity between these two documents indicates that they were penned by the same person and addressed to the same person. However, is there evidence which specifically points to Luke as the author of the Gospel of Luke and Acts? Indeed, there is. Such evidence is found in the so-called "We Sections."

"We Sections" refers to sections of Acts where the author writes in the first person plural ("we").[59] This means that the author was a traveling companion of Paul during portions of his missionary journeys. The "We Sections" help us identify the author in the following ways:

a. The start of the "We Sections"—Acts 16:10 reads, "After Paul had seen the vision, *we* got ready at once to leave for Macedonia, concluding that God had called *us* to preach the gospel to them." So, the author is with the Apostle Paul immediately after the Macedonian vision, when Paul leaves Troas and travels westward on his 2nd missionary journey.

b. The "We Sections" stop when Paul is imprisoned at Philippi.

c. The "We Sections" begin again with Acts 20:6ff. This means that our author *was not present* with the Apostle Paul when he ministered in Thessalonica, in Berea, in Athens, in Corinth, and in Ephesus.

d. The "We Sections" continue for the rest of the Book of Acts. The author travels with the Apostle Paul to the capital of the empire, Rome (Acts 27:1).

The internal evidence indicates that our author was a traveling companion of Paul. Can we conclude that this person was Luke? Colossians 4:14, Philemon 24, and 2 Timothy 4:11 all state that Luke is present with Paul. Since Mark was not present with the Apostle Paul after his first missionary journey, he cannot account for the "We Sections." Also, all persons mentioned in Acts 20:4 went on before the Apostle Paul (see also Acts 20:5). However, the "We Sections" continue after this point. By the process of elimination then, Luke alone explains the "We Sections" of Acts.

All of this means that Luke met the Apostle Paul somewhere in the area of Troas (Acts 16:8) in about the year AD 51. Was he the Macedonian man of the "Macedonian Vision"? (Acts 16:9)

B. External Evidence

As with Matthew and Mark, the early church fathers are unanimous in their support of Lukan authorship. For example, Irenaeus, Clement of Alexandria, Origen and Tertullian all agree that Luke is the author of not only the Gospel but the Book of Acts as well. In fact, Tertullian quotes and alludes to the Gospel of Luke over 500 times in his writings.

---

59. Edward Schweizer, *The Good News According to Luke,* (Atlanta: John Knox Press, 1971) 6.

C. Additional Notes Concerning Authorship

The "prologue" (1:1-4) reveals the following:

1. Luke's vocabulary and writing style are the closest to classical Greek in the New Testament [60] Only the anonymous Epistle to the Hebrews matches the eloquence and superiority of Luke's Greek.

2. Luke was not an eyewitness to the life and ministry of Jesus.

3. Paul refers to Luke as a physician (cf. Colossians 4:14). The Gospel of Luke evidences more medical terminology than the other Gospels.[61] Luke is usually more descriptive of diseases and physical ailments than the other Gospels (cf. Luke 4:38, 5:12).

In conclusion, the author of the Gospel of Luke and Acts is an intelligent, highly accomplished writer. He was a traveling companion of Paul, and a physician by trade. All of these descriptions point to Luke as the author of both works.

II. DATE

The following should be observed:

1. Since Acts 1:1 refers to "the former treatise," then Luke must have been written prior to the Book of Acts.

2. Luke 1:1 states that others have attempted to write gospels. The oral period of the apostles is coming to a close and the codification of the Gospels has begun.

3. The temple (which was destroyed in AD 70) appears to be standing at the close of Acts.

4. Luke was present with Paul prior to his execution in AD 64.

5. The historical and political context is 1st century and not 2nd century.[62]

Estimates have ranged from a conservative dating of AD 60 to a liberal dating as late as AD 115.[63] It is possible that Luke was written circa AD 60.

---

60. Marshall, *Luke,* 40.
61. Harris, *New Testament,* 116.
62. Ibid., 22.
63. Harris, *Luke,* 22-24.

PART 2—CENTRAL THEMES

The target audience of the author directly relates to the central themes he presents. For example, Luke is addressed to the non-Jewish world and a central theme of Luke is God's love for Gentiles.[64] The aged Simeon was led by the Spirit into the Temple to prophesy that Jesus will be a light to the Gentiles (2:27-32). This theme of God's loving care for the Gentiles is especially evident in the healings of the Lord. Jesus notes that even though there were many widows in Israel, Elijah was sent only to a widow in Sidon. Similarly, even though there were many lepers throughout Israel, only Naaman the Syrian was healed during the ministry of Elisha (4:25-27). When asked to describe a good neighbor, Jesus spoke the parable of the Good Samaritan (10:30-37). Finally, even though Zacchaeus was Jewish, he had made himself into a Gentile because he was a chief tax collector. Yet, Jesus sought him out and blessed him with His special presence (19:1-8). Although Zacchaeus was a sinner, Jesus clearly said that he too was a son of Abraham and that salvation had come to his house (19:9-10).

In conclusion, one could say that the central theme of the Gospel of Luke is simply the gospel of grace to all humankind. The love of God is not limited to the traditional covenant people of Israel. God's unmerited favor was displayed during the Old Testament covenant and is presently being displayed in the life and ministry of God's Son, Jesus Christ. In short, God is no respecter of persons, and freely gives His love, grace, and mercy to all who will receive it, whether they be Jew or Gentile.

---

1. The Gospel of Luke is written primarily to:
   a. Gentiles
   b. Romans
   c. Jews

2. Luke is noted for emphasizing the:
   a. role of women and children
   b. Roman persecution of Jesus
   c. Old Testament prophecies that point to the Messiah

---

64. Harris, *New Testament*, 120.

PART 3—STRUCTURE AND CONTENT

I. GENERAL STRUCTURE OF LUKE

In that Luke can be classified as one of the "Synoptic Gospels," the general structure need not be repeated here. Let it suffice to say that Luke follows the "kerygmatic framework" evidenced in the Gospel of Mark. In other words, Luke has patterned his gospel after the simple outline of the life of Jesus found in the early Christian preaching. Note the parallelism between the structure of the Gospel of Mark and the preaching of Peter in Acts.

II. DIFFERENCES IN THE STRUCTURE

A. The Birth Narratives

The first major difference in the structure of Luke can be found in the birth narratives. Luke pays more attention and gives more space to the childhood narratives of Jesus and John the Baptist than any other gospel.[65] The birth of John is recorded only by Luke. He portrays the birth narratives from the perspective of the mothers (Mary and Elizabeth) rather than the fathers (Joseph and Zechariah). No doubt this reflects Luke's special concern for the place of women in the gospel story. It should also be noted here that the genealogy of Jesus is traced back to Adam rather than to Abraham and David as was the case in Matthew. Luke clearly wants to emphasize the humanity of Jesus Christ with regard to all humans, rather than the peculiar Jewishness of Jesus. Neither Matthew nor Mark record anything about the birth of John the Baptist, but Luke records the event in detail. It is obvious to Luke, the physician, that births have a very important place in the economy of God.

B. Revelation

The preceding point concerning Luke's interest in the birth narratives reveals that for Luke all events are considered to be part of God's divine revelation. God reveals himself in time and space and therefore the events of time and space reveal God as well. Luke 3:1-3 states:

> *In the 15th year of the reign of Tiberius Caesar—when Pontius Pilate was governor of Judea, Herod tetrarch of Galilee, his brother Philip tetrarch of Iturea and Traconitis, and Lysanias tetrarch of Abilene—during the high priesthood of Annas and Caiaphas, the word of God came to John son of Zechariah in the desert. He went into all the country around the Jordan, preaching a baptism of repentance for the forgiveness of sins.*

This shows that Luke joins the life and ministry of Jesus to history in order to show that, although Jesus is the divine Savior, he is also a man among men who lived in space and time just like every person does.

---

65. Ibid., 67.

C. Unique Parables

The major structural difference between the Gospel of Luke and the other Gospels occurs in 9:51-18:14. This section is not found in any other gospel.[66] In these nine chapters, Luke tells about the life and teachings of Jesus as he travels from his ministry in Northern Galilee to the holy city of Jerusalem. The section contains many parables unique to the Gospel of Luke. For example, the parable of the Good Samaritan is found only here (10:28-37). The parable of the Rich Fool (12:13-21) and the parable of the Fruitless Fig Tree (13:6-9) are unique as well. The parable of the Marriage Feast (14:7-14) and the parable of the Great Supper (14:15-24) are contained only here. The parables of the Lost Coin and the Prodigal Son are also part of his unique contributions (15:8-10; 11-32). And finally, the parable of the Unjust Steward (16:1-13), the parable of the Rich Man and Lazarus (16:19-31) and the parable of the Pharisee and the Publican (18:9-14) round out this special section which can only be found in the Gospel of Luke.

The parable of the Pharisee and the Publican may indicate Pauline influence on Luke's production of the gospel because this is the only place in all of the Gospels that the word "justified" can be found. Since Luke was a close traveling companion of the Apostle Paul, it is very likely that his speech and theology would "rub off" on Luke.

D. The Trial and Crucifixion of Christ

The Gospel of Luke contains some significant additions to the trial and crucifixion of Christ. For example, Jesus' comfort of the Apostle Peter is found only in this gospel (22:31-32). The fact that Luke was a physician may have led him to be the only evangelist to record that Jesus' sweat was as great drops of blood (22:43, 44). Jesus' appearance before Herod (22:4-16) and his address to the women of Jerusalem (23:27-31) are also unique to this gospel.[67] Finally, the repentant thief on the cross is a unique contribution of Luke as well (23:39-43).

E. Resurrection

The Lukan gospel contains unique material concerning the resurrection.[68] All resurrection appearances are near or in Jerusalem. Unlike the other Gospels, the resurrected Lord does not appear to his disciples in Galilee. Again, many Gentiles would have known of Jerusalem, but not of Galilee and Nazareth. Also, if we did not have the Gospel of Luke, the story of the two men on the road to Emmaus would not have been recorded.

---

66. Guthrie, New Testament, 97.
67. Tenney, New Testament, 183.
68. Ibid.

PART 4—GENERAL CHARACTERISTICS

A careful study of the Gospel of Luke reveals that there are four general characteristics.[69]

I. IT IS COMPREHENSIVE

Luke is the longest gospel. This gospel begins with the birth of John the Baptist and ends with a reference to the Ascension. Apart from Mark 16:8 ff. (which does not appear in the earliest manuscripts) Luke is the only gospel that records the Ascension of our Lord.

II. IT IS UNIVERSAL

Luke is writing to the *world*. Angels speak peace to all persons of goodwill (2:14). Simeon prophesies that Jesus will be a light to the Gentiles (2:32). Luke emphasizes that all men are created equal (9:54, 10:33, 17:16).

III. IT IS DOCTRINAL

Luke is careful to preserve central doctrines of the faith.[70] Luke states that the central mission of the Lord was to save the lost (19:10). It is the only gospel that explicitly uses the word "justified" (18:9). Luke's understanding of the Spirit, or his *pneumatology*, is the most developed of the Gospels. He has more references to the Holy Spirit than the Gospels of Mark and Matthew combined.[71] All major characters in Luke, including Jesus, are empowered by the Holy Spirit (1:15, 41, 67, 4:1).

IV. IT IS HISTORICAL

Luke is not simply giving some mystical presentation of the Son of God.[72] Although Jesus was the Son of God, he lived in space and time just like everyone else does (1:5, 2:1, 3:1 & 2).

Discuss the significance of the name "Theophilus" and the two ways in which the name can be understood.

---

69. Guthrie, *New Testament,* 90-92.
70. Tenney, *New Testament,* 184.
71. Morris, *Luke,* 44.
72. Tenney, *New Testament,* 201.

How do the "We Sections" of Luke relate to the question of authorship?

PART 5—SPECIAL LUKAN CHARACTERISTICS

I. A SOPHISTICATED WRITING STYLE

Luke 1:1-4 is closest to classical Greek in the New Testament. Only the Epistle to the Hebrews contains such polished Greek. Also, the complexity of Luke's writing style is evidenced in the four songs he records. All of these have become great hymns of the church.[73] They are:

A. *The Magificat*

Mary praises the Lord when she is told that she will conceive of the Holy Spirit (1:46-55).

B. *The Benedictus*

This is the song of Zechariah, the father of John the Baptist, after the birth of his son and after he has been called John. The Lord allowed Zechariah to speak again and he broke forth in song unto the Lord (1:67-79).

C. *Gloria in Excelsis Deo*

The angels announced the birth of Jesus to the shepherds in song (2:14).

D. *Nunc Dimittis*

These Latin words literally mean "now dismiss." This is the prayer/song of Simeon after he saw the baby Jesus in the temple (2:28-32).

II. THE ROLE OF WOMEN AND CHILDREN

Luke is careful to record Jesus' affirmation of the women of his day. He mentions the word "woman" 43 times. Matthew and Mark combined only used "woman" 49 times. The special material about Mary and Elizabeth underscores his care of women. Also, Luke's detailed description of the women at the tomb should be noted as well (23:55-56, 24:1-11).

With regard to children, Luke records more about the childhood of Jesus and John the Baptist than any other gospel. He alone records that Jesus disputed with the scribes in the temple at the age of 12 (2:38-50). On three occasions Luke notes that Jesus heals or raises from the dead *an only child* (7:12, 8:42, 9:38). Matthew and Mark record that children were being brought to Jesus, but Luke says *infants* were brought to be blessed by Jesus (18:15-17).

III. LUKE CHAMPIONS OUTCASTS AND SINNERS

Luke records an immoral woman anointing Jesus' feet with her tears (7:36-48). The stories of Zacchaeus the tax collector (19:1-10) and that of the repentant thief (23:39-43) are found only in Luke. He continually exalts the value of the poor and the oppressed and speaks against the rich and powerful (cf. 7:42-43, 12:13-21).

---

73. Guthrie, *New Testament,* 93.

IV. THE PRAYERS OF JESUS

Luke records nine prayers of Jesus, seven of which are unique to Luke. Each is associated with an important event in the life of Christ, such as his baptism (3:21), before his transfiguration (9:29), and prior to his crucifixion (23:34 & 46).

V. GOSPEL OF JOY

The songs in Luke are an indication of the spirit of joy present in this Gospel (1:14, 44 & 47). Throughout Luke, people are leaping for joy, laughing, and being happy (6:21-23, 15:23, 32).

SELF TEST:

1. T or F   Luke is the only Gospel to record the birth of John the Baptist.

2. T or F   Luke is not concerned about the prayers of Jesus.

3. T or F   Luke has no musical interest.

4. T or F   Luke contains the simplest Greek in the New Testament.

5. T or F   Luke champions women, children, outcasts and sinners.

6. T or F   All of the resurrection appearances in Luke take place in Galilee.

7. T or F   Of all the Gospels, Luke alone uses the word "justified."

----

1. List three of the "special emphases" of Luke:

     a. _____

     b. _____

     c. _____

2. List three ways that the structure of Luke differs from the other Gospels:

     a. _____

     b. _____

     c. _____

LESSON 6—THE GOSPEL OF JOHN

Part 1	Background Information
Part 2	Central Theme
Part 3	The Unique Structure of John
Part 4	Special Emphases
Part 5	Unique Characteristics of John

OVERVIEW

The Gospel of John is not part of the "Synoptic Gospels." His approach and structure are totally different from that of Matthew, Mark, and Luke. He does not begin with the life of Jesus in Bethlehem. Rather, he opens with words about the preincarnate *logos*. A chronological presentation of the life of Jesus is not a top priority for John. He is more interested in the theological significance of miraculous *signs* of the Lord and structures his gospel around seven major signs.

John is able to use simple words like "light," "word," "flesh," etc. to communicate profound theological principles. On a linguistic level, John's gospel is simple, but on a theological level it is very complex.

John is able to accommodate traditional Jewish themes to a Greek mindset, without allowing Greek thought to determine the content of his message. In fact, his gospel can be viewed as a *polemic* ("argument against") certain aspects of Greek philosophy.

John desires to present Jesus as the Incarnate Word; God in the flesh. As God, Jesus performed extraordinary miracles, each having special theological significance. The overall purpose of John's theology is to lead one to faith.

OBJECTIVES

- Discuss the authorship of John.
- Explain the unique structure of the Gospel of John.
- Clearly state the central themes of the Gospel of John.
- List three special emphases of John.
- Relate the date of John to authorship.
- List four unique characteristics of John.

HELPS FOR LEARNING AND REMEMBERING

1. Use a highlighter pen to help impress material on your memory.

2. Read your notes aloud as you review. This technique employs the principle of *neural traces*. Each thought wears a pathway or "neural trace" in your mind. The more a thought goes through the mind, the deeper and wider the pathway becomes. The deeper and wider the pathway is, the easier it is to retrieve that particular thought.

3. View John as an artist who paints with words, rather than an architect who builds according to clearly drawn plans. This may help you cope with the different structure in John.

4. Look for John's special use of numbers, particularly seven and three. Knowing that John will arrange his material in series of seven or three will help you master the material.

KEY WORDS

Prologue	*agapao*	*paraklete*	qualitative
Logos	polemic	discourse	*emunah*
Kosmos			

PART 1—BACKGROUND INFORMATION

I. AUTHORSHIP

The name of the Apostle John is not found anywhere in the gospel. Yet with regard to authorship, note the following:

A. Internal Evidence

John 1:14 and 19:35 indicate that the author was an eyewitness to the historical Jesus and the crucifixion. In the place of "the Apostle John," we find the phrase, "the disciple whom Jesus loved" (13:22-25), who in fact is the one bearing witness in this gospel. This beloved principle was the disciple who was very close to Jesus at the Last Supper (21:20). But exactly who is "the beloved disciple"?[74]

Throughout the Gospel of John, this beloved disciple has a close association with the Apostle Peter. In the Synoptics, John is a close associate of Peter (Mark 5:37, 9:2, 14:33). Also, in the Gospel of John, John the Baptist is simply called "John." This may indicate that the author knew that he would have been known by another title, that is the Apostle John. John 20:2-8 speaks of the beloved disciple coming to faith upon entering the empty tomb. The one most likely to remember this precise moment would be the disciple himself. Thus, the author of the gospel and the beloved disciple appear to be one and the same person (cf. 21:20, 24, 25; 13:22-25).

But why would John refer to himself as "the disciple whom Jesus loved"? Would it not have appeared conceited to refer to oneself as the disciple whom Jesus loved? Perhaps such a reference is, in fact, an act of humility. One might recall that Jesus referred to James and John as the 'sons of thunder" (Mark 3:17). The Apostle John may have been continually amazed that Jesus could love such a one as himself. There can be no question that the Apostle John was thoroughly impressed with the unmerited favor of God. The Greek word *agapao* literally means "the divine love of God." This Greek word appears 21 times in 1 John alone, which is more than any other book of the New Testament. In the light of all of this, the phrase "the beloved disciple" is indeed fitting for the Apostle John.

B. External Evidence

Irenaeus was the first to identify the Apostle John as the author of the fourth gospel. In his *Against Heresies*, Irenaeus states that the Apostle John authored the fourth gospel while in Ephesus during the reign of Trajan (AD 98-117).[75] Eusebius, the early church historian, indicates that Irenaeus got his information from Polycarp, who was a disciple of the Apostle John. Tertullian, Clement of Alexandria, and Origen also state that the Apostle John is the author of the gospel.[76]

---

74. Leon Morris, *The Gospel According to John,* (Grand Rapids: Eerdmans, 1971) 9 ff.
75. John R.W. Stott, *The Letters of John,* (Grand Rapids: Eerdmans, 1988) 18.
76. Ralph P. Martin, *New Testament Foundations: A Guide for Christian Students,* vol. 1 (Grand Rapids: Eerdmans, 1975) 277.

II. DATE

The date of composition is directly related to the issue of authorship. Estimates range from the fall of Jerusalem in AD 70 to the last quarter of the 2nd century, (AD 175).[77] However, a vast majority of scholars accept a date between AD 90 and AD 110. Indeed, early Christian tradition indicates that John lived to be quite old, and therefore would have been alive at the turn of the 2nd century.

---

77. Tenney, *New Testament,* 191-92.

PART 2—CENTRAL THEME

The atypical structure of John relates to the central theme. Usually the major purpose of a literary work is stated near the beginning, but the key to John's gospel is near the end. John 20:30-31 states, "Jesus did many other miraculous *signs* in the presence of his disciples, which are not recorded in this book. But these are written that ye may *believe* that Jesus is the Christ, the Son of God, and that believing ye may have *life* in His name." For John, *signs* communicate theological truths which are designed to lead to *faith* and ultimately result in *eternal life*. So, the central theme of this gospel is *belief*.

Some form of the term "to believe" is used 98 times in John. By "belief," John does not mean intellectual assent, but the Jewish concept of *emunah*.[78] This word refers to a trusting heartfelt relationship between two persons. So, when John speaks of "belief," he is referring to a wholehearted reliance upon the integrity of God, making the principles of trust and commitment central to an understanding of John.

Briefly give the arguments for and against the Johannine authorship of the fourth gospel.

78. Martin Buber, *Two Kinds of Faith* (London: Routledge and Kegan Paul LTD, 1951).

PART 3—THE UNIQUE STRUCTURE OF JOHN

John did not use the "synoptic framework" as evidenced in Matthew, Mark, and Luke. The major differences in the outline and content of John can be summarized as follows:

I. THE PROLOGUE

The term *prologue* literally means "foreword." The foreword of the Gospel of John consists of the first 14 verses. It truly is amazing that the central doctrines of the Christian faith have all been encapsulated in these few verses. These include:

A. The Pre-existence of Christ (1:1). This is not explicitly mentioned in any other gospel.
B. Jesus is co-eternal with the Father (1:1, 14.) He is equal in power and glory.
C. Jesus is co-Creator (1:4, 5, 9). He is the source of all life (1:3, 4) both physical and spiritual.
D. Jesus is superior to John the Baptist (1:6-8).
E. Jesus actualized the plan of salvation in history (1:10-11).
F. Faith in Jesus affects spiritual regeneration (1:12). It also incorporates one into God's family.
G. The incarnation (1:14). "God with us."

In some ways, the rest of the Gospel of John is simply an unfolding and elaboration of the theological concepts presented in the prologue.

II. THE SEVEN SIGNS

John structures his gospel around seven significant signs which communicate profound spiritual truths. These signs are as follows:[79]

A. The changing of water into wine (2:1-11). This was the first miracle performed by the Lord in the Gospel of John. The key word here is "quality." John wishes to demonstrate that Jesus, as the Son of God, is not limited by the quality of anything or substance.

B. The healing of the nobleman's son (4:46-54). One might recall that the nobleman requested that Jesus simply speak the word and that his son would be healed. In fact, Jesus sends the man home assuring him that his son has been restored. This miraculous sign demonstrates that the power of Jesus is not limited by space.

C. The healing of the lame man (5:1-9). This story speaks of a lame man who had been paralyzed for 38 years. Nevertheless, in spite of this long and torturous history, the man is immediately healed by the Lord (5:5, 8-9). This experience demonstrates that Jesus is not limited by time.

D. The feeding of the 5,000 (6:1-14). This particular miracle demonstrates that the power of God in Christ is not limited by quantity.

---

79. Tenney, *New Testament*, 192.

E. Walking on the water (6:16-21). In this instance, Jesus is represented as having power over the environment. He is not limited by natural law.

F. The healing of the blind man (9:1-12). Jewish religious tradition maintained that all illness and deformities were directly attributable to sin. The Jewish religious leaders at the time of Jesus wanted to know whose sin had caused this blindness. Jesus gave a startling response. He claimed that personal sin was not the cause here. He indicated that disease and weakness are simply consequences of living in a fallen world. This miracle shows that Jesus has power over the misfortunes of this life.

G. The raising of Lazarus (11:1-46). The theological significance of this miracle is apparent. The greatest threat to human existence is physical death. This particular sign demonstrates that Jesus is not limited by the power of death.

One can readily see how different the Gospel of John is from that of the Synoptics. It may be that John was very familiar with the Gospels that already existed. Perhaps he wanted to supply what was lacking in those Gospels and to present the story of Jesus in a fresh new way. Although John made unique contributions to the gospel tradition, he also left out large portions of the traditional gospel material. For example, he omitted much of the Galilean ministry, almost all of the parables of Jesus, and freely admits that he had been selective in presenting the miracle stories of the Lord (20:30).

PART 4—SPECIAL EMPHASES

The three special emphases of John are:

I. PERSONAL FAITH

The central importance of faith in Jesus has already been discussed.[80] John stressed a wholehearted commitment to the person and work of the Lord Jesus Christ. In fact, the name "Jesus' is mentioned some 252 times in John alone.[81]

II. DEITY OF CHRIST

The central doctrine of John is the deity of Christ, which is not only evidenced by the seven signs, but also by the seven "I am's." They are:[82]

A. I am the bread of life (6:35, 48). Jesus supplies everything necessary for spiritual life. Jesus does not say that he gives bread, but that he *is* bread. His own person and being are the source of *spiritual nourishment.*

B. I am the light of the world (8:12). Jesus probably spoke these words during the Feast of Tabernacles. During this feast, there was a tremendous lighting ceremony in the Court of the Women. Jesus is the source of true *spiritual illumination.*

C. I am the door (10:7). The imagery of a door certainly communicates the idea of access. Only Jesus provides *access* into the presence of God himself.

D. I am the good shepherd (10:14). The death of the shepherd was to be avoided. Yet Jesus intentionally died for the sheep. The doctrine of the *atonement* is clearly evidenced here.

E. I am the resurrection (11:25). This statement *puts death in its proper perspective.* For the believer, death is no longer a period, but simply a pause.

F. I am the way, the truth, and the life (14:6). Jesus is *the only way* to the Father. He is the only one who can provide genuine spiritual life for the believer. In a way that seems very intolerant to modern ears, Jesus boldly claimed that no one comes to the Father except through him.

G. I am the vine (15:1). The principle of *vital connection* is present here. One must be intimately connected with Christ by faith to receive the spiritual nourishment that grants eternal life.

III. ETERNAL LIFE

---

80. Martin, *New Testament Foundations,* 282.
81. Morris, *Theology of the New Testament Theology,* 225.
82. Tenney, *New Testament,* 197.

The central goal of the gospel is life. The word *life* does not simply mean "endless days," for life is not to be understood in quantitative terms. Rather, John is speaking of a qualitatively new life. The believer experiences the power of the Kingdom of God in this present world. One does not simply have a long life, but one experiences a totally new kind of existence in Christ.

It is clear that John recorded the seven signs to demonstrate the *power* of God in Christ. The purpose of the "I am's" is to reflect the *deity* of Jesus Christ. The desired result is that one will *believe in* Jesus and *receive* eternal life.

1. What is the significance of signs in the Gospel of John?

2. List the seven major signs of John:

a. _____

b. _____

c. _____

d. _____

e. _____

f. _____

g. _____

3. List the seven "I am's" of John:

. _____

b. _____

c. _____

d. _____

e. _____

f. _____

g. _____

PART 5—UNIQUE CHARACTERISTICS OF JOHN

The unique characteristics of John are:

I. THE LOGOS DOCTRINE

The Logos doctrine is only found in John.[83]   In that Jesus is the Word, he is the pre-existent, personal and eternal communication of God. John's Logos doctrine has both a Greek and a Hebrew connection. The Greeks called the creation the *kosmos*, which literally means "the adornment." The Greeks concluded that there must be some type of "divine reason" which accounts for the order and beauty of creation. This rational principle was called the "Logos."

Yet for the Jew, the Word communicated "the self-expression of God." It was through the Word of the Lord that the heavens and earth were created (Genesis 1-3). It was through the Word that God communicated himself to his people.

For both the Jews and the Greeks the "Logos" is the very starting point of all things. In that the Word was with God (Jesus is co-eternal with the Father) the Logos doctrine emphasizes both the transcendence (John 1:1) and immanence of the Lord (1:14).[84]   John 1:14 *does not* say that the Logos became human, but that the Logos became *flesh*, strongly emphasizing the Incarnation of Christ. Also, the verb "became" is in the aorist or past tense. It refers to a particular action at one single point in time. John is referring here to the Virgin Birth of our Lord Jesus Christ.

II. JESUS' TEACHING ON THE HOLY SPIRIT

Although Luke has more references to the Holy Spirit than Matthew and Mark combined, John records more of Jesus' own personal words concerning the Holy Spirit. A prime example is Jesus' conversation with Nicodemus (3:1 ff). True believers worship the Father in Spirit and in truth (4:24). The most complete gospel description of the person and work of the Holy Spirit is given in John 14:16-26. John records that Jesus refers to the Spirit as the "Comforter" or *paraklete*, literally "one called alongside of."[85]   Jesus portrays the Holy Spirit as "the Spirit of truth" who comes to the aid of the Christian (14:17).

III. SPECIAL VOCABULARY

John repeatedly uses simple words like *world, life, light, darkness, work, flesh,* and *know* to communicate extraordinary theological principles.[86]   "Darkness" does not mean an absence of light, but rather it means wickedness. When Jesus says that he came to do the "work" of the Father, he means that he came to execute the will of God. To "know" the Father means that one has a vital relationship with God. So, John is gifted at giving special spiritual theological meaning to ordinary vocabulary.

---

83. Barclay M. Newman and Eugene A. Nida, *A Translator's Handbook on the Gospel of John* (New York: United Bible Societies, 1980) 7.

84. Morris, *Theology of the New Testament*, 227.

85. Martin, *New Testament Foundations*, 285.

86. Tenney, *New Testament*, 198.

IV. PERSONAL DISCOURSE

"Discourse" means personal conversations that the Lord had with individuals in John (Nicodemus, the woman, at the well, Pilate, etc.).[87] There are 27 such private interviews between Jesus and individuals in the fourth gospel.

SELF TEST:

1. The Gospel of John:
    a. is one of the Synoptics.
    b. frequently uses the word "miracle."
    c. uses some form of the word "belief" nearly 100 times.
    d. all of these
    e. none of these

2. It was noted that:
    a. the seven "signs" point to the divinity of Jesus.
    b. the seven "I am's" point to the divinity of Jesus.
    c. "eternal life" is to be understood in qualitative rather than quantitative terms.
    d. all of these
    e. none of these

3. It was noted that the "Logos" doctrine:
    a. is found in other Gospels.
    b. is derived solely from Greek roots.
    c. emphasizes both the transcendence and immanence of the Lord.
    d. A & B
    e. B & C

4. John's gospel:
    a. has more of Jesus' teaching on the Holy Spirit than any other gospel.
    b. is able to use simple words to communicate profound theology.
    c. contains more personal discourse of the Lord than any other gospel.
    d. all of these
    e. none of these

---

87. Ibid., 199.

SECTION 3:

THE BOOK OF ACTS

Lesson 7	Background Information
Lesson 8	An Historical Overview of Acts
Lesson 9	Important Sermons and Speeches

SECTION OVERVIEW

One of the societal difficulties that we experience today is the sense of rootlessness. That is to say, in many ways a genuine appreciation of the past is lacking in our contemporary society. As a result, many do not have a sense of continuity or historical perspective. In turn, a genuine self-understanding and true comprehension of one's place in time goes wanting. Opportunities to learn from the past are lost. Adopting successful patterns and methods from our forefathers in order that we might plan for the future is a rare occurrence. We live for the moment and "modernity" is the byword of the day.

Fortunately, Luke did not suffer from this modern malady. He fully understood the consequences of neglecting to observe the successes and failures of the early church. The Lord had not returned as quickly as expected. It appeared that the church was in the world to stay for a while. So now what? What was the mission of the church? Who will record the story of the birth, growth and development of the early Christian believers? What evangelical purposes can be accomplished in telling the story of the church?

Luke meets all of these challenges and addresses these questions in the Book of Acts. Let us now examine this monumental work; the proper sequel to the Gospel of Luke.

BLANK PAGE

LESSON 7—BACKGROUND INFORMATION

Part 1	The Similarity Between the Gospel of Luke and Acts
Part 2	The Date of Acts
Part 3	A General Outline
Part 4	The Importance of Acts
Part 5	Central Themes

OVERVIEW

It is important to keep in mind that Acts is the sequel to the Gospel of Luke. Look for interrelationships between Luke's gospel and this historic work. For example, what theological principles in Luke are further developed in Acts? Does Luke have a theological agenda directing his treatment of the church? Is his concern for the poor, the outcast, and the sinners also evidenced in Acts? Is Luke an *apologist* (a defender of the faith) or a *polemicist* (a destroyer of heresy)?

Since Acts is the sequel to Luke, the authorship has already been discussed. Yet the dating of Acts is important. Was Acts written during the 1st century or the 2nd? With regard to structure, what type of organizational principles does Luke use? How does Luke use the geographic expansion of the church to direct his story? What role does the "church growth motif" play here? It is to these questions and others that we now turn.

OBJECTIVES

- Completely describe the similarity between the Gospel of Luke and the Book of Acts.
- Argue for a 1st century date for the Book of Acts.
- Present a general outline for the entire Book of Acts.
- Describe the importance of Acts.
- List the central themes of Acts.

HELPS FOR LEARNING AND REMEMBERING

1. A map of the 1st century will help in understanding the geographic context of Acts.
2. A map which traces the missionary journeys of Paul will also help.
3. An apostolic chronology will help in ordering the events of Acts.
4. The importance of structure and organization cannot be overemphasized. A grasp of the geographic and chronological context will help. When did Pentecost occur? When was the first persecution of the church? When was the Apostle Paul called into the ministry? A rapid reading of Acts and the development of a brief outline of each chapter will help you follow Luke's story.

KEY WORDS

Hebraisms	apologetics	apocalyptic
Church growth	*martures*	kerygma
Jerusalem Council	Lingua Franka	polytheism
Heilsgeschichte		

PART 1—THE SIMILARITY BETWEEN THE GOSPEL OF LUKE AND ACTS

I. AUTHORSHIP

This has been discussed under the Gospel of Luke (refer to previous notes).

II. THE SIMILARITY BETWEEN LUKE AND ACTS

A. "The Former Treatise" (1:1)

This is a reference to the Gospel of Luke. Both works are addressed to the same person, Theophilus. So, the similarity of Luke and Acts actually begins in the very first verse of Acts. Acts is the sequel to the gospel and is addressed to the same individual.

B. The Role of the Holy Spirit

For Luke, the church is a Holy Spirit empowered movement. The Holy Spirit is involved in every major event in Acts, and every influential person is inspired by the Spirit.

C. Similar Literary Style

Both Luke and Acts emphasize history. God has revealed Himself in space and time. For these reasons, the people, cultures, and historical context of both Luke and Acts are extremely important. Also, Luke and Acts frequently contain many Hebraisms. This means that Luke is fond of including Jewish phrases, practices, and thought forms in his gospel and Acts. Finally, Luke makes many references to the LXX in both works. In other words, he makes frequent use of the Septuagint. Once again, the LXX or Septuagint refers to the Greek translation of the Hebrew Old Testament.

D. The Fulfillment of the Jewish Faith

This is a very important point. Luke is careful to note that Christianity is not simply some subset of Judaism. The early Christian movement is not to be understood as simply a sect of Judaism. Rather, Christianity is a fulfillment and continuance of God's plan for humankind.

E. De-emphasize Apocalyptic

Both Luke and Acts emphasize history and de-emphasize apocalyptic. If you will recall, apocalyptic emphasizes the sudden catastrophic intervention of God which brings this present world to an end. For Luke, Christianity is in the world to stay, at least for a while. This aspect of Luke in Acts can be seen in his tendency to anchor the story of the church in a thoroughly worldly setting. For example, in Acts Luke mentions 32 countries, 54 different cities, nine Mediterranean islands, and 95 individuals. Of the 95 persons, 62 are not mentioned anywhere else in the New Testament, and 27 of the 95 are non-believers. For Luke, the church is thoroughly involved with the people and places in this present life.

PART 2—THE DATE OF ACTS

The historical, geographical, and political atmosphere of Acts is definitely first century and not second century.[88] There is no mention of the destruction of the temple which took place in AD 70. Luke consistently represents the Roman Empire and its officials as non-hostile toward Christianity. Despite the many charges laid against Christians in the Gospel of Luke and in Acts, no Roman official condemns any leader of the church, including Jesus Christ. Pilate found Jesus not guilty and Paul is not condemned by Gallio, Felix, or Festus. It is clear that the Romans are not the ones persecuting the church. Rather, Luke represents the Jews as the real enemies of the faith. And by way of contrast, the Roman state is often represented as protecting the Apostle Paul from his own people (Acts 21:32, 22:25-29; 23:16-24). We know that an official Roman persecution of the church broke out in AD 64 under Nero. Therefore, the Book of Acts must have been written prior to AD 64. It is estimated that the Apostle Paul arrived in Rome in around AD 60-61. In that Paul was imprisoned in Rome for two years, and the Book of Acts ends with the Apostle Paul freely preaching the gospel under those conditions, Acts may well have been written around AD 63-64.

Discuss the similarities between the Gospel of Luke and the Book of Acts:

---

88. F.F. Bruce, *The Book of Acts,* (Grand Rapids: Eerdmans, 1988) 10-11.

PART 3—A GENERAL OUTLINE

I. A GEOGRAPHICAL OUTINE

A. The Church in Jerusalem (chs. 1-7)

This represents the earliest *Jewish* stage in the church's development.

B. The Church throughout Israel (chs. 8-12)

The church is in a transitional phase, breaking out of its Jewish ethnocentricity, becoming a multi-cultural, multi-ethnic spiritual movement.

C. The Church among the Nations (chs. 13-28)

The church is predominately Gentile, and the internationalization of the church is well underway.

II. THE ECCLESIASTICAL FRAMEWORK

With regard to the *ecclesiastical* framework, Luke divides Acts into six major sections, each covering about five years.[89] Each section concludes with a summary verse emphasizing *church growth*.

A. The Church in Jerusalem (1:1-6:7)

This section records the start of the church in Jerusalem, focusing on Peter's preaching and the outpouring of the Holy Spirit at Pentecost. The summary verse is Acts 6:7 and reflects Luke's "church growth motif."[90]

B. Transition from Jewish to Gentile (6:8-9:31)

The transition from a predominately Jewish church to a Gentile mission is noted here. The theme of "witness" (a legal term from the Greek *martures*, meaning "to witness or testify") is explicitly mentioned 28 times in Acts.[91] Jewish hostility increases and culminates with the *martyrdom* of Stephen (6:8-7:60). Yet Phillip witnesses to the Samaritans and the Ethiopian eunuch, and the persecutor Paul is converted to the faith. The summary verse (9:31) emphasizes the comfort of the Holy Spirit, thus underscoring Lukan *pneumatology*.

---

89. James Hastings, *A Dictionary of the Bible,* (New York: Charles Scribner's Sons, 1911) 421.

90. French L. Arrington, *The Acts of the Apostles,* (Peabody, Massachusetts: Hendrickson, 1988) xxxvi.

91. Charles W. Carter and Ralph Earle, *The Acts of the Apostles,* (Grand Rapids: Zondervan, 1973) 10-11.

C. The Spread of Antioch (9:32-12:24)

The church has spread to Antioch of Syria (*not* Antioch of Pisidia in south central Asia Minor). Through the preaching of Peter, Cornelius and his household are converted. Gentiles are officially admitted into the church indicating Christianity is not a sect of Judaism. The summary verse (12:24) shows Theophilus that Christianity is a Spirit-inspired movement that cannot be stopped.

D. Paul's First Missionary Journey (12:25-16:5)

This section records Paul's first missionary journey.[92]   The first missionary team (Paul, Barnabas, and Mark) were commissioned from the church in Antioch. Jewish Christianity is overshadowed by Gentile Christianity, and Jewish distinctives are threatened. As a result, some Jews sought to force the Gentiles to be circumcised and obey the law of Moses. The first general council [the Jerusalem Council (cf. Acts 15)] ruled that Gentiles were accepted on the basis of faith alone, and not by becoming proselytes to Judaism. This momentous decision established two important principles:

> 1. Although Jewish Christianity was in the minority, Jerusalem is still the headquarters for the whole church.

> 2. The internationalization of the church was preserved. One's ethnic identity has no bearing upon becoming a child of God. The summary verse (16:5) states that the church grew in faith and numbers. This tremendous crisis was overcome, and the growth of the church was unhindered.

E. Paul's Second and Third Missionary Journeys (16:6-19:20)

This section covers Paul's second and third missionary journeys. The central event in this section is Paul's Macedonian vision.[93]   The church spreads westward into Europe and establishes Christianity as the future moral and religious paradigm for Europe and the United States. Paul establishes churches in Philippi, Thessalonica, Corinth, and Ephesus. The summary verse (19:20) speaks of the growth of the Word.

F. The Church in Rome (19:21-28:31)

This last section describes how the church established a beachhead in the capital itself. Paul is arrested in Jerusalem, spends two years in prison at Caesarea and finally is imprisoned for another two years in Rome. He is living in his own hired household, being held under house arrest. Visitors can come and go, and he is allowed to preach the gospel freely.[94]   The summary verse (28:31) ends with the word "unhindered." Even under these severe circumstances, the power of the gospel is unhindered.

---

92. Tenney, *New Testament,* 258 ff.
93. Arrington, *Acts,* 165 ff.
94. Bruce, *Acts,* 511.

PART 4—THE IMPORTANCE OF ACTS

Luke has made five major contributions in the Book of Acts. They are:

I. A LINK BETWEEN THE GOSPELS AND THE EPISTLES

The Book of Acts serves as a link between the gospel records concerning the life and ministry of Jesus, and the letters or epistles of the apostles.[95] It is hard to imagine what a study of the New Testament would have been like without the Book of Acts. When one would have finished studying the four Gospels, the very next book encountered would have been the Epistle to the Romans. One would have been faced with the puzzling dilemma of reconstructing the entire history of the church from Jerusalem to Rome. How did the church spread from a small, completely Messianic Jewish movement centered in Jerusalem, to a multi-ethnic, multi-lingual, multi-cultural spiritual movement which embraced a large portion of the Roman Empire? The Book of Acts is important because it answers these questions.

II. A HISTORY OF THE SPREAD OF THE CHURCH

Acts supplies a history of the spread of the church from Jerusalem to Rome.[96] It should be emphasized that the extraordinary success of the early church was due to the person and work of the Holy Spirit. In recording the growth of the church, Luke has also supplied a thorough going pneumatology. Acts is important because it shows us how the Holy Spirit worked in the early church.

III. INSIGHT INTO EARLY CHRISTIAN WORSHIP

Although 1 & 2 Corinthians and Galatians grant some insight into early Christian worship, Acts also tells us about methods of evangelism and even leadership models in the church.[97] In this way, Acts supplies a pattern for life and conduct in the church.

IV. INSIGHT INTO EARLY CHRISTIAN PREACHING

Acts records the speeches and sermons of the early church. We have Peter's sermon at Pentecost, Stephen's speech prior to his martyrdom, and sermons by Paul. These first sermons reveal the *kerygma*, or the early Christian preaching. They also present the theology and principles of the first believers.

V. BIOGRAPHICAL MATERIAL ON KEY CHURCH LEADERS

The Book of Acts gives additional information about the personality and character of prominent early Christian leaders. The first 12 chapters of Acts concentrate on the personality of Peter. In this phase of Luke's story, Peter is the predominant Christian leader guiding and directing the ministry of the church from Jerusalem to Antioch in Syria. However, for the rest of Acts, Paul is

---

95. Arrington, *Acts,* xxxi.
96. Bruce, *Acts,* 8.
97. Morris, *Theology of the New Testament,* 193, 196, 212.

clearly the dominate character. For Luke, Paul is the super apostle.[98] He is the apostle to the Gentiles. He is the central figure in God's plan for the nations. In addition to these two major apostles, the Book of Acts introduces many other significant persons. For example, in Acts we are introduced to such important leaders as Barnabas and Mark, Silas, Priscilla and Acquila, Timothy and others. Without the Book of Acts, we would have very limited information on such persons.

TRUE/FALSE:

1. T or F   Throughout the Book of Acts, the Roman Empire is represented as being hostile to the church.
2. T or F   The "church growth motif" is a major theme of Acts.
3. T or F   According to Luke, every Christian must be a martyr (see *martures* in 1:8).

---

98. Bruce, *Acts,* 14-16.

PART 5—CENTRAL THEMES OF ACTS

The three major themes of Acts are:

I. THE THEME OF WITNESS

Acts 1:8 states, "But you will *receive power* when the *Holy Spirit* comes on you; and you will be my *witnesses* in Jerusalem, and in all Judea and Samaria, and to the ends of the earth." This serves as a blueprint for the rest of Acts.[99] Luke's story is simply an unfolding and development of Acts 1:8.

First, it is extremely important for Luke to communicate that every work of God is empowered by the Holy Spirit. Secondly, the theme of "witness" is central and appears some 20 times in Acts. God is leaving a clear and unmistakable witness of his person and work in the world. Finally, the geographical and ethnic expansion of the church is presented here. The church started in Jerusalem as a thoroughly Jewish spiritual movement. Yet through early Christian Hellenists such as Stephen and the Seven (Acts 6:1-6), the church spread throughout Judea to the north. Through workers such as Phillip the evangelist, non-Jewish persons such as Samaritans and the Ethiopian eunuch were converted. Finally, full-blown Gentile missionaries carried the gospel to the uttermost parts of the earth.

II. THE THEME OF APOLOGETICS

Apologetics refers to the defense and promotion of the faith.[100] It is a legal term which speaks of a lawyer defending a particular case in court. For Luke, Christianity is on trial, and he presents a defensible case for the faith.

A central point of his defense is to show Theophilus that the church is not politically dangerous to Rome. No Christian leader is condemned by any Roman official. Both Jesus and all of the apostles are pronounced innocent (Acts 3:13-17, 16:37 ff., 18:14, 25:8). The civil unrest which often accompanied Christianity was not due to the Christians, but to the resistance of the Jews.

III. THE THEME OF CHURCH GROWTH

Luke is careful to note the Jewish roots of Christianity, but demonstrates that Christianity is *a fulfillment* of God's plan of salvation.[101] The gospel is not an ethnic or nationalistic religious movement, but good news for all people. The gospel has universal implications and cosmic applications.

---

99. Ibid, 36.
100. Arrington, *Acts,* xxxvi.
.101 Ibid.

1. Name at least two important points that the Gospel of Luke and the Book of Acts have in common.

2. List three reasons why the Book of Acts is so important for our understanding of the New Testament.

3. Briefly explain Luke's "apologetic" as set forth in the Book of Acts.

4. Briefly discuss why Acts 1:8 is so central to an understanding of the Book of Acts.

LESSON 8—AN HISTORICAL OVERVIEW OF ACTS

Part 1	An Apostolic Chronology
Part 2	Paul's Missionary Journeys

OVERVIEW

Luke presents God as entering into our world and working his will within the confines of human history. Thus, particular times, events, persons, and places are all part of divine revelation. Indeed, Luke could be described as a "historical" theologian. Events that seem mundane, like births or who was ruling Rome at the time, are of theological importance to Luke. Therefore, this lesson will focus on two major areas: major events in Acts and the significance of Paul's missionary journeys.

OBJECTIVES

- Produce a brief apostolic chronology of the 1st century church.
- Be able to give a brief outline of Paul's activities and accomplishments on each of his missionary journeys.

KEY WORDS

Pentecost   Judaizers   Epicureans
Antioch of Pisidia salvation history Stoics

PART 1—AN APOSTOLIC CHRONOLOGY

The following apostolic chronology provides a panoramic view of the major events in Acts.[102]

I. BIBLICAL CHRONOLOGY

A. The Outpouring of the Holy Spirit (AD 29-30)

On the 50th day after Passover (hence *Pentecost*, meaning "50th"), the Holy Spirit was poured out upon the church (Acts 2:1-4).

B. The Martyrdom of Stephen (AD 33-36)

The church had grown to such an extent that it drew violent opposition from Orthodox Judaism. This is the first example of many instances of Jewish persecution of the church in Acts.

C. The Conversion of the Apostle Paul (AD 35-36)

The conversion of the Apostle Paul can be determined with certainty. Shortly after his conversion, Paul escaped from King Aretas of Damascus (cf. Acts 9:1-8, 25; 2 Cor. 11:32). Secular records indicate that King Aretas was in power from AD 34 to AD 37. Paul's conversion must have occurred during this period, probably around AD 35-36.

D. Paul's First Missionary Journey (AD 46-48)

Paul's first missionary journey took place soon after Herod's death, about AD 44 (cf. Acts 12:21-23), and therefore spanned a period from about AD 46 to AD 48.

E. Jerusalem Council (AD 49)

At the close of Paul's first missionary journey, the question of receiving Gentiles into the church became an extremely divisive issue. The first general council of the church convened in about AD 49-50 to resolve this conflict.[103]

F. Paul's Second Missionary Journey (AD 49-53)

On his second missionary journey, Paul pastored in Corinth. During this period, Paul appeared before the Roman governor, Gallio (18:12-18). Archaeologists have uncovered an inscription near Corinth stating that Gallio was in power during the 12th year of Claudius Caesar.[104] Gallio ruled in Corinth from AD 51 to 52. Since Paul pastored in Corinth for 18 months, this would mean that Paul's second missionary journey dates from AD 49 to 53.

---

[102] Tenney, *New Testament,* 133.
[103] Bruce, *Acts,* 282 ff.
[104] Carter and Earle, *Acts,* 271.

G. Paul's Third Missionary Journey (AD 53-56)

Acts 19:8-10 records that Paul stayed in Ephesus for about two years and three months, and then continued on to Jerusalem. Figuring two years and three months from AD 53, plus time for the trip to Jerusalem, Paul's third missionary journey covered the period from AD 53 to 56.

H. Paul's Imprisonment in Caesarea (AD 56-58)

Paul appeared before Felix, who reigned in Caesarea from AD 52-56 (cf. Acts 24). Since Paul was imprisoned for two years, he must have been in Caesarea from AD 56-58. From there he was taken to Rome.

I. Paul's Journey to Rome (AD 59-60)

Paul's journey from his imprisonment in Caesarea to the capital is recorded in 27:1-28:14. This marks the final phase of Luke's record of the church.

J. Paul's Roman Imprisonment (AD 60-63)

Paul lived in Rome for two years in his own hired household, under house arrest (28:30). This would mean that Paul was in Rome from AD 60 until the early years of AD 63.[105]

II. CHURCH TRADITION

The following is not part of the biblical record, but is derived from church tradition.

A. Paul's Release from Prison (AD 63)

B. Continued Missionary Work to Spain (AD 64-67)

C. Paul's Second Roman Imprisonment and Execution (AD 67-68)

---

[105] The history of the early church ends with the 28th chapter of Acts. As previously mentioned, it closes with the image of Paul receiving guests in Rome, and freely preaching the gospel of Jesus Christ, no person hindering him. Therefore, the Book of Acts does not record the martyrdom of the Apostle Paul. There are some events in the Pastoral Epistles which are not included in the Book of Acts. There are some movements of the Apostle Paul, such as to the island of Crete, which cannot be found in Luke's record in Acts. This leads some to believe that upon his first hearing before Caesar, Paul was acquitted of all charges laid against him. That is, Paul was released for a brief period of time, continued his missionary work and was once again recaptured and finally killed by the Romans. (Tenney, *New Testament,* 133).

PART 2—PAUL'S MISSIONARY JOURNEYS

I. PAUL'S FIRST MISSIONARY JOURNEY

A. The Commissioning of the First Missionary Team (13:1-2)

Luke gives us insight into an early Christian worship service.[106] The first missionary team (Barnabas, Paul and John Mark) is commissioned through an inspired utterance of the Holy Spirit (13:1,5). Although Barnabas is mentioned first as a matter of priority, Paul will soon eclipse all other missionary characters. John Mark, the cousin of Barnabas and the author of the Gospel of Mark, probably established small prayer groups, and helped disciple newly founded leadership in the churches.

B. Elymas the Sorcerer

For Luke Christianity is superior to all of the primitive powers of the Mediterranean world. In this case, the power of gospel overcomes Elymas the sorcerer.[107] But, this *power encounter* demonstrates that Christianity is more powerful than the pagan magic of the day (13:6-12).

C. John Mark's Departure

In Acts 13:13, John Mark abandons Paul and Barnabas at Perga.[108] The reason for Mark's departure is not clear, but Paul did not deem it justified. The desertion of John Mark will cause a rift between Paul and Barnabas, eventually leading to the breakup of the first missionary team (15:36-41).

D. Paul and Barnabas Minister in Pisidian Antioch (13:14)

The experience in Pisidian Antioch (*not* Antioch of Syria) is significant because Paul and Barnabas explicitly state that they will go to the Gentiles (13:46).[109] Within God's economy (or *salvation history*), it was necessary to preach to the Jews first. Yet after continued resistance, Paul and Barnabas sense the freedom to go directly to the Gentiles.

E. Confusion at Lystra (14:5-19)[110]

Due to the process of hellenization, the Greek language became the *lingua franca* or "common language" of the known world. But the people of Lystra were speaking their local dialect, and Paul and Barnabas did not know they were preparing to sacrifice to them (14:11). They thought Barnabas was Zeus (or in the Roman system, Jupiter) and that Paul was Hermes (or Mercury).

---

[106] Carter and Earle, *Acts,* 174.
[107] Arrington, *Acts,* 133-34.
[108] Bruce, *Acts,* 250-51.
[109] Ibid., 265.
[110] Arrington, *Acts,* 141-43.

Something of the personality and physical stature of Paul and Barnabas may be learned here. Zeus is consistently represented as a large, silent person. On the other hand, Hermes is the small, fleet-footed messenger of the gods (from whence the word *hermeneutics* is derived). Paul may have been small in stature and very articulate, while Barnabas may have been large and not very talkative.

The fickle nature of the people can be seen in this incident. When Paul and Barnabas convinced them that they were not gods, the people of Lystra began to stone them (14:14-20).

II. PAUL'S SECOND MISSIONARY JOURNEY

Paul's second missionary journey is marked by a renewed westward expansion of the gospel, and the growth of the missionary team.

A. The First Church Council

The Gentile population of the church rapidly outstripped the Jewish membership.[111] In order to maintain their Jewish distinctives and control, ultra Orthodox Jews sought to force all Gentile converts to become Jewish proselytes.

If these *Judaizers* had succeeded, the fledgling church would have been hopelessly divided and probably would not have survived as a vibrant spiritual movement. Fortunately, through the testimony of Peter (15:6-11), and Paul and Barnabas" report (15:12), James ordered that the Gentiles be accepted on the basis of faith alone (15:13-35).

B. Disagreement between Paul and Barnabas

The break-up of Paul and Barnabas over Mark forced Paul to take on a new traveling companion (15:39-41).[112] Silas was an excellent choice because he was respected by the Jewish leadership in Jerusalem, and he also was a Roman citizen. His Roman citizenship would have permitted him to travel freely throughout the world, and his respect in Jerusalem would strengthen their relationship with the mother church. Also, Timothy (a half-Jew), joins the missionary team at this point (16:1-3).

C. The Macedonian Call

Not only does Paul's Macedonian vision demonstrate his spiritual sensitivity, but it had profound effects upon the western world and culture.[113] Instead of the gospel going east into Asia, the gospel goes west into Europe. Also Acts 16:10 marks the beginning of the "we" sections indicating Luke has joined the missionary team at this point.

---

[111] Bruce, *Acts,* 282-96.
[112] Carter and Earle, *Acts,* 223-24.
[113] Bruce, *Acts,* 306-07.

D. The Conversion of Lydia

The rest of the 16th chapter contains several *power encounters*.[114] The first concerns the conversion of Lydia at Philippi. Lydia was a business woman from Thyatira (16:14). She sold a purple dye extracted from a mollusk. It was extremely expensive and could only be worn by the nobility. So, Lydia was an influential business woman who was in contact with powerful people. Her conversion represents the first European Gentile convert.

The second major power encounter concerns the exorcism of the *Pythoness* (16:16-24). The Greek text states that a slave girl was possessed of the "spirit of Pytho," considered to be the mouthpiece of the god Apollo. Through the power of the Holy Spirit, Paul casts out this spirit of divination which ends her career as a fortune teller. Again, the power of the gospel is stronger than the evil forces of the Mediterranean.

The third major power encounter focuses on the supernatural deliverance of Paul and Silas from prison and the conversion of the Philippian jailer (Acts 16:13-34). The power of God vindicates his servants and brings a jailor to salvation.

E. The Bereans

In marked contrast to the obstinate resistance of the Jews, the Bereans seriously considered the message of Paul and Silas (17:5-11).[115] The Bereans were more noble than the Thessalonians (17:5-9), and searched the scriptures to see if what Paul said was true (17:11).

F. Paul in Athens

Athens was the center of Greco-Roman intellect and philosophy.[116] While in Athens, Paul confronted two schools of philosophy, the *Stoics* and the *Epicureans*.

Zeno, of the 4th century BC, often taught in a portico supported by columns or *stoa*, hence the name "Stoics." He taught that one should live consistently with nature and cultivate a spirit of self-sufficiency. Even today the word 'stoic" refers to an unemotional, detached approach to life.

Epicures, also of the 4th century BC, taught that pleasure or freedom from pain was the chief aim in life. The Epicureans believed that one should eat, drink, and be merry, for tomorrow one might die.

Acts 17:22-34 indicates that both the Stoics and the Epicureans believed Paul was preaching "strange gods"; perhaps one called "Jesus' and the other called "the Resurrection."

G. Paul in Corinth

Aquila and Priscilla join Paul here and he takes a Nazarite vow (18:1-3; cf. also Numbers 6:1-21).[117] This vow was often taken prior to a long and hazardous trip. The hair was completely cut

---

[114] Arrington, *Acts,* 169-70.

[115] Carter and Earle, *Acts,* 250-51.

[116] Bruce, *Acts,* 330-44.

off and would not be cut again until the journey was completed. The hair would then be offered unto God in the temple (Acts 18:18). In Acts, Luke presents Paul as a good law-abiding Jew, but in Galatians and Philippians, Paul emphasizes his freedom from the law and Jewish ceremony (Galatians 3:1-14; Philippians 3:1-10).

H. Paul Visits Ephesus

At this time, Paul stayed only a short while in Ephesus and then sailed directly on to Jerusalem, landing in Caesarea (18:21-23). This was the last leg of Paul's second missionary journey, covering some 1,500 miles, and reveals how brief Luke can be.

---

[117] Arrington, *Acts,* 182 ff.

III. PAUL'S THIRD MISSIONARY JOURNEY

A. Paul Revisits the Churches[118]

As part of Paul's missionary strategy, he sought to remain in contact with the churches either through personal visits or letters.

B. Return to Ephesus[119]

This visit lasted over two years and Paul had a tremendous influence on Ephesus. First, he brought the full gospel to some disciples who had only received John's baptism (19:1-7). Secondly, the influence of witchcraft was severely curtailed in Ephesus (19:18-19). Ephesus was a center for the magical arts and known for its temple to Diana, (considered to be one of the seven wonders of the ancient world). Diana was the goddess of the hunt and love. An astronomical quirk of nature reinforced the Diana cult in Ephesus. A meteor landed in the vicinity of Ephesus, and many of the Ephesians assumed that the chief of all gods, Zeus, had sent them an image of Diana (19:35). The silversmith's guild produced small replicas of Diana.

Paul's ministry in Ephesus completely undermined two basic industries: witchcraft and the worship of Diana. As a result, the Ephesians rioted. Somewhat humorously, Luke notes that many did not know why they were rioting (19:32). The political and civil leaders of Asia, being the friends of Paul, sought to protect Paul from their own people (note the apologetic theme).

C. Farewell to the Ephesians

Acts 20:16-17 indicates that Paul summoned the Ephesian elders to Myletus in order to save time.[120] But the sending of messengers and additional travel would not have saved time. Perhaps because of the turmoil in Ephesus, Paul did not want to risk imprisonment and thus would "save time" by not being thrown in jail.

His farewell speech marks the end of his ministry in the East (20:25, 38; Romans 15:24).

D. Paul is Warned

Upon arriving in Tyre, the Spirit speaks and warns Paul not to go to Jerusalem.[121] Yet the Lord *had already* informed him that difficulties and imprisonment await him in every city (20:23-24). So the warning in Tyre was not the first time the Spirit spoke to him about future sufferings.

---

[118] Carter and Earle, *Acts,* 275.
[119] Bruce, *Acts,* 362 ff.
[120] Ibid., 369.
[121] Arrington, *Acts,* 211.

Yet Paul feels he must go up to Jerusalem despite the warning of hardship and imprisonment. In Caesarea, Agabus prophesies in Old Testament fashion (recall 11:27), binding his own hands and feet with Paul's belt (21:11).

E. Arrival in Jerusalem[122]

James, the half-brother of the Lord, warns Paul that false rumors have been circulating throughout Jerusalem, namely that he is requiring Jews to forsake the law and abandon all Jewish customs. In order to relieve the concerns of the ultra-orthodox Jewish Christians, James advises Paul to take a Nazarite vow (Numbers 6:1-20) and to pay the expenses for four others.[123] For the sake of unity, Paul agrees.

Yet unbelieving Jews from Asia claim that Paul has taken a Gentile into the temple, an act punishable by death (21:28). The ensuing riot leads to Paul's arrest (21:33) and Paul is never free again for the rest of Acts. He was transported to Caesarea and ultimately to Rome, being imprisoned for two years in each place.

Match the appropriate missionary journey of Paul with the events listed below:

1—Paul's first missionary journey
2—Paul's second missionary journey
3—Paul's third missionary journey

A. _____ The first general council of the church.

B. _____ Paul confronts Elymas the sorcerer.

C. _____ The gospel undermines idolatry and witchcraft in Ephesus.

D. _____ John Mark abandons Paul and Barnabas in Patmos.

E. _____ Paul preaches to the Epicureans and Stoics in Athens.

F. _____ Paul is arrested in Jerusalem and transferred to Caesarea.

G. _____ Paul is stoned at Lystra.

---

[122] E. Earle Ellis, *Pauline Theology: Ministry and Society,* (Grand Rapids: Eerdmans 1989) 87 ff.
[123] Bruce, *Acts,* 406-07.

LESSON 9—IMPORTANT SERMONS AND SPEECHES

Part 1	Peter's Sermon at Pentecost
Part 2	Stephen's Sermon
Part 3	Peter's Sermon to Cornelius
Part 4	The Sermons of Paul

OVERVIEW

Apart from the Gospels, Acts alone records the *kerygmatic* presentations (sermons and speeches) and theology of early Christian leaders such as Peter, Stephen and Paul. Peter preaches about the historical Jesus (2:22-24), Stephen reviews the entire *Heilsgeschichte* (or 'salvation history") of God (7:1-53) and Paul stresses grace and justification by faith (13:39). Additionally, these sermons reveal the different methods employed in proclaiming the gospel [compare Paul's words in the synagogue (13:16-20) with his sermon at Mars Hill (17:16-34)]. But the impact the sermons had on the establishment and development of the church is the most important factor here. Through Peter's preaching thousands were converted at Pentecost (2:41) and Gentiles were officially welcomed into the church (10:1-48). Stephen provided a valuable critique of Judaism and thus helped formulate the distinct identity of the church (7:51-53). The internationalization of the church was largely the result of Paul's preaching (14:1-28, 16:1-20:38).

OBJECTIVES

- Briefly describe the content of Peter's sermon at Pentecost.
- State the theological significance of Stephen's sermon.
- State the theological significance of Peter's sermon to Cornelius.
- State the major theological points contained in each of Paul's sermons.

PART 1—PETER'S SERMON AT PENTECOST

The major parts of Peter's sermon are:

I. AN EXPLANATION OF PENTECOST (2:14-21)

Peter quotes Joel 2:28-32. when explaining the outpouring of the Holy Spirit with the evidence of speaking in tongues.[124] He views Pentecost as an eschatological fulfillment of prophecy marking the last days of this world. The old age is passing away and the new age is pouring into the present experience of the church.

II. THE KERYGMA (2:22-36)

This is the first example of the *kerygma*, or "early Christian preaching." This first presentation of the gospel contains four major points:

A. The age of fulfillment has arrived (2:14-21)

God's plan has reached a pivotal point. The time has come for everyone to act decisively with regard to the claims of the Lord.

B. Jesus Affirmed by God (2:22-24)

The miracle-working power of Christ combined with the atoning benefits of his death demonstrate his special place in God's plan.

C. Affirmed by Scripture (2:25-36)

The Old Testament citations show that all of the messianic prophesies have been fulfilled in the person and work of Jesus Christ.

D. Repent, Believe and Receive (2:37-39)

In that the kingdom has reached a crisis, and all messianic prophecies have been fulfilled in Jesus, there is only one alternative left: repent, believe on Jesus and receive the Holy Spirit (cf. also 3:12-36). However, one should recall that this *kerygmatic* preaching formed the synoptic framework for the first three Gospels.

---

[124] Arrington, *Acts,* 25 ff.

PART 2—STEPHEN'S SERMON

Stephen was one of the seven Hellenistic Jews appointed to care for the Greek-speaking Jewish Christians (6:1-7).[125] He was the spiritual leader of the Hellenistic Jewish Christian sector of the church. Although he only appears in Acts 6 and 7, he has an extraordinary impact on the early church, including the Apostle Paul. He delivers the lengthiest sermon in Acts, starting with Abraham and continuing through the crucifixion of Christ (7:1-53). Stephen makes two major points:

I. GLORY FOLLOWS PRESENCE

Stephen argues that God has never been restricted to one land, people, or material building.[126] During the Exodus, the tabernacle followed the presence of God and not the other way around. God's presence is not restricted to the Temple in Jerusalem. He compares the excessive veneration of the Temple to the worship of the golden calf (Exodus 32:1 ff). This implies that the desire to restrict God's presence to a material building is idolatry.

II. TRUE PROPHETS ARE PERSECUTED

The Jewish people have always persecuted the true prophets of God, so it is only fitting that they would also reject their own Messiah.[127] The very suffering of the Lord is a sign that he was divinely appointed of God.

Stephen points out the spiritual truths concerning God's presence and the nature of true worship. He represents the transition from a purely Jewish Christian church to a multi-national, multi-racial church.

---

[125] Bruce, *Acts,* 129-60.
[126] Carter and Earle, *Acts,* 103.
[127] Ibid., 104.

PART 3—PETER'S SERMON TO CORNELIUS (10:34-43)

Although Stephen and the Hellenists were making inroads into non-Jewish evangelization, this is Luke's "official" introduction to Gentile missions.[128] Just prior to this sermon in Acts 10, Peter receives an extraordinary vision (10:9-16). A large sheet or tarp was lowered on three separate occasions from heaven. It was full of a mixture of animals which were ceremonially clean and unclean. Peter is commanded of the Lord to kill and eat, but on each occasion, he refuses to do so. His refusal is based upon ceremonial purity regulations (10:9-14). However, rather than be commended of the Lord for his religious scruples, the Lord rebukes Peter and informs him that he should not call anything that God has created unclean (10:15). In time, Peter realizes that the vision is speaking of the mixture of Jews and Gentiles in the church. God is helping Peter to understand that all people are created equal, and that there should be no racial division in the body of Christ. As part of this extraordinary revelation, Peter is sent to the house of Cornelius and given an opportunity to preach the gospel. Cornelius was "a God-fearer." This means that he was a Gentile who feared and reverenced the God of the Jews. Nevertheless, he did not fully obey the law of Moses with regard to purity regulations, and he refused to submit to circumcision. In other words, he was not a Jewish proselyte. Peter's sermon to Cornelius consists of two major points. They are as follows:

A. The salvation of God is not confined to any one race (10:34).

B. The conversion of Cornelius and all of his household was the official opening of the door of the church to the Gentiles (10:46-48, 11:1-18, 15:6-11).

---

[128] Arrington, *Acts,* 110-14.

PART 4—THE SERMONS OF PAUL

I. PREACHING TO THE JEWS

Paul's first sermon in Acts is addressed to a Jewish audience. In Antioch of Syria, Paul preaches to the Jews (13:16-39). This particular sermon follows the general form of the *kerygma* which has been previously discussed on several occasions. However, Paul's special emphasis on justification by faith and not on works of the Law can be clearly seen in his words here.

II. PREACHING TO THE GENTILES

Paul's second major sermon, and perhaps one of the most interesting sermons in Acts, is to the Athenians on Mars Hill (17:22-34).[129] It is fascinating to see how Paul adapts the manner in which he presents the gospel to his audience. The content of the message is the same, but the mode of delivery is different. Since the pagan Greeks and philosophers would have known little or nothing about the experience of the Jews and the revelation of God in the Old Testament, Paul is not able to work from the scriptures in convincing them of the lordship of Jesus Christ. Rather, he employs a totally different approach. The four major divisions of his sermon in Athens are as follows:

A. God is pre-eminent and universal

Paul begins by presenting philosophical concepts about God (17:17-27). "God" communicates the "ultimate," or "the one and only." Logically there can be only one God who is preeminent over all. In this way, Paul attacks *polytheism* (a belief in many gods). Secondly, he appeals to the universal consciousness of God (17:27-28).

B. Accommodation and contextualization

He does not quote the Old Testament since his audience is mostly unfamiliar with it. Instead, Paul speaks of Greek poets. Even Greek poets understand that we are all the children of God (17:28).

C. Idolatry is foolish

If God cannot be confined to any one place and we are his special creations, how foolish it is to worship the creation of our own hands (17:29).

D. Special Revelation

Paul begins to speak of the final judgment, individual repentance, and the resurrection of the dead (17:30-31). The resurrection was particularly difficult for the Greek mind to accept. Many Greeks viewed salvation as a deliverance from the material body. To claim that the body would also be redeemed was offensive to Gentile thinking.

---

[129] Bruce, *Acts,* 332 ff.

Overall, Paul's appeal to the Athenians was rejected. Yet he did convert some influential persons to the faith (17:34).

There are only two other instances where Paul is represented as preaching the *kerygma* in Acts. Paul preaches the gospel to Festus (26:19-23), and is briefly noted as preaching the *kerygma* upon his arrival in Rome (28:23-24).

Match the speaker with the sermon he preached.

1—Peter
2—Stephen
3—Paul

a. _____ He gave a thorough-going critique of the temple and the Law in this sermon.

b. _____ He preached to Cornelius, who was a "God-fearer."

c. _____ He preached on Mars Hill and based his sermon on logic and the revelation of God in nature.

d. _____ In his sermon he compared the temple to the golden calf mentioned in Exodus.

e. _____ He was the first Christian preacher to set forth the *kerygma* that provided the literary structure for the Synoptic Gospels.

f. _____ He argued that, since the tabernacle in the Old Testament followed the presence of God, then God could not logically be restricted to the Temple in Jerusalem.

g. _____ The message of this sermon was greatly influenced by the vision of the clean and unclean beasts lowered in a sheet.

SELF TEST:

1. Luke and Acts:
      a. are addressed to the same person
      b. have similar writing styles and vocabulary
      c. both emphasize history
      d. all of these
      e. none of these

2. The Book of Acts is important because it:
      a. serves as the link between the Gospels and the epistles
      b. gives us insight into early Christian worship
      c. emphasizes apocalyptic
      d. A & B
      e. B & C

3. In Acts:
      a. the Romans are officially persecuting the church
      b. the *church growth motif* is important
      c. Paul is the 'super apostle"
      d. A & B
      e. B & C

4. Luke:
      a. expresses the key to Acts in 1:8
      b. uses apologetics to defend Christianity
      c. understands that Christianity is a sect of Judaism
      d. A & B
      e. B & C

5. It was noted that:
      a. Pentecost was celebrated 50 days after Passover
      b. Paul was the first Christian to be martyred
      c. the meeting in Acts 15 was called the "General Assembly"
      d. all of these
      e. none of these

6. Which came first?
      a. the conversion of Paul
      b. the conversion of Cornelius
      c. the outpouring of the Holy Spirit

1—Paul's first missionary journey

2—Paul's second missionary journey

3—Paul's third missionary journey

a. _____   The first general council of the church

b. _____   The gospel undermines magic in Ephesus

c. _____   Paul preaches to the Epicureans and Stoics in Athens.

d. _____   Paul is arrested in Jerusalem and sent to Caesarea.

e. _____   Paul is stoned at Lystra.

----

1. T or F   Stephen was the first *apostle* to be martyred.

2. T or F   Luke was a traveling companion of Paul from the time of Paul's conversion.

3. T or F   The "Macedonian Vision" was instrumental in the gospel moving westward.

4. T or F   The leader of the Jerusalem Council was Peter.

5. T or F   Paul cast out a 'spirit of Pytho" at Philippi.

SECTION 4:

THE EPISTLES OF THE APOSTLE PAUL

Lesson 10	Introductory Material
Lesson 11	Romans
Lesson 12	1 Corinthians
Lesson 13	2 Corinthians
Lesson 14	Galatians
Lesson 15	Ephesians
Lesson 16	Philippians
Lesson 17	Colossians
Lesson 18	1 Thessalonians
Lesson 19	2 Thessalonians
Lesson 20	1 Timothy and Titus
Lesson 21	2 Timothy
Lesson 22	Philemon

OVERVIEW

We are now leaving the period of the oral presentation of the gospel and a history of the beginnings of the church and are entering into the period of the established churches. In this section, we will concentrate on the letters that Paul sent to the churches throughout the Roman Empire.

The 13 epistles of Paul form nearly half of the New Testament canon. Even more remarkable, some of Paul's epistles have been lost (cf. 1 Corinthians 7:1; 2 Corinthians 7:12; Colossians 4:16). Apart from the person and work of Jesus, Paul and his letters have done more to establish Christian thought and practice than any other Christian figure.

Before one can fully understand Paul's writings, one must come to understand something about the man behind the letters. What follows will be a brief overview of his personality, spirit, and vision.

BLANK PAGE

LESSON 10—INTRODUCTORY MATERIAL

Part 1	A Brief Biography of the Apostle Paul
Part 2	Personal Characteristics of the Apostle Paul
Part 3	The General Form of Paul's Epistles
Part 4	Additional Characteristics

OVERVIEW

Paul's life as an orthodox Jew affected his understanding of God and how he communicated that understanding. Even the place of his birth, Tarsus, exposed Paul to thoughts and philosophies which he would not have experienced in Jerusalem. Finally, Paul's violent reaction to the early church made an indelible impression upon him.

The different contexts that Paul found himself in also affected his writing. For example, the model church at Philippi permitted him to write in a very joyous and positive manner. But the severe threat to the gospel in Galatians led Paul to write in a militant way. The confusion in Corinth required Paul to write with clarity about the doctrines of the faith.

Thus a brief biography of Paul, a study of his personality, and the form of his letters will follow.

OBJECTIVES

- Present a brief biography of Paul.
- List six characteristics of the Apostle Paul.
- Outline the general form of Paul's letters.

HELPS FOR LEARNING AND REMEBERING

1. Be fully aware that you are entering a completely new phase in the study of the New Testament. Also, the distinct flavor of each of Paul's epistles should be firmly established.

2. Fully focus on each and every individual epistle, establishing "mental boundaries" which distinguish one from the other.

3. A good evangelical commentary on each epistle may serve as a reference.

KEY WORDS

Amanuensis   encyclical   benediction

PART 1—A BRIEF BIOGRAPHY OF THE APOSTLE PAUL

The major events of the Apostle Paul's life and ministry are:

I. BIRTHPLACE

Paul was born in Tarsus (Acts 9:11, 21:39, 22:3) being one of the most important cities in Asia Minor.[130] Tarsus was an educational center during the first century. So, Paul grew up in a very cosmopolitan, Hellenistic environment. He would have been familiar with Greco-Roman education, philosophy and literature. This great wealth of experience and knowledge helped Paul in communicating the gospel cross culturally.

II. TRAINED AS A PHARISEE

Paul was a Pharisee and a son of a Pharisee (Acts 23:6), this being the strictest sect of the Jews. Acts 22:3 indicates that Paul studied at the feet of Gamaliel in Jerusalem. Philippians 3:5 states that Paul knew he was from the tribe of Benjamin. Although Paul was born and raised in Tarsus, he was a Jew, embracing the most conservative form of Judaism of his day.[131]

III. ROMAN CITIZENSHIP

Paul was a Roman citizen *by birth* (Acts 22:28). Roman citizenship was often bestowed upon a family for some great deed done for the Empire.[132] In that Paul's parents were Hebrew, and he did not purchase his Roman citizenship, then someone in Paul's family must have done some great deed for Rome. Roman citizenship granted freedom of movement and a right to trial before a Roman court.[133]

IV. PERSECUTOR OF THE CHURCH

Paul violently persecuted the early church. Yet while going to Damascus, Paul was confronted by the risen Lord (Acts 9:1-20). This supernatural revelation of Jesus profoundly changed Paul and is recorded twice more in Acts (22:1-16, 26:1-20).

The dramatic conversion of Paul underscores the *special grace* he received, which served as the basis for his apostolic authority and mission to the Gentiles.[134]

V. COMMISSIONED DIRECTLY BY THE LORD

At the time of his conversion, Paul did not consult with any of the apostles. Rather, he went into "Arabia" for a period of three years (Galatians 1:17,18). Paul, therefore, is not a product of the Jerusalem apostles.[135] He received his calling, gospel, and divine commission directly from the Lord.

---

[130] Harris, *New Testament*, 200-201.
[131] Ibid., 200.
[132] Marshall, *Acts*, 274-75.
[133] Haenchen, *Acts*, 500.
[134] Tenney, *New Testament*, 248-50.
[135] Cole, *Galatians*, 52-53.

VI. APOSTLE TO THE GENTILES

Soon after his conversion, Paul joined the church in Antioch, thus identifying with Hellenistic Christianity (Acts 13:1,2). While in Antioch, Paul received his call to the Gentiles.

VII. IMPRISONED AND SENT TO ROME

Paul's arrest in Jerusalem, transport to Caesarea and then to Rome has already been covered. These events demonstrate how Paul used his Roman citizenship and how the Roman judicial system actually protected the apostle from the Jews.

VIII. SUMMARY

From this brief biography we can draw the following conclusions. Paul was thoroughly familiar with both the Gentile and Jewish worlds of the first century. His Roman citizenship gave him freedom of travel and the right to trial. His radical independence from the Jerusalem apostles granted a unique authority to his calling and mission. Paul used all of these factors for the spread of the gospel and the formulation of the faith.

PART 2—PERSONAL CHARACTERISTICS OF PAUL

In order to understand Paul's theology and mission, one must come to know the man behind the letters. The following are six major characteristics of the Apostle Paul:[136]

I. STRONG SENSE OF CALLING

The Damascus Road experience is continually reflected throughout all of his epistles (cf. Romans 1:1-6). He maintains that he has been called by God and that his message was received by direct revelation (Galatians 1:12).

II. STRONG SENSE OF AUTHORITY

Paul argued that since God had called him, he had the authority to actualize that calling in the church and the world. Paul sets forth his authority even in churches he did not start or visit, and Paul viewed his apostolic authority as universally binding (Romans 1:1 ff., Colossians 1:1). When the Corinthians and Galatians rejected his authority, Paul strongly reaffirms his place in the body of Christ.

III. STRONG LOVE FOR HIS CONVERTS

Paul's apostolic authority is only matched by his compassion (Philippians 1:3-8). He even expresses an extraordinary love and care for the Corinthians (1 Cor. 13, 2 Cor. 7:7).

IV. STRONG CONVICTIONS

Paul possessed clarity of mind which did not yield to peer pressure or popular opinion. He strongly opposed the notion that Gentiles must be circumcised and obey the law of Moses in order to be saved. Yet he had Timothy circumcised so that he might minister to the Jews (Acts 16:1-3). When the Judaizers insisted that Titus must be circumcised to be saved, Paul refused (Galatians 2:3,4). When Peter's hypocrisy indicated that the Gentiles were not full members in the church, Paul confronted him to his face (Galatians 2:15). Whether the issue was marriage (1 Cor. 9), the Lord's Supper (1 Cor. 11), or the resurrection (1 Cor. 15), Paul consistently expresses his convictions by demonstrating the spiritual principles upon which they are based.

V. PHYSICAL ENDURANCE

When one considers the tremendous accomplishments of the Apostle Paul in the light of the hardship he suffered, he must have been in excellent physical condition (2 Cor. 11:23-28).

VI. EXTRAORDINARY SPIRITUAL EXPERIENCES

Paul was a man of extraordinary spiritual experiences (2 Cor. 12:1-5). Acts reveals that Paul had visions, performed exorcisms and healings. Yet Paul never pointed to these experiences as a matter of personal pride, but as means for furthering the gospel.

---

[136] Guthrie, *New Testament*, 386-91.

In conclusion, we see that Paul's calling and authority are interrelated. He was directly called by God and hence his authority transcends all human institutions and offices. Nevertheless, he had a strong love for his converts. His love for God and the church instilled in him a strong sense of convictions. His physical constitution was well suited to the task of preaching the gospel in the first century world. Finally, although he had tremendous spiritual experiences, they never served as a source of pride or boasting.

PART 3—THE GENERAL FORM OF PAUL'S EPISTLES

Paul wrote letters or epistles to remain in contact with the churches. The following presents the general form of his epistles:[137]

I. INTRODUCTION

Paul followed the Greco-Roman form of letter writing. That is, he identifies himself, goes on to identify the addresses and then extends grace and peace to the recipients (cf. Romans 1:1-7).

II. THE BODY OF THE EPISTLES

This comprises the text of Paul's epistles. The body is divided into two major parts:

A. Doctrinal matters

The first half of Paul's epistles is generally concerned with doctrinal and theological matters (Romans 1-11).

B. Practical or ethical exhortations

The second half of Paul's epistles is concerned with the practical application of Christian doctrine and theology. In this section, believers are told how to actualize their faith in Christ (Romans 12-15).

III. THE CLOSING OF THE EPISTLE

Paul usually closes each epistle with a spiritual benediction or words of blessing (Romans 16:25-27).

---

[137] Ibid., 390.

PART 4—ADDITIONAL CHARACTERISTICS

I. USE OF AN *AMANUENSIS*

Paul uses an amanuensis or a male scribe (cf. Romans 6:22) and signed the epistle to demonstrate its authenticity (2 Thessalonians 3:17, Galatians 6:11).[138]

II. DUPLICATE COPIES

Several of his letters contain similar sections, and it is possible Paul may have kept copies and used them on later occasions (compare 1 Cor. 12 with Romans 12:4-9).

III. USE OF THE SEPTUAGINT

Although Paul was a Hebrew, and was fluent in the Hebrew language, he preferred to quote from the Septuagint.[139] You will recall that the Septuagint, or the *LXX*, is the Greek translation of the Hebrew Old Testament. He probably chose to quote from the Greek translation because he was writing to predominantly Gentile churches, as they may have had some familiarity with the Greek Old Testament.

Once again, it should be noted that Paul wrote all of his letters in the Greek language. Since Greek was the *lingua franca* this would have insured a wide circulation.

IV. PARAPHRASES

Paul rarely gives a verbatim quotation, often choosing to paraphrase the Old Testament. Perhaps he is quoting from memory, not having a prepared text before him at the time of writing.

V. ENCYCLICALS

Some of Paul's epistles are encyclicals. That is, Paul intended these letters to be circulated among various churches. Galatians 1:2 indicates that this epistle was written to the *churches* (plural) of Galatia. Also, Colossians 4:16 states that the Colossians are to share their epistle with the Laodicians, and the Laodicians are to share their epistle with them.

Give a brief biography of the Apostle Paul, listing the major events and influences in his life:

---

[138] Leon Morris, *The Epistle to the Romans*, (Grand Rapids: Eerdmans, 1988) 543.
[139] Tenney, *New Testament*, 113.

SELF TEST:

1. The Apostle Paul was:
   a. a Sadducee
   b. born and raised in Jerusalem
   c. a Roman citizen
   d. all of these
   e. none of these

2. Paul:
   a. was taught the gospel by Peter, James, and John
   b. wrote every word of each of his epistles
   c. used an amanuensis in writing his epistles
   d. all of these
   e. none of these

3. Paul:
   a. wrote doctrinal matters first and practical matters second in his letters
   b. quoted from the Hebrew Massoretic text and not from the Greek Septuagint
   c. often paraphrases Old Testament quotes
   d. A & C
   e. B & C

4. Paul:
   a. occasionally wrote 1 letter to be read by several churches
   b. reused portions of 1 epistle to write another epistle
   c. ends his epistles with a benediction
   d. all of these
   e. none of these

LESSON 11—ROMANS

Part 1	Background Information
Part 2	Origin of the Church in Rome
Part 3	Expanded Outline
Part 4	Racial Composition

OVERVIEW

The epistle to the Romans is one of the most important books of the New Testament Apart from the Gospels, this single book has done more to shape Christianity than any other book of the New Testament [140] With regard to Christianity, Romans contains all of the major doctrines of the Christian faith. Indeed, Romans has been described as a compendium, or a collection, of the major doctrines of faith. These central tenets of the faith are set forth in a very orderly form by Paul in Romans. Although Romans may not constitute a 'systematic theology" of Christian doctrines, it certainly presents the most important truths of the church in an orderly fashion.

In Romans, Paul addresses the central question of how one must be saved. He goes on to discuss the very important principle of sanctification. The Spirit-filled life occupies a large portion of this epistle. One of the most difficult problems, the present status and destiny of Israel (ch. 9-11), is addressed in Romans as well. Paul ends his great epistle with practical exhortations on how to live the Christian life.

Not only has Romans been influential in shaping the contours of Christianity, it has been most influential in shaping the thought and theology of major Christian theologians.[141] For example, the great 4th century church father and theologian Augustine, was brought to faith through a reading of Romans. Augustine is considered by many church historians as being the very first Christian systematic theologian. No doubt the epistle to the Romans played a major role in his organization and systemizing of Christian doctrine. The Protestant Reformation itself in some degree can be attributed to the epistle to the Romans. Martin Luther, the great reformer, realized the significance of being justified by faith alone, apart from works of the law, by his study of Romans. John Bunyan, the author of *Pilgrim's Progress*, notes that he was inspired by Romans to write this great work. John Wesley, the one who started the great holiness revival in England, which ultimately led to the founding of the Methodist church, felt his heart 'strangely warmed" when he simply read Luther's preface to Romans.

These factors demonstrate that Romans occupies an important place, not only in the New Testament, but also in the history of the church and the development of western civilization.

OBJECTIVES

- Give the background information for Romans.
- Discuss the possible origin of the church at Rome.
- Sketch a brief outline of Romans.

---

[140] Morris, *Romans*, 1.
[141] Anders Nygren, *Commentary on Romans*, (Philadelphia: Fortress, 1949), 3.

- Discuss the racial composition of the Roman church.
- Summarize the conclusions drawn from your study of Romans.

HELPS FOR LEARNING AND REMEMBERING

1. Be aware of the specific purpose or occasion of Romans.

2. Jot down the various doctrines presented in Romans.

3. Note the structure and progression of Paul's argument.

4. Purchase a good evangelical commentary on Romans.

KEY WORDS

Adam/Christ parallel	special revelation	*hagioi*
General revelation	Judaizing	polemical

PART 1—BACKGROUND INFORMATION

I. AUTHORSHIP

A. Internal Evidence

The very first verse identifies Paul as the author. What we read in Romans is in harmony with the Acts account (compare Romans 15:19, 24-28, 32; Acts 19:21, 20:16; 1 Cor. 16:1).

In many ways, Romans is perhaps the "most Pauline" of Paul's epistles.[142] The vocabulary and writing style are thoroughly Pauline. Central Pauline doctrines, such as justification by faith, sanctification in the Spirit and the church as the body of Christ, are present throughout Romans. All of this supports the traditional view that Paul is in fact the author of the Romans.

B. External evidence

The early church fathers unanimously support Pauline authorship. Clement of Rome (AD 90-100) quotes from Romans as if it is Pauline. Irenaeus and Tertullian clearly state that Paul is the author.

In conclusion, both the internal evidence and external evidence clearly support Pauline authorship.

II. DATE

From Romans, we gather that Paul has completed his work in Asia, plans to bring the collection to the poor saints in Jerusalem, and continue on to Rome.[143] This means that the epistle must have been written on Paul's third missionary journey, just prior to his trip to Jerusalem. Since we know Paul was imprisoned in Rome in about AD 60 and had spent two years previous to this time in jail in Caesarea, Paul must have penned Romans sometime late in the year of AD 56 or early 57.

III. PURPOSE FOR WRITING

Paul's reason for writing Romans has been the subject of much debate. It is clear from the scriptures that Paul sincerely desired to go to Rome and then onward to Spain. Yet since he did not found the church in Rome, nor had he ever visited that church, why would he write to the Romans about his future plans? There are three general theories concerning why Paul wrote to the Romans.[144]

---

[142] Charles Hodge, *Commentary on the Epistle to the Romans*, (Grand Rapids: Eerdmans, reprint 1964) 9.

[143] C.G. Moule, *The Epistle of St. Paul to the Romans*, (London: Hodden and Stroughton, 1896) 1.

[144] Morris, *Romans*, 7.

A. Establish a Center for Evangelism

Paul's field of evangelism was extending further westward. As noted above, he desired to preach the gospel in Spain. Therefore, he needed a new center or home base for his ministry. Antioch of Syria was located too far to the east for evangelism in Spain. Paul desired to establish a relationship with the church in Rome so that the church might sponsor him on his journey westward. If the Roman church was to serve as his base camp for launching out westward, they needed to know what Paul believed and what he taught (Romans 15:24). This theory proposes that Paul penned the epistle to the Romans to establish a relationship with that church, inform them of his gospel, and seek their support for his continued missionary enterprises westward.

B. Confront Error

Paul was perhaps writing *polemically* to undermine the Judaizers *before* they arrive in Rome. You will recall that the word "polemical" relates to an aggressive attack against heresies which threaten the church. The Judaizing heresy sought to force the Gentiles to be circumcised and obey the law of Moses. This theory suggests that Paul is writing to undermine the influence of the Judaizers in Rome before they destroyed the church there. This would explain why Paul speaks of the importance of living by faith and not by works, the relationship between Jews and Gentiles and the present status and destiny of Israel (cf. Romans 9-11).

C. Pastoral

A third theory suggests that Romans is actually a pastoral letter. That is, Paul is writing as a pastor to meet the personal needs of the Christians in Rome. In fact, Paul seems to have quite a bit of knowledge about the difficulties in the church at Rome, although he had never visited them personally. For example, he writes about the weak and the strong in Romans 14 and 15. He writes about the controversy over eating meats dedicated to idols. He also clarifies the relationship of the Christian to the civil government in Romans 13. This theory states that Paul was motivated by pastoral concerns to pen the epistle to the Romans.

It may be that Paul had no one single purpose in writing his epistle to the Romans. The reason for Paul writing his epistle to the Romans might be all of the above. Nevertheless, if one had to choose a single theory, the first option seems to fit the overall context. Indeed, Paul had finished evangelizing in the east and was seeking to evangelize further westward into Spain. He naturally would have needed a new missionary headquarters located further to the west. What better church to serve this purpose than the church in Rome?

PART 2 -THE ORIGIN OF THE CHURCH IN ROME

As previously noted, Paul did not start the church in Rome nor had he yet visited the church there. Yet it is clear from Romans 1:8 that the church in Rome was started at a very early date and had grown to considerable size and notoriety. In fact, Paul said that their faith was spoken of throughout the world. The question remains as to just how such a thriving vibrant church got started in the capital city of the empire. There are 3 major theories concerning the origin of the church in Rome.[145]

I. ROMAN CATHOLIC TRADITION

Roman Catholic tradition states that the Apostle Peter moved to Rome and started the church there. He then became the first bishop of Rome and hence the first Pope. However, the New Testament shows that Peter was the apostle to the Jews and ministered primarily in and around Jerusalem. It will be shown that the predominant people group in the Roman church was Gentile, not Jewish. Finally, it would be strange for Paul to write a letter to the Romans and not mention the Apostle Peter. In summation, the theory that Peter started the church in Rome has no biblical nor historical base.

II. PILGRIMS RETURNING FROM JERUSALEM

Acts 2:10 records that among the many pilgrims who were visiting Jerusalem on the day of Pentecost, there were Roman Jews and proselytes. If some of these were among the 3,000 saved on the day of Pentecost, they may have been the founders of the church in Rome. After receiving Christ in Jerusalem, they would then return back to Rome and start house churches there (cf. Acts 2:41). This would explain how the church in Rome got started at a very early date.

III. PAUL's CONVERTS

If the church in Rome had been started by Roman Jews and proselytes who were saved on the Day of Pentecost, how could Paul give so many personal greetings to the Romans in Romans 16? In fact, in this chapter, Paul sends 26 personal greetings to the saints there. How could Paul know so many of the members in the Roman church, if he had yet visited there?

It is possible that some of Paul's own converts started the church in Rome. If believers from Corinth, Ephesus, and Philippi traveled to Rome and started the church there, Paul would have been personally acquainted with such persons. Acts 18:2 states that Acquila and Priscilla were from Rome and no doubt returned to Rome.

In conclusion, the most viable options are the second and third. It is not impossible that Roman Jews and Gentile proselytes were converted at Pentecost. These persons could have returned to Rome and started a church there, but this would not explain the many personal greetings that Paul gives in Romans 16. In the final analysis, the last option seems to be the most probable.

---

[145] John Murray, *The Epistle to the Romans*, (Grand Rapids: Eerdmans, 1965) xvii.

PART 3—AN EXPANDED OUTLINE

The following constitutes an expanded outline of Romans.

I. INTRODUCTION (1:1-17)

Paul identifies himself as the author (1:1), and addresses the recipients of his epistle (1:7). He also states the *general purpose* of the letter [to bless and affirm the *hagioi* (saints) (1:11)]. But the *central theme* of the entire epistle is justification by faith (1:16-17).

II. THE NEED FOR JUSTIFICATION (1:18-3:20)

Paul demonstrates this universal need in two ways:

A. All Gentiles under Sin (1:18-32)

The Gentiles are condemned because they *deliberately* refused to receive the revelation of God in nature (*general revelation*).

B. All Jews under Sin (2:1-3:20)

All Jews are condemned because they failed to live up to the law contained in the written Word (*special revelation*).

The universal problem of sin is stated in 3:23, "All have sinned and fallen short of the glory of God."

III. THE ANSWER TO THE SIN PROBLEM (3:21-4:25)

Paul makes two central points:

A. Justification by Faith (3:21-28)

It follows that if the Gentiles are condemned apart from the law and the Jews are condemned with the law, then justification must have a different basis (faith alone).

B. Abraham and David as Examples (4:1-8, 9-22)

Before the law of Moses and the practice of circumcision, Abraham believed God and it was credited to him for righteousness (4:3). David claims the highest state of blessedness afforded by the law is when God *refuses* to impute sin.

IV. THE RESULT OF JUSTIFICATION BY FAITH (5:1-8:39)

A. Peace with God (5:1, 10-11)

God's wrath against sin fell on Christ, and hence is no longer directed towards those who are justified by faith, reconciled by grace, and received the atonement.

B. Adam/Christ Parallel (5:12-21)

Just as the first man Adam was responsible for the sin problem, so too is the second man Adam responsible for the deliverance from sin.

C. Sanctification through Christ by the Holy Spirit (6:1-8:11)

Paul argues that it is not enough to be justified by faith and saved through grace. Rather, we must actualize or "incarnate" the life of Christ in this world. Justification by faith is inseparable from true sanctification.

D. Joint Heirs with Christ (8:12-30)

Because we have been adopted into the family of God, we are co-heirs with Jesus Christ, and destined to share in his future glorification.

E. Divine Assurance (8:31-39)

The extraordinary grace of God in Christ, and the continual empowering of the Spirit secure our relationship with the Father.

V. GOD's WISDOM AND FREEDOM IN REJECTING ISRAEL (9:1-11:36)

Paul's treatment of the present status and future destiny of Israel can be divided into 3 general categories:

A. Romans 9

Many Jews argued that as the people of God, God *had* to express his grace and mercy to them. Paul maintains that God has the freedom to determine who his chosen people are and who will receive his promises. Paul states that *racial Israel* is not the *spiritual Israel* of God (9:6).

B. Romans 10

Paul teaches that God was not unrighteous in rejecting Israel, because she went about to establish her own righteousness, rather than accepting the righteousness that comes by faith alone (10:2-3).

C. Romans 11

Paul notes that the righteous use of God's liberty resulted in the salvation of the Gentiles. Furthermore, the *true Israel* of God, *the remnant*, will be saved and inherit the promises (11:1-5).

VI. THE ETHICAL INSTRUCTIONS AND EXHORTATIONS (12:1-15:33)

As previously noted, the first half of Paul's letters is devoted to doctrinal issues, while the second half is devoted to ethical exhortations.

A. Romans 12

This is clearly parallel to Paul's teaching on sanctification in Romans 6. By using imagery from the temple, believers are described as living sacrifices, holy unto God.

B. Romans 13

Paul claims that all powers ultimately find their source in God, and that civil government is God's way of establishing order in the world. The Christian is to live by the law of the land.

C. Romans 14:1-15:33

Paul deals with the interrelationship between the strong and the weak. The strong are those who are spiritually mature and have a healthy conscience. The weak are those who have an over-sensitive conscience and are scrupulous about insignificant things. Paul's counsel is that the strong should be sensitive to the weak, and the weak should respect the freedom of the strong.

VII. PERSONAL GREETINGS AND CONCLUSIONS (16:1-27)

Paul states his desire to go to Spain and welcomes their assistance. He greets 26 persons by name, perhaps those previously converted under his ministry. The final two verses contain a beautiful *doxology* or "words of praise" to God.

In summary, the above outline demonstrates that Paul wrote this epistle with 3 basic questions in mind. These questions are:

> 1. How can a sinful person be set right with God?
> 2. What is the significance of Israel's history, her present status, and her future destiny?
> 3. How can one who is justified by faith live out the practical Christian life?

In response to these 3 questions, Paul develops 3 major themes. These three major themes are:

> 1. The just shall live by faith through grace apart from works of the law.

2. Being racially Jewish does not guarantee a place in the covenant. Racial Israel is not the same as the spiritual Israel of God. The true Israel will be saved and God's promise will be kept.

3. Continual consecration as living sacrifices actualizes salvation in the world.

Discuss the internal and external evidence for Pauline authorship of the Book of Romans:

PART 4—RACIAL COMPOSITION OF THE CHURCH AT ROME

An understanding of the racial composition of the church aids in interpretation. For example, why did Paul speak so much about the law and the destiny of Israel? Why is he concerned about the relationship of the weak and the strong? Finally, why does Paul address the Christian's relationship to the state? All of these questions relate in some way to the racial makeup of the Roman church. There are two primary options:[146]

I. PREDOMINANTLY A JEWISH CHURCH

Those who hold that the Roman congregation consisted primarily of Jewish Christian believers make reference to Paul's use of the Old Testament. They argue that Paul's frequent Old Testament citations would have made sense only to those who were thoroughly familiar with God's revelation in the Jewish scriptures. Also, Paul speaks of Abraham as "our father." Of course, we know that Abraham was the father of the Jews. Finally, the long and extensive treatment of the present role and future destiny of Israel in Romans 9-11 indicates that Paul is vitally concerned with Jewish affairs in the church. All of these factors seem to point to a predominantly Jewish congregation at Rome.

II. PREDOMINANTLY A GENTILE CHURCH

Romans 1:13 states that Paul desires to have fruit among the Romans even as among other Gentiles. This statement seems to indicate that the Roman church is mainly a non-Jewish church. And even though Romans 9-11 focuses on Israel, Paul frequently mentions the Gentiles in this context as well. The Gentiles are warned that they should not boast against the Israelites (11:17-25). Finally, in his closing remarks, Paul is proud of his ministry to the Gentiles (15:9-13, 16).

Although the exact racial composition of the church at Rome can never be determined, it can be safely concluded that the Roman congregation was a mixed congregation. In other words, there were both Jews and Gentiles in the church at Rome. All things considered, more than likely the Gentiles were in the majority and the Jewish Christians formed a smaller, yet significant minority.

True/False:

1. T or F   Most modern scholars question Pauline authorship of Romans.
2. T or F   Paul's epistle to the Romans was written on his first missionary journey.
3. T or F   Church history supports the Roman Catholic belief that Peter started the church in Rome.
4. T or F   Paul was the one who founded the church in Rome.
5. T or F   In Romans, Paul argues that the Jews are saved.
6. T or F   In Romans 13, Paul teaches that Christians must not submit to the Roman state.
7. T or F   Romans 16 indicates that although Paul had never visited Rome, he had many personal acquaintances there.
8. T or F   The evidence indicates that the Roman church was primarily a Jewish church.

---

[146] R.C.H. Lenski, *The Interpretation of St. Paul's Epistle to the Romans*, (Minneapolis: Augsburg, 1936) 17.

List the three major theories which seek to explain Paul's purpose for writing Romans:

a. _____

b. _____

c. _____

SELF TEST:

1. With regard to the section in this course guide entitled "Background Information" it was learned that:
     a. most modern scholars question Pauline authorship of Romans
     b. Romans was written near the end of Paul's 3rd missionary journey
     c. Paul founded the church in Rome
     d. all of these
     e. none of these

2. The Book of Romans shows that:
     a. Paul believes that all of racial Israel will be saved
     b. the church in Rome was a predominantly Jewish church
     c. even though Paul had never visited Rome, he had many personal acquaintances there
     d. A & B
     e. B & C

3. Paul's *primary* reason for writing Romans was:
     a. doctrinal (to correct heresy)
     b. pastoral (to solve local problems)
     c. evangelistic (to secure a new missionary headquarters
     d. all of these
     e. none of these

4. It was noted that:
     a. Paul parallels his teaching on sanctification in Romans 12 with his words in chapter 6
     b. Paul parallels the person/work of Adam with the person/work of Christ (ch. 5)
     c. true justification is inseparable from true sanctification
     d. all of these
     e. none of these

5. In Romans, we can see that:
     a. Jews are condemned because they rejected the *general revelation* of God
     b. Gentiles are condemned because they rejected the *special revelation* of God in His Word
     c. Abraham was justified by faith before the coming of law and circumcision
     d. all of these
     e. none of these

BLANK PAGE

LESSON 12—1 CORINTHIANS

Part 1	Background Information
Part 2	The Historical Context
Part 3	Central Problems in the Corinthian Church
Part 4	Expanded Outline

OVERVIEW

1 Corinthians is radically different from Romans. Unlike Rome, Paul founded the church in Corinth, pastured it for 18 months, and established subsequent leadership through Apollos (Acts 18:1-11, 24-28). Also, the Corinthian church was experiencing severe difficulties. The Corinthians formed parties and factions around Paul, Apollos, Cephas, and even Christ (1:10-16). They exalted human wisdom above faith and grace and were thoroughly lacking in love (1:17-2:16, 13:1-13). There was gross sexual immorality and incest among the members of Corinth (5:1-12, 6:12-20). The Corinthians were suing one another (6:1-11) and completely misunderstood the nature of Christian marriage (7:1-39). They were thoroughly insensitive to the feelings of the weak, especially with regard to food sacrificed to idols (8:1-13, 10:1-22). Indeed, some of the Corinthians were presently engaging in idolatrous practices (10:14-22, 27-30). Their worship services were in disorder, especially with reference to the Lord's Supper (11:1-34). They were abusing the gifts of the Spirit (12:1-31, 14:1-40). Finally, some were denying the physical resurrection of the dead (15:1-58).

By grappling with these serious problems, Paul gives us many theological insights and practical directives in living the Christian life. Herein lies the importance of 1 Corinthians: it serves as a manual for basic Christian doctrines and practical Christian living.

OBJECTIVES

- Discuss the background information for 1 Corinthians.
- Explain the significance of the historical context.
- Discuss the major problems of the Corinthian church.
- Outline the major portions of 1 Corinthians.
- Summarize the central message of Paul in 1 Corinthians.

HELPS FOR LEARNING AND REMEMBERING

1. 1 Corinthians is not the most organized of Paul's epistles, so keeping separate note cards, extensive outlining and immediately writing down questions which address the text will help in controlling the material.

2. Paul is very disturbed when writing 1 Corinthians. By understanding the spirit in which Paul wrote, perhaps the content will be more comprehensible.

3. Jot down ways in which Paul's words in 1 Corinthians relate to the contemporary church. Making a contemporary application of the text will aid in understanding and memorization.

4. Develop a series of Bible studies from 1 Corinthians. This will help you to "own" what Paul says in this great epistle.

KEY WORDS

Libertinists	isthmus	Isthmian games
Hagioi	athletic motif	agape feast
Aphrodite	quasi-gnosticism	peloponnesus
Gnostics	Acrocorinth	agora

PART 1—BACKGROUND INFORMATION

The history of Corinth, the philosophical and intellectual environment, the religious milieu, and even its geographic location helped create the problems at Corinth. The following background information is vital to understanding 1 Corinthians.

I. AUTHORSHIP

1 Corinthians is a very "Pauline" epistle. The vocabulary, writing style, and themes are thoroughly Pauline. Our study of the authorship is divided into two divisions. They are:[147]

A. Internal Evidence

Acts tells us that Paul founded the church, pastured for 18 months and corresponded with them throughout their development (Acts 18:1-28). Paul's name is attached as the author (1 Cor. 1:1) and mentioned in several other places (1 Cor. 1:12-13, 3:5). Themes such as the body of Christ, the gifts of the Spirit, the freedom of the Christian, and the physical resurrection of the dead are thoroughly Pauline.

B. External Evidence

Recent excavation has uncovered the "Gallio Stone."[148] This stone inscription states that Gallio was the proconsul in Corinth from AD 51-52. Since Paul appeared before his judgment seat, Paul must have been in Corinth at this time (Acts 18:12).

The early church fathers are in complete agreement concerning Pauline authorship. When Clement of Rome wrote the Corinthians (AD 93-97), he quotes from 1 Corinthians as if Paul is the author.[149] Irenaeus (AD 130-202) makes frequent reference to 1 Corinthians as if Paul is the author.

II. DATE

Paul actually wrote four letters to the Corinthians, two of which have been lost. The sequence of his correspondence is as follows:[150]

A. "The Previous Letter"

1 Corinthians 5:9 speaks of a previous letter, which apparently addressed sexual immorality. Some theologians believe that 2 Corinthians is a "composite document" and the 2 Corinthians 6:14-7:1 is a fragment of the "previous letter." However, we have no literary proof that 2 Corinthians is a composite document.

---

[147] Donald S. Betz, "The First Epistle of Paul to the Corinthians," *The Beacon Bible Commentary*, vol. 8 (Kansas City: Beacon Hill, 1968) 295.

[148] Tenney, *New Testament*, 234-35.

[149] Betz, *1 Corinthians*, 295.

[150] Guthrie, *New Testament*, 424 ff.

B. 1 Corinthians

1 Corinthians 1:11 indicates that Paul received an oral report from Chloe's household stating that the church was split into factions. Paul also receives a written report containing questions about marriage and interpersonal relationships (cf. 7:1). Paul's response to these two reports constitutes what we know as 1 Corinthians. It was probably written from Ephesus around AD 55-56 (compare 16:1-8 with Acts 19:22, 20:1-3).

C. "The Tearful Letter"

Paul's second visit to Corinth was a painful one (2 Cor. 2:1). He was rejected and publicly humiliated before the church. From Troas, Paul wrote a very harsh letter of rebuke ("The Tearful Letter," cf. 2 Cor. 2:4, 7:8).

D. 2 Corinthians

Titus (the bearer of "The Tearful Letter") informed Paul that, *for the most part*, "The Tearful Letter" worked (2 Cor. 7:5). The Corinthians repented and once again recognized Paul's special place in their church (2 Cor. 7:6,7). Upon receiving this good news, Paul wrote what we know as 2 Corinthians.

In conclusion, Paul wrote at least four letters to the Corinthians: The Previous Letter, 1 Corinthians, The Tearful Letter, and 2 Corinthians. All of these letters were written in the mid-fifthies AD.[151]

---

[151] Gordon Fee, *The First Epistle to the Corinthians*, (Grand Rapids: Eerdmans, 1987), 15.

PART 2—THE HISTORICAL CONTEXT

An understanding of the historical context of Corinthians is imperative for a proper interpretation.

I. HISTORY

Corinth (originally "Ephyra" meaning *look out* or *vantage point*) may have been inhabited as early as 2,000 BC. It was called "Ephyra" because of its strategic location on the *isthmus* (a narrow strip of land with water on two sides connecting two larger land regions) joining the southern *Peloponnesus* (with the mainland to the north). In 146 BC, the Romans totally destroyed Corinth, but Julius Caesar, realizing its strategic location, rebuilt it in 46 BC.[152] In a sense, Corinth was a relatively new city at the time of Paul, and may have inspired Paul's "building motif" in 1 Cor. 3:9-15.

Corinth was also the cite of the "Isthmian games" (second only to the Olympics) and may have led Paul to develop his "athletic motif" (cf. 1 Cor. 9:24-27).[153]

II. NATURE OF THE CITY

A. Militarily Strategic

Its location permitted the defense of both the Aegean and Adriatic coasts. An attacking army from the east, west, north or south would have to pass through Corinth.[154]

B. Economically Strategic

All commerce traveling north, south, east or west must pass through Corinth and of course the Corinthians charged high custom taxes. Also, because the waters around the Peloponnesus were dangerous, merchants would transport their ships overland down the streets of Corinth on rollers.

C. Culturally Pluralistic

As a port city, Corinth experienced the vices of a highly mobile and pluralistic society.[155] Immorality and pagan philosophies and religions were rampant. The temple of *Aphrodite*, the "goddess of love," located on the *Acrocorinth* (or highest point) with its thousand temple prostitutes did not help matters.[156] The great wealth of Corinth was spent on vice and corruption. To corrupt the morals of another was to "Corinthianize" that person.[157] God called Paul to start a church in such an environment.

---

[152] Tenney, *New Testament*, 289.
[153] Fee, *1 Corinthians*, 2.
[154] Guthrie, *New Testament*, 421.
[155] Harris, *New Testament*,
[156] Fee, *1 Corinthians*, 2.
[157] Ibid.

PART 3—CENTRAL PROBLEMS IN CORINTHIAN CHURCH

In his introductory remarks (1:1-9) Paul identifies himself and states that the Corinthians are in fact sanctified in the Lord. He calls them *hagioi*, which literally means 'saints." This is significant considering the terrible spiritual and moral problems that many of the Corinthians are going through. However, in an objective sense, the holiness and righteousness of Jesus Christ is imputed to all those who are in Christ Jesus (1:30). Three major problems are dealt with in 1 Corinthians:

I. DIVISIONS IN THE CHURCH

The Corinthian church was a very divided church. An extremely carnal spirit was literally tearing that portion of the body of Christ apart. This spirit of divisiveness took many different forms. The Corinthians created parties or factions around Paul, Apollos, Cephas, and Christ (1:11-13) each representing a distorted understanding of the faith.[158]

A. The Paul Party

These persons no doubt distorted his doctrine of justification by faith, viewing it as a license to sin. They abused Christian freedom, and hence were termed the Libertinists.

B. The Apollos Party

The "Apollos Party" were infatuated with secret wisdom and eloquence in speech (1 Cor. 1:17-2:16). Acts 18:24-26 tells us that Apollos was an Alexandrian Jew, who was eloquent in speech and mighty in his use of the scriptures. Alexandria was located in North Africa and was a center for the allegorical method of interpretation. This method viewed the literal understanding of scripture as the most primitive or elementary level of interpretation. It held that everything in scripture had a deeper or more hidden meaning. Perhaps Apollos applied the allegorical method of interpretation of the scriptures with his speaking ability. This thoroughly impressed the Corinthians, and some may have misconstrued Apollos' message and method. That is to say, they formed a faction or subset of the church in his name.

C. The Cephas Party

More than likely this subgroup was composed of Jewish Christians. They saw Peter as promoting a strict observance of the law and the keeping of Jewish purity regulations. This group would have been characterized by an excessive legalism and an obsession with rituals and ceremonies.

D. The Christ Party

Paul does not deal with this particular party in Corinth. He simply mentions its existence. However, his silence here should not be interpreted as endorsement. Paul has included this party as simply another example of the carnal divisiveness which pervades the church. It may well be that such persons in the Christ party claimed an exclusive relationship to Jesus Christ,

---

[158] Guthrie, *New Testament*, 443.

and that they were superior to all other believers in the church. Perhaps they did not recognize any human authority in the church but only pledged allegiance to the exalted Lord.

II. GROSS IMMORALITY

Fornication, incest, and idolatry were present in the Corinthian church (5:1-13; 6:14-20, 8:1-13, 10:14-29). Also, some Corinthians were in a habit of suing one another (6:1-8).

III. DOCTRINAL HERESY

The Corinthians managed to misunderstand every major doctrine of the church: they failed to grasp God's plan for marriage (7:1-40); they viewed the Lord's Supper as any other festive meal or banquet (11:23-34). The exercise of spiritual gifts became a matter of carnal pride and arrogance rather than a means to exalt God and serve the church (12:1-31, 14:1-40).

In conclusion, Paul wrote this epistle to set the church in order. They took some things lightly; Paul called it sin. They asked about doctrine, and he called them back to the central principles of the faith.

PART 4—AN EXPANDED OUTLINE

The following is an expanded outline of 1 Corinthians.

I. THE INTRODUCTION (1:1-9)

Despite their many problems, Paul continually considers them *hagioi* or "saints." In an *objective sense*, they are holy "in Christ Jesus" (cf. 1:30).

II. DIVISIONS (1:10-4:21)

Refer to the discussion above. Additional comments are:

A. Divisions over Personalities (1:10-16)

Paul *does not* endorse any one of these parties, even the Christ party. Paul's joining of baptism and divisiveness may indicate that some are baptizing in their name, trying to gather personal adherents (cf. 1:14-16).

B. Divisions concerning False Wisdom (1:17-2:16)

The misplaced emphasis on esoteric wisdom indicates the presence of *quasi-gnosticism* (or beginning Gnosticism) in Corinth.[159] Full blown Gnosticism did not exist until the first quarter of the 2nd century. Paul counters this heresy by stating that carnal wisdom is man-centered and not God-centered (1:19-29). Paul claims that the crucified Messiah is in fact the wisdom of God and the power of God, but this is spiritually discerned (1:24, 2:14). Some of Paul's opponents criticized the simplicity of his message and method. Yet Paul claims that he deliberately avoided eloquent words, so that the gospel might be validated through the demonstration of the Spirit (2:4).

C. Divisions over False Judgments (4:3-13)

Some of the Corinthians have judged the sufferings of Paul as weakness (4:3) and as a sign of being inferior to the other apostles (4:8-13). Paul states that the only judgment that counts is the judgment of the Lord (4:4). Paul does not even judge himself (4:3).

III. IMMORALITY IN THE CHURCH (5:1-6:20)

The following are two examples of grave sin in Corinth.

A. Fornication and Incest (5:1-15)

The Corinthians are actually proud of such sins. This indicates that their arrogance is *theologically informed*. The Gnostics viewed the spirit as essentially distinct from the body, so what one did in the body could not affect one's spirit. The Corinthians were proud of their belief that deeds done in the body were irrelevant to the condition of one's spirit. Paul rebukes

---

[159] Fee, *1 Corinthians*, 5, 11.

the church for not taking action against this sin and instructs them to excommunicate the evil brother (5:2-13).

B. Believers are going before Heathen Judges (6:1-20)

Paul's objection to lawsuits in the church is based on two principles. First of all, a public lawsuit between two believers is a terrible testimony before the world (6:6). Secondly, Paul argues that believers are thoroughly qualified to settle such matters within the church, because they will judge the world and angels (6:3-4). Paul states that it would be better to suffer loss than to bring shame upon the church (6:7).

IV. MARRIAGE (7:1-40)

It is clear that Paul is responding to a letter the Corinthians sent to him (cf. 7:1). The words, "It is good for a man not to marry" belong to the Corinthians and not the Apostle Paul, for Paul endorses marriage (7:1-7). One can remain single if one has "the gift," and this can facilitate ministry (7:6-10, 28). Widowed believers should marry believers, as should all Christians, for it is not God's will that one be unequally yoked (2 Cor. 6:14, 7:39). A believer is not to divorce an unbelieving spouse, yet if the unbeliever wishes to leave, then the believer is free (7:12-16). The birth of the church presented the apostolic leaders with situations and conditions which were not addressed by the historical Jesus. Under the leadership of the Spirit, Paul uses his apostolic authority to give guidance and counsel concerning such situations (7:25, 40). Yet throughout chapter 7, Paul is careful to note the distinction between his own personal advice and an explicit commandment of the Lord (7:10, 12, 25).

V. MEAT SACRIFICED TO IDOLS AND IDOLATRY (8:1-13, 10:14-29)

Paul addresses two major issues. They are:

A. The Agora

The open marketplace or *agora* (also called "the shambles") consisted of different stalls which sold various items and foods (10:25).[160] Store owners frequently offered up a portion of the food as a sacrifice to an idol. Some Corinthians (the "weak") had very sensitive consciences and believed that eating such meat would spiritually defile them. Yet some (the "strong") realized that this food was harmless.

Paul sides with the strong explaining that eating meat offered to an idol will not affect one spiritually (8:1-13). But Christian love constrains one to be sensitive to the consciences of the weak (8:7).

B. Idol Worship and Shared Meals

The *Libertinists*, or those who practiced an "all things are lawful" philosophy (6:12, 10:23), led some Corinthians to attend idol feasts as a matter of social interaction.[161] But Paul argues

---

[160] Tenney, *New Testament*, 292.
[161] Guthrie, *New Testament*, 424.

that this constitutes a religious experience and is not simply a matter of fellowship. Paul's main point is that Christian communion is absolutely incompatible with idol feasts (10:14-21). Just as Christian communion establishes a spiritual connection between the believer and Christ, idol feasts establish a spiritual connection between the participants and demonic powers.

VI. THE CHARACTER OF THE APOSTLE PAUL IS ATTACKED (9:1-27)

The Corinthians questioned:

A. The Legitimacy of Apostleship (9:1-2)

Since Paul had not been a disciple of the historical Jesus, his opponents argue that he is not a true apostle of the Lord.[162]

B. Lifestyle and Finances (9:4-8)

The other apostles married and were supported by the church. Paul was single and worked with his own hands. The Corinthians viewed this as inappropriate for a true apostle.

C. Paul's Explanations (9:12, 15, 19-23)

Paul explains that he has forfeited all these privileges for the purpose of advancing the gospel.

VII. WORSHIP SERVICES ARE IN DISORDER (11:2-3, 19-23)

The disorder in Corinth was evidenced in three major ways:

A. Social Relationships (11:4-13)

The social custom of the day was for women to wear a veil on their head in public.[163] Yet in the name of Christian liberty, some of the Corinthians women were casting off the veils during the worship services. Paul saw this as a deliberate rejection of God's ordering of the sexes in society (11:16).

B. Abuse of the Lord's Supper (11:20-34)

Paul gives three central principles:

1. Paul teaches that a fellowship meal or *Agape feast* is not the same as the Lord's Supper (11:20-23).[164]

---

[162] Ibid., 422.
[163] Fee, *1 Corinthians*, 496.
[164] Betz, *1 Corinthians*, 418.

2. Christian tradition has established the pattern of the Lord's Supper, and this is universally binding on the church (11:23-26).[165]

3. Paul warns that there are serious consequences for abusing the Lord's Supper, even sickness and death (11:27-34).

C. Abuse of the Gifts of the Spirit (12:1-31, 14:1-39)

It appears that some of the "super spirituals" were competing with one another, trying to out-prophesy or continually speak in tongues.[166] For the sake of order, Paul gives three guidelines:

1. Paul argues that the trinity is diverse, but unified. Similarly, the gifts of the Spirit are diverse, yet they are also unified. Paul gives the human body as an example of the principle "unity in the midst of diversity" (12:4-14).

2. Paul states that carnal pride has no place in the body of Christ, and that God had ordained every member for a particular purpose. The more gifted members are not to reject the less gifted ones. There is no room for boasting as if one owned the gifts (12:15-19).

3. The gifts of the Spirit should edify the body of Christ, unify the church, and bring the lost to salvation (12:30-31, 14:1-39).

The most important thing is that everything be done decently and in order (14:40). The most valuable thing is not spiritual gifts or knowledge, but faith, hope, and love (13:8-12).

VIII. SOME DENY THE BODILY RESURRECTION (15:1-58)

The Gnostic tendencies in Corinth led some to deny the physical resurrection. Paul sets forth the following points:

1. The physical resurrection is a historical fact which has been preserved by the tradition of the church (15:1-11).

2. A denial of the resurrection completely undermines the Christian faith (15:12-19).

3. Christ's resurrection has destroyed the powers of sin and death (15:20-28, 51-58).

4. The nature of the resurrected body makes it fit for a heavenly existence (15:37-41, 51).

5. A seed must die to yield a plant; a body must be buried to be raised.

6. There is an essential connection between a seed and a plant and there is an essential connection between our present body and our future glorified body.

---

[165] Fee, *1 Corinthians*, 545 ff.
[166] Ibid., 575-76.

7. Our present body is mortal (designed to live in this life), but our future body is spiritual (*not made of spirit*, but designed to live in a heavenly environment).

IX. CONCLUSION (16:1-24)

A. The Collection (16:1-4)

In an attempt to improve the relationship between the Gentile and Jewish church, Paul organized a collection. The Corinthians were not meeting their obligation, and Paul exhorts them to finish what they started.

B. Endorsement of Faithful Ministers (16:10-15)

Paul recommends Timothy, Apollos, and Stephanas.

C. Final Greetings (16:19-24)

Paul's closing words correspond to our contemporary practice of including a salutation at the end of a letter.

True/False:

1. T or F   The authorship of 1 Corinthians is seriously disputed.
2. T or F   The record in the Book of Acts supports Pauline authorship of 1 Corinthians.
3. T or F   1 Corinthians may in fact be "2 Corinthians" and 2 Corinthians may be "4 Corinthians."
4. T or F   The Corinthians confused the "Agape feast" with the Lord's Supper.
5. T or F   The Corinthians were most attracted to the "power gifts."

----

1. The city of Corinth was located on:
    a. an island
    b. an isthmus
    c. a river

2. The word "Acrocorinth" means the:
    a. lowest point
    b. highest point
    c. middle point

----

1. List the three major problems of the Corinthian church which Paul addresses:

    a. _____

    b. _____

    c. _____

2. List the three types of divisions found in Corinth:

a. _____

b. _____

c. _____

SELF TEST:

1. It was noted that:
      a. 1 Corinthians may really be "2 Corinthians" and 2 Corinthians may be "4 Corinthians"
      b. "Ephyra" meant "look out"
      c. the "Isthmian games" may have inspired Paul's "athletic motif"
      d. all of these
      e. none of these

2. This lesson taught that:
      a. the phrase "all things are lawful" belonged to the "Libertinists"
      b. the Gnostics rejected the value of the material world
      c. Corinth was located on an island
      d. A & B
      e. B & C

3. With regard to the Corinthian problems, it was noted that:
      a. Paul endorsed the "Paul party" and the "Christ party"
      b. the Corinthians were boasting about the case of incest in their church
      c. the Corinthians criticized Paul for doing manual labor
      d. B & C
      e. A & B

4. With regard to the introductory material, it was noted that Corinth's geographic location:
      a. was militarily advantageous
      b. was economically advantageous
      c. facilitated moral corruption
      d. all of these
      e. none of these

5. With regard to the problems at Corinth, it was taught that:
      a. Paul affirmed the position of "the weak"
      b. the Corinthians confused the "Agape feast" with the Lord's Supper
      c. Paul argued for unity amidst diversity
      d. A & B
      e. B & C

LESSON 13—2 CORINTHIANS

Part 1	The Importance of 2 Corinthians
Part 2	The Opponents of the Apostle Paul
Part 3	Accusations against the Apostle Paul
Part 4	Paul's Response to the Accusations
Part 5	Major Themes Addressed

OVERVIEW

You will recall from the introductory material on 1 Corinthians, that 2 Corinthians is more than likely the fourth letter that Paul wrote to the Corinthians. It appears that just prior to writing 2 Corinthians Paul wrote what has come to be known as "The Tearful Letter." Paul had written a very harsh letter to the Corinthians rebuking them for their resistance and carnality. From 2 Corinthians we can learn that for the most part the "Tearful Letter" was effective (a good number of the Corinthians have repented and reaffirmed the authority and place of the Apostle Paul in their lives and in their church). Nevertheless, pockets of resistance still remain. 2 Corinthians is designed to deal with these obstinate church members. Here Paul sets forth the model of the true Christian minister and develops the theme of reconciliation.

OBJECTIVES

- Explain the importance of 2 Corinthians.
- Describe the personal nature of 2 Corinthians.
- Identify the opponents of Paul in 2 Corinthians.
- Discuss the accusations brought against Paul.
- List and describe Paul's response to these accusations.
- Discuss conclusions drawn from your study of 2 Corinthians.

HELPS FOR LEARNING AND REMEMBERING

1. Take note of the differences between 2 Corinthians and 1 Corinthians. This will help you not to confuse the two epistles.

2. Note the difference in the *tone* of 2 Corinthians as compared with 1 Corinthians. The theme of reconciliation and personal transparency are characteristic of 2 Corinthians.

3. 2 Corinthians has been overshadowed by 1 Corinthians. Make an effort to give this epistle its due.

4. As you read through the epistle, take notes on the central themes which arise. This will help organize your thoughts concerning the content of 2 Corinthians.

5. Have a good evangelical commentary on hand. You might want to refer to it in your studies.

KEY WORDS

Reconciliation   Judaizers   ecclesiastical

PART 1—THE IMPORTANCE OF 2 CORINTHIANS

The importance of 2 Corinthians focuses on the following:

1. 2 Corinthians forms a sequel to Paul's first epistle to the Corinthians. In other words,   it allows us to see what effect Paul's correspondence had upon this particular church.

2. This Corinthian epistle is of a more personal nature than 1 Corinthians.[167] It gives us deep insight into the personality and ministry of the Apostle Paul.

3. 2 Corinthians is important because it gives us a clear picture of Christian ministry. Paul describes Christian ministry as basically the service of a new covenant (3:1-18). Also, in this regard, 2 Corinthians demonstrates Christian ministry as involving great responsibility and suffering (4:1-12).

4. The epistle gives us additional insight into the future state of the believer (5:1-4). This particular section is important because it is not identical to what Paul says in 1 Corinthians 15. Nevertheless, it compliments some of the concepts presented in Paul's previous correspondence concerning the future state.

5. 2 Corinthians emphasizes the blessings of being a cheerful giver.[168] Paul presents a theology of Christian giving in this epistle. He notes that the Macedonians are a great example of Christian giving (8:1-3). He also emphasizes that Jesus Christ is our example in giving (8:9). Finally, Paul stresses that ultimately one reaps what one sows (9:6-10).

---

[167] Tenney, *New Testament*, 301.
[168] Guthrie, *New Testament*, 447.

PART 2—THE OPPONENTS OF THE APOSTLE PAUL

Two Corinthians seems to be addressed to two groups in the Corinthian church.[169] As previously indicated, the majority of the Corinthians have repented of their errors (2:6-7, 7:6-7). Nevertheless, a minority continued to oppose the Apostle Paul and his ministry (10:2, 10-12). For this reason, Paul's defense of his apostleship is particularly strong in 2 Corinthians (10-13).

But who exactly were Paul's opponents in Corinth at this time? 2 Corinthians 11:22-23 gives some insight here. The opponents of the Apostle Paul in 2 Corinthians were apparently Jews who claim to be ministers of Christ. They may well have been Judaizers. These were Jews who had some affiliation with Christ yet were requiring Gentiles to follow the law of Moses and be circumcised. 2 Corinthians 11:23 ff. indicates that these troublemakers were not prepared to do pioneer work on their own. Rather they had infiltrated the church at Corinth and were capitalizing upon the work of Paul and Apollos. Not only were they not prepared to do the groundwork of founding the church, but they did not want to suffer for the sake of Jesus Christ and the gospel. It also appears that they used letters of recommendation from other churches in order to gain access to the congregations of the Apostle Paul. In conclusion, Paul's opponents at Corinth more than likely were Judaizers. They were incorporating aspects of the Old Testament law into the Christian faith. They were not prepared to do pioneer work, nor suffer for Jesus Christ. Rather, they commandeer the fruit of other person's labor and gain access into congregations through letters of recommendation.

---

[169] F.F. Bruce, "1 and 2 Corinthians," *The New Century Bible Commentary*, (Grand Rapids: Eerdmans, 1971) 172-74.

PART 3—THE ACCUSATIONS AGAINST THE APOSTLE PAUL

The opponents of Paul have brought at least seven accusations against him and his ministry.[170] They are:

I. PAUL WAS NOT SPIRITUAL

They accused Paul of walking according to the flesh (10:2). The opponents promoted standards of spirituality, and judged Paul as failing these standards.

II. PAUL WAS A COWARD

They contend Paul was a coward who hid behind powerful letters. Yet, when Paul was present, he was weak and fearful (10:10). It may be that Paul's opponents were confusing his dependence upon the grace of God with weakness and fearfulness.

III. PAUL WAS MENTALLY UNSTABLE

The precise basis for this accusation (5:12-13) is unclear. Perhaps it had something to do with Paul's ministering style or the manner in which he evidenced the gifts of the Spirit. At any rate they questioned the sanity of the Apostle Paul.

IV. PAUL WAS GREEDY

They accused the Apostle Paul of becoming rich by taking advantage of the Corinthians (7:2). They had slanderously accused the Apostle Paul of exploiting the Corinthians. Of course, this accusation is patently unfounded since Paul accepted no contribution from the Corinthian church.

V. PAUL WAS NOT A TRUE APOSTLE

Paul's apostleship was attacked (11:15, 12:11-12). The Judaizers no doubt would have claimed a special relationship to the Jewish sector of the church. Particularly, they would have claimed a special connection with the Jerusalem apostles. These apostles were the disciples of the historical Jesus and Paul was not. Therefore, they deemed he was not a true apostle.

VI. PAUL HAD NO LETTER OF RECOMMENDATION

They note that no church had sent a letter of recommendation for the Apostle Paul (3:1). As previously noted, they gained access into Paul's congregation by letters of recommendations. Of course, since Paul founded the churches in Corinth, he would not have had a letter of recommendation, neither did he need a letter of recommendation.

---

[170] Philip E. Hughes, *The Second Epistle to the Corinthians*, (Grand Rapids: Eerdmans, 1962) xvii-xviii.

VII. PAUL WAS BOASTFUL AND PROUD

They considered Paul's defense of his apostleship (10:8, 13, 14) as carnal pride. But he boasted in his weakness and suffering, and not in his accomplishments. It is clear that the opponents of the Apostle Paul were prepared to say anything which would undermine his person, character, and influence in the Corinthian congregation.

PART 4—PAUL'S RESPONSE TO THE ACCUSATIONS

Paul responded to his opponents in two ways:[171]

I. HE EXPOSES THE TRUE CHARACTER OF HIS OPPONENTS

A. They Claimed the Work of Others

Paul pointed out that his accusers promoted themselves and sought honor on the basis of another person's work (10:15-18). In other words, they were interested in satisfying their egos by claiming the accomplishments of the Apostle Paul.

B. They Set their own Standards

Paul's opponents had lowered God's spiritual standard to their own level (10:12). They were comparing themselves among themselves rather than comparing themselves to the standard of God. In so many words, they have promoted themselves as God, determining what is acceptable and what is unacceptable. In essence, this was idolatry.

C. They Proclaimed a Different Gospel

Paul claimed that his opponents were false apostles, in fact were preaching a totally different gospel (11:13-15). His point was that they had no genuine ecclesiastical authority and that their message did not communicate salvation.

D. They Lived Immoral Lifestyles

The true nature of his opponents is evident in their immoral lifestyle (12:20-21). Their evil conduct was simply a manifestation of the corruption of their hearts. What is particularly distressing is that in the midst of their immorality they remained unrepentant (13:2).

II. HE DEFENDED HIS CHARACTER AND MINISTRY

Paul's defense of his character and ministry can be divided into six areas. They are:

A. The Fruit of His Ministry

Paul claimed that he needed no letter of recommendation, but that the Corinthians themselves were his letter of recommendation (3:2-3). Paul's point here is that the fruit of his ministry is the defense of his ministry. His place in the kingdom of God is to be judged on the basis of what God has done through him.

---

[171] Guthrie, *New Testament*, 447.

B. His Personal Conduct

In the sincerity of his heart, Paul claimed that his personal conduct was impeccable (4:2). This was no idle boast, nor carnal pride. It was simply a matter of record. Through the grace of God in Christ, and the power of the Holy Spirit, Paul had lived a godly life in this world.

C. His Willingness to Suffer

The integrity of Paul's ministry is demonstrated in his willingness to suffer for the gospel (6:4-6, 11:23-28). This demonstrates the selflessness of the Apostle Paul. He was not in the ministry in order to advance or benefit himself. His willingness to suffer for the gospel demonstrated that his utmost concern was for the promotion of the kingdom of God, and not for the promotion of himself.

D. His Extraordinary Spiritual Experiences

Paul had many supernatural experiences in the Lord (12:1-5). The false apostles in Corinth were impressed with extraordinary experiences in the Spirit. Perhaps it would be more accurate to say that they were infatuated with ecstatic experiences in the Spirit. To counter the charge that Paul is carnal, lacking the power of the Spirit in his life, Paul was forced to share with them his extraordinary experiences in the Spirit.

E. Divine Affirmation

Paul claimed that God had confirmed his apostleship through the working of miracles in his life and ministry (12:11-12). The miracle working power of the kingdom in the life and ministry of the Apostle Paul represented God's thorough-going endorsement of his apostleship.

F. He Preached the Gospel Free of Charge

Paul had preached the gospel freely to the Corinthians, not accepting any payment. Paul's point here is that he was not interested in their money, nor was he interested in benefiting from the Corinthian church. Incredibly, some of the Corinthians claimed that the reason Paul would not accept financial support was that he was too proud and arrogant. Paul used irony and sarcasm in refuting such a ludicrous charge (11:7-11).

PART 5—MAJOR THEMES ADDRESSED

In summarizing 2 Corinthians, there are three major themes addressed. They are:

I. THE SUPREMACY OF THE NEW COVENANT

2 Corinthians presents a clear picture of the early Christian ministry. Paul explains that he, and indeed every single believer, is ministering in a new covenant (3:7-18). In a way which sounds very similar to the epistle of Hebrews, Paul argues that the new covenant is far superior to the old. Additionally, Paul explains that service in the new covenant involves great responsibility and suffering (4:1-12). The integrity of one's life and ministry becomes evident in this type of environment. He who selflessly promotes the things of God is endorsed by God.

II. ADDITIONAL INSIGHT INTO THE FUTURE STATE

2 Corinthians grants additional insight into the future state (5:1-5). Although Paul's presentation here is somewhat different from that given in 1 Corinthians 15, he maintains that God has prepared a glorified body for us.

III. THE PRINCIPLE OF SOWING AND REAPING

Paul teaches that generosity and hospitality lie at the heart of the Christian gospel. He notes that the Macedonians are a great example of Christian living (8:1-3). Nevertheless, the greatest example of Christian giving must be attributed to our Lord Jesus Christ. He gave himself completely in utter self-sacrifice for the redemption of humankind (8:9). Finally, Paul sets forth the spiritual principle of sowing and reaping (9:6-10). He who sows sparingly will reap sparingly, and he who gives generously shall also receive abundantly from the Lord.

True/False:

1. T or F   Some of the Corinthians accused Paul of making himself rich from the ministry.
2. T or F   Paul notes that his accusers are "building on another man's foundation."
3. T or F   Some Corinthians claimed that Paul was a coward and mentally unstable.
4. T or F   Paul charged a fee for preaching the gospel in Corinth.

----

1. The _____ were more than likely the opponents of Paul in 2 Corinthians.
2. In emphasizing the supremacy of the New Covenant in 2 Corinthians, Paul's words sound very similar to the epistle to the _____.

----

1. List the 3 major themes addressed by Paul in 2 Corinthians:
   a. _____

   b. _____

   c. _____

2. Recall the six ways in which Paul defends his ministry and personal integrity:

a. _____

b. _____

c. _____

d. _____

e. _____

f. _____

SELF TEST:

1. It was noted that:
    a. *all* of the Corinthians repented at the "Tearful Letter"
    b. Paul's opponents were probably Judaizers
    c. Paul is more personal in 2 Corinthians than in 1 Corinthians
    d. A & B
    e. B & C

2. Paul's opponents claimed that:
    a. he was a coward
    b. he was insane
    c. he was greedy for money
    d. all of these
    e. none of these

3. With regard to Paul's opponents it was learned that they:
    a. did not claim a special relationship to the Jerusalem apostles
    b. were not able to obtain any letters of recommendation
    c. were impressed with supernatural experiences
    d. A & C
    e. B & C

4. Again, it was noted that:
    a. Paul viewed suffering as a sign of apostleship
    b. Paul claimed the Corinthians as his letter of recommendation
    c. Paul accepted financial support from the Corinthians
    d. A & B
    e. A & C

5. With regard to major themes, the lesson states that:
    a. a superior covenant involves greater responsibility and suffering

b. Paul's teaching on the resurrection in 5:1-5 is different from, but not contradictory to what he says in 1 Corinthians 15:3 ff.

c. the principle of sowing and reaping relates to the theme of Christian giving

d. all of these

e. none of these

LESSON 14—GALATIANS

Part 1	Background Information
Part 2	Central Themes
Part 3	Expanded Outline

OVERVIEW

In many ways, Galatians serves as a condensed version of Paul's theology, and in this sense, the epistle to the Galatians can be viewed as a prelude to Paul's epistle to the Romans.[172] This is because Galatians contains Paul's central doctrines of justification by faith through grace in Jesus Christ. In Galatians, Paul clearly proclaims that there is a righteousness of God which is totally distinct from the law. Paul teaches that circumcision has no spiritual value for the Christian. In fact, God has now revealed that there is no distinction whatsoever between Jews and Gentiles as far as God's plan of salvation is concerned. Finally, human will and obedience to the law are not enough to properly live the Christian life. On the contrary, one must be filled with the Holy Spirit to continually live in a manner pleasing to the Lord. The very infilling with the Spirit testifies that the Gentiles are also the children of God. The manifestation of the fruit of the Spirit is simply part of the normal Christian life.

Although Paul's epistle to the Galatians parallels Romans, its tone is completely different. Paul is clearly displeased with the situation in Galatia. They have been drawn away by Judaizers and are on the verge of falling from grace. Paul's tone is militant and even hostile at times. This is the only epistle of Paul's which contains no thanksgiving in the introduction. Paul's concern for the Galatians drives him to speak with clarity and force. Nonetheless, his anger is fueled by a love for their souls. As a father chastens his children when they are careless and expose themselves to danger, so too Paul chastens the Galatian Christians for yielding to the Judaizers.

Our study will reveal that Galatians is indeed one of the most passionate of all of Paul's epistles. In drawing the Galatians back to orthodoxy, Paul sets forth the central doctrines of the faith and appeals to the common experience of the Holy Spirit.

OBJECTIVES

- List the major points of the "north and south Galatian theories."
- Discuss the central purpose of Galatians.
- Outline the major portions of Galatians.
- Summarize the major themes of Galatians.

---

[172] John Eadie, *A Commentary on the Greek Text of the Epistle of Paul to the Galatians*, (Grand Rapids: Zondervan, 1894), 1, vii.

HELPS FOR LEARNING AND REMEMBERING

1. Make notes on how the themes of Galatians parallel Romans. By comparing the two, the theological contributions of each can be remembered.

2. A map of the Mediterranean world as it existed at the time of Paul will become important when discussing the destination of the epistle.

KEY WORDS

Hetero	polemic	hupocrisis
Allegory	*allon*	*anathema*
Paidagoge		

PART 1—BACKGROUND INFORMATION

I. AUTHORSHIP

As with Romans and 1 & 2 Corinthians, the authorship of Galatians is not disputed. Again, it is among the most Pauline of all Paul's epistles. The internal and external evidence is as follows:

A. Internal Evidence

Paul clearly identifies himself as the author of this epistle at the beginning and at the end of the letter (1:1, 5:2).[173] The writing style, themes, and vocabulary of Galatians are typically Pauline. For example, words like righteousness, justification, law, works, and faith are all used repeatedly throughout the epistle to the Galatians. With regard to typical Pauline themes, justification by faith apart from works of the law and circumcision is a major theme of Galatians.

Our study of Romans has already revealed that this theme forms the core of Paul's theology. Finally, Paul's personality is clearly evidenced in this epistle. His love for his converts is set forth in 4:19. Nevertheless, his love is a mature love and he does not hesitate to rebuke them as his children in the Lord (3:1). He is vitally concerned for their souls and fears that they may fall from grace. As in the Corinthian epistles, Paul fervently defends his apostleship (1:1). He strongly challenges anyone who questions his apostolic appointment (5:11-12, 6:17).

In summary, there is not internal evidence which casts Pauline authorship in doubt. Paul identifies himself as the author, the vocabulary and themes are thoroughly Pauline, and the man behind the epistle is clearly the Apostle Paul.

B. External Evidence

The only external evidence that we have addressing Pauline authorship of Galatians is the testimony of the early church fathers. As you will recall, the early church fathers represent that authoritative leadership of the church immediately after the apostolic age. The early church fathers unanimously support Paul as the author of Galatians. For example, Origen, Ignatius and Tertullian all allude to Galatians as written by the Apostle Paul.

II. DATE AND DESTINATION

The date and destination of Galatians are essentially intertwined. This is true because the term "Galatia" may refer to two separate regions in Asia Minor. These two separate regions yield the "North Galatian theory" and the "South Galatian theory."[174] An explanation of the theories follows.

---

[173] Herman Riddenbos, *St. Paul's Epistle to the Churches of Galatia*, (Grand Rapids: Eerdmans, 1953) 13.
[174] Guthrie, *New Testament*, 405 ff.

A. The South Galatian Theory

The word "Galatia" is interpreted to mean the Roman *provincial* designation for the territories held in Southern Asia Minor (the areas of Pisidia, Phyrgia, and Lyconia). Paul established churches in this region on his first missionary journey. If Galatians was destined to South-central Asia Minor, then it must have been written around AD 49, one year prior to the Jerusalem Council of Acts 15.[175]

B. The North Galatian Theory

The term "Galatia" had another meaning at the time of the Apostle Paul. It also referred to ethnic Galatia. Ethnic Galatia referred to the ancient kingdom of the Gauls which was located in North-central Asia Minor. Acts 16:6 and 18:23 tell us that Paul passed through North-central Asia Minor on his 2nd and 3rd missionary journeys. The Acts account does not explicitly state that Paul established churches in North-central Asia Minor, although it does say that he met some brethren there. If one interprets Galatia to mean North-central Galatia, then a later date must be assigned to the epistle to the Galatians. The North Galatian theory holds that the epistle was written from Corinth near the end of his 3rd missionary journey to the churches in North Galatia sometime around AD 56 or 57. This would mean that Paul's epistle to the Galatians was written some 6-7 years after the noted Jerusalem Council.[176]

Both theories have merit, but if Galatians was written on Paul's 2nd or 3rd missionary journeys, then we must reckon with the following: You will recall that the Jerusalem Council settled the issue of accepting Gentiles into the church. James, the moderator of the Council, did not require the Gentiles to be circumcised and issued an encyclical letter to that effect. In Galatians, Paul is fighting the Judaizers. These are Jewish "Christians" who are trying to make the Gentile believers obey the law of Moses and be circumcised. If Paul had written the epistle to the Galatians after the Jerusalem Council, it seems strange that he would not have mentioned the decision of that council. For after all, the Jewish leadership in Jerusalem did agree with the Apostle Paul on this vital point. Secondly, Peter's hypocrisy in Galatians 2:11 ff. is more easily explained if it occurred prior to the Jerusalem Council. It is difficult to believe (though not impossible) that Peter would separate himself from the Gentile believers after the apostolic leadership in Jerusalem had definitively decided that there was no distinction between Jews and Gentiles in the church. Finally, the Book of Acts does not explicitly state that Paul established churches in North-central Galatia. On the contrary, it clearly evidences Paul's founding of churches in South-central Galatia. The South Galatian theory with a date of AD 49 seems to be a more plausible position.[177]

---

[175] R.A. Cole, *The Epistle of Paul to the Galatians*, (Grand Rapids: Eerdmans, 1970) 20-23.

[176] Guthrie, *New Testament*, 450-52.

[177] William M. Ramsay, *A Historical Commentary of St. Paul's Epistle to the Galatians*, (Grand Rapids: Baker, 1979) 6.

PART 2—CENTRAL THEME

The central theme of Galatians is stated in 1:6-7. Judaizers (Jewish "Christians") were teaching that the Galatians could not be saved by the grace alone, but had to be circumcised and obey the law of Moses.[178] This completely undermined the doctrine of salvation by grace through faith in Jesus, and struck at the very heart of Paul's law-free gospel to the Gentiles.

In 1:6-7 Paul says, "I marvel that you are so soon removed from him that called you into the grace of Christ unto *another* gospel which is not *another*; but there be some that trouble you and would pervert the Gospel of Christ." Paul uses two different words for the word "another" (cf. NIV translation).[179] The word "another" is verse six is *hetero* and literally means "qualitatively different." Paul is saying that *the Judaizers are teaching a qualitatively different gospel* from the one that he preached. The word for "another" in vs. 7 is *allon*, refers to another of the same kind, but in a different form. Paul did not object to a different form of the same message, but he vehemently reacted against a totally different message.

Paul's intense anger is evidenced in 1:8-9. Paul says that if anyone, even an angel from heaven, should preach a qualitatively different gospel than what he preached, then they are *anathema*, "condemned of God."[180]

The Judaizers have come to the Galatians for only one reason: they want to take away their liberty in Christ and bring them into bondage (2:4-5). The Judaizers were making the cross of Christ worthless, and completely destroying the grace of God in the church (2:21).

The central theme of Galatians is very *polemic* in nature (destroying false ideas and heresy). Paul will settle for nothing less than complete salvation through grace apart from works of the law (5:1).

The Judaizers realized that the personality, character, and doctrine of Paul must be destroyed in order to make progress in Galatia churches.[181] Paul continually defends his apostleship and authority throughout the epistle (1:11-12).

---

[178] William Barclay, *The Letters to the Galatians and Ephesians*, (Philadelphia: Westminster, 1959) 1.

[179] Daniel Arichea and Eugene A. Nida, *A Translator's Handbook on Paul's Letter to the Galatians*, (Stuttgart: United Bible Societies, 1976) 12-13.

[180] Ridderbos, *Galatians*, 49.

[181] Barclay, *Galatians and Ephesians*, 1.

PART 3—EXPANDED OUTLINE

Paul realized that he must present a highly organized defense to refute the Judaizers. Indeed, the thematic organization of Galatians is evident, being constructed around 3 major arguments: biographical, theological, and practical. An expanded outline of Galatians is as follows:

I. INTRODUCTION

A. Salvation by Faith through Grace (1:1-5)

Galatians 1:1-5 is not the typical writing style of Paul. These verses are very short and to the point, as if Paul is anxious to get to the subject as quickly as possible. Paul expresses no thanksgiving here.[182] Paul's anger and concern are immediately communicated in this very curt, thankless introduction.

B. The Occasion for Writing (1:6-10)

Paul immediately takes the offensive, attacking the perverters of the gospel and pronouncing a divine curse on their heads. They are to be *anathema*, which means "cursed of God."

The word *anathema* originally meant "dedicated" and was used by the Romans to describe the dedication of a soldier to Caesar. The Jews used it to describe sacrifices dedicated to God. Thus *anathema* came to mean that which is the object of divine wrath. Paul claimed that anyone who twists and undermines the gospel is to be condemned to hell. This sounds too severe, but it demonstrates the gravity of the situation in Galatia.

II. THE BIOGRAPHICAL ARGUMENT

As noted about, Paul used several methods to defend his law-free gospel to the Gentiles. Here Paul points to his own personal experience as an example of the gospel of grace. His argument consists of three major life experiences. They are:

A. The Result of Direct Revelation (1:11-24)

Paul was not converted by the Jerusalem apostles, nor by hearing early Christian sermons. On the contrary, he experienced grace on the Damascus road, and the content of the gospel was directly communicated to him, independent of all Christian witnesses.[183] Paul received direct revelation from God, indicating his authority and commission are completely independent of the apostles and their messages.

B. An Independent Message (2:1-10)

The Jewish leadership recognized and affirmed Paul's special place in the kingdom of God (2:1-10). Thus, Paul asserts his radical independence from the Jewish leadership, yet notes their complete acceptance of him. He was not a maverick doing his own thing.

---

[182] Cole, *Galatians*, 37-38.
[183] Ridderbos, *Galatians*, 62-66.

C. Uncompromising Apostolic Authority (2:11-21)

Paul's direct confrontation with Peter in Antioch proves that even apostolic pressure will not undermine the doctrine of justification by faith (2:11-21).[184] Peter's table fellowship with Gentiles demonstrated that he accepted them as equal partners in the gospel. But when men from James arrived from Jerusalem, Peter *gradually* began to distance himself from the Gentiles. Paul uses the imperfect tense (denoting continuous action in past time) to describe the gradual but continual distancing of Peter from the Gentiles.[185] In this, Peter communicated that Gentiles were not true members of the church. Paul confronted Peter before the whole church for his *hypocrisy*. The word *hupocrisis* literally means "to speak from beneath the mask" and was taken from Greek theater. It described the actors as they spoke from beneath their masks between performances. What they said often did not match the mask they were wearing. Peter's actions were equivalent to 'speaking from beneath a mask."

III. THE THEOLOGICAL ARGUMENT

Paul presents four major parts of his theological argument for justification by faith. They are:

A. Prior Experience (3:1-5)

The experience of the Holy Spirit testifies that the Galatians have been fully incorporated into the church.[186] The Galatians received the Holy Spirit on the basis of faith, not works of the law. If God grants his Spirit on the basis of faith, why are they now trying to gain acceptance with God on the basis of works?

B. Abraham's Justification (3:17)

The Judaizers were claiming that only the children of Abraham (Hebrews) can partake of the covenant blessings. The Gentiles must become proselytes to Judaism in order to be saved. Paul notes that Abraham was justified by 430 years *prior to* the giving of the law (Gen. 15:6),[187] making it chronologically impossible for Abraham to be justified through the law. Anyone who has faith like Abraham is his child.

C. Purpose of the Law (3:24)

Paul claims that the law was not given to save but was a "school master" or *paidagoge* leading us to Christ (3:24).[188] The Greek "pedagogue" was a household slave entrusted with the tutoring of the master's children. The pedagogue was known for harsh discipline and unyielding demands. Yet his purpose was to lead the child to maturity. Paul is saying that the law was a stern taskmaster which was designed to lead us to maturity in Christ. Why are

---

[184] Cole, *Galatians*, 72.

[185] Arichea and Nida, *Galatians*, 41.

[186] Eadie, *Galatians*, 219.

[187] Ridderbos, *Galatians*, 135-36.

[188] Arichea and Nida, *Galatians*, 81.

the Gentiles wanting to revert to the days of immaturity, and submit themselves to a strict taskmaster like the law?

D. Joint Heirs with Christ (4:21-5:1)

Paul develops an elaborate allegory (from *allegorein* meaning "to speak in an allegory") to communicate the freedom of the gospel.[189] Each part of an allegory has its own special significance. Hagar stands for the slave woman which coincides with Mt. Sinai, both symbolizing bondage to the law. Sarah represents the free woman, paralleling Mt. Zion in Jerusalem. Both Sarah and Mt. Zion are symbolic for the freedom of the gospel. Paul's point is that the Galatians have not been born to Hagar to be enslaved by the law of Mt. Sinai. But rather, they have been born of Sarah and enjoy the glorious freedom of the gospel on Mt. Zion in Jerusalem.

IV. THE PRACTICAL ARGUMENT

Paul draws points from practical living to support justification by faith. His practical argument consists of four major parts:

A. The Curse of the Law (5:1-12)

Paul argues that circumcision brings one under the condemnation of the law (5:1-12). If the Galatians allow themselves to be circumcised, they are obligated to keep *the entirety* of the law, and everyone under the law is cursed of God (1:10,13).

B. The Fulfillment of the Law in Love (5:13-26)

Those who are led by the Spirit fulfill the law by loving God and neighbor (5:13-26). Through the infilling of the Spirit, the believer evidences the fruit of the Spirit, and in doing so, fulfills the intent of the law (5:22-23).

C. Love Bears One Another's Burdens (6:1-6)

The fulfillment of the law is evidenced in love, particularly, bearing one another's burdens in Christ.[190]

D. True Righteousness (4:10, 5:6, 6:17-18)

Paul's final point is that those who depend on the law and circumcision are not walking in the Spirit but are in the flesh. The Judaizers simply wanted to make converts to Judaism and were not interested in the welfare of the Galatians. Paul proved his sincerity by bearing about in his body the scars of Christ (6:17-18).[191]

True/False:

---

[189] Ibid., 111.
[190] Cole, *Galatians*, 170 ff.
[191] Barclay, *Galatians and Ephesians*, 62.

1. T or F   The North Galatian theory supports an early date for the writing of Galatians.
2. T or F   The South Galatian theory supports a late date for the authorship of Galatians.
3. T or F   The Judaizers were teaching a *hetero* or "qualitatively" different gospel from the one preached by the Apostle Paul.
4. T or F   Paul does not hesitate to condemn the troublemakers in Galatia to he (*anathema*) (1:8-9).
5. T or F   The word "polemic" means to build up the Christian faith.

6. T or F   With regard to his message and calling, Paul emphasizes his independence from the Jerusalem apostles.
7. T or F   The word "hypocrisy" means "to speak from beneath the mask."
8. T or F   *Paidagode* means a 'schoolmaster."
9. T or F   Paul argues that the law brings a curse and explains the nature of that curse through the Hagar/Sarah analogy.

----

1. List the types of arguments set forth by Paul in Galatians:

a. _____

b. _____

c. _____

SELF TEST:

1. With regard to "background information," the lesson noted that:
    a. the "North Galatian theory" supports an early date for Galatians
    b. the "South Galatian theory" supports a late date for Galatians
    c. Acts states that Paul started several churches in south Galatia
    d. A & C
    e. B & C

2. In fighting the Judaizers, it was learned:
    a. that they taught a *hetero* (qualitatively the same) gospel as Paul
    b. that the word *polemic* means to build up the faith
    c. that Paul "anathematizes" the Judaizers
    d. all of these
    e. none of these

3. It was learned that Paul:
    a. stresses his dependence on the Jerusalem apostles
    b. was taught the content of the gospel by other Christians
    c. clearly expresses thanks for the faith of the Galatians as he does in other epistles
    d. all of these
    e. none of these

4. Paul argues that:
    a. the experience of the Spirit testifies that the Galatians are the children of God
    b. Peter spoke "from beneath the mask"
    c. the law was a *pedagogue* leading us to Christ
    d. all of these
    e. none of these

5. Paul:
    a. uses allegory to defend the law-free gospel to the Gentiles
    b. states that if one keeps part of the law, then one must keep all of the law
    c. taught the Spirit-filled Christian keeps the intent of the law by loving one's neighbor
    d. all of these
    e. none of these

LESSON 15—EPHESIANS

Part 1	Background Information
Part 2	Central Themes
Part 3	Outline and Content

OVERVIEW

The epistle to the Ephesians has been called the "Royal Epistle" because it expresses the pre-eminence of Christ in such eloquent terms. Paul proclaims that Christ is above all, through all, and in all. There is no name, nor power, or any other entity which is more powerful than that of the Lord Jesus Christ.

The church also shares in the glory and power of Jesus Christ. Paul describes the church as the body, building, and bride of Christ. Paul teaches that the church is already experiencing heaven to some degree. Yet this heavenly existence must be expressed in practical living (the church has been called to holiness).

The epistle to the Ephesians presents two major themes: the absolute superiority of Christ, and the unique identity of the church.

OBJECTIVES

- Discuss the authorship, date, and purpose of Ephesians.
- List and describe the two central themes in Ephesians.
- Give a definition of the church as presented in Ephesians.
- Present an outline of Ephesians.

HELPS FOR LEARNING AND REMEMBERING

1. Clearly focus on the unique aspects of Ephesians. This will help you to distinguish the contribution of Ephesians from the other epistles you have studied.

2. Seek to make the epistle to the Ephesians come alive for you in your studies; that is, try to enter into the first century world of the Ephesian church. As you continue to study, you will realize that the newborn church at Ephesus is coming under the attack of false teachers and heretics, and Paul is struggling to retain the cardinal principles of the faith in the midst of that portion of the body of Christ. If you keep this first century situation in mind, the burden of this epistle is more likely to become impressed in your mind.

3. When questions arise concerning Ephesians, quickly jot them down as you study along. If your study reveals answers to these questions, then simply write the answers down immediately. In this way by the end of your study of Ephesians, you will have a list of good questions and answers regarding the subject at hand.

4. A major part of learning is building vocabulary. If you encounter any new words, look them up in a dictionary and write down the word and the definition on a flash card. By building your

vocabulary you will increase your potential to communicate to those who the Lord has entrusted to your care.

5. Always be prepared to jot down sermon titles, outlines, and subjects for Bible studies which might arise as you study Ephesians. Do not wait until you have completed the material to write down these ideas. If you do, you may find that they are difficult to recall. Jot them down now! You can develop them later when time allows. Remember, the goal of our studies is to help disciple our people in the Lord. In this way, the overall strength and vitality of the church will be enhanced.

KEY WORDS

Angeology	Christology	Muratorian Canon
Amanuensis	ecclesiology	doxology
Pleroma	peripateo	in the Heavenlies
Akrogonios	polemically	

PART 1—BACKGROUND INFORMATION

I. AUTHORSHIP

Computer analysis identifies 44 words in Ephesians which are not found elsewhere in Paul's epistles. This leads some to reject Pauline authorship of Ephesians.[192] There are some peculiarities in sentence structure as well. For example, Ephesians 1:3-10 is a single continuous sentence in the Greek text (cf. also 1:15-23).[193] Paul usually writes in much shorter, clearer segments.

Such points become extremely important when comparing Ephesians with Colossians. Indeed, Ephesians is very similar to Colossians, indicating that they may have been written at the same time.

A. Internal Evidence

Paul's name appears twice as the author (1:1, 3:1). Despite the unique vocabulary present, there is much vocabulary which is clearly Pauline (cf. 2:5-9, 4:4-12).[194] The fact that Paul may have written Colossians at the same time may have influenced his writing style. An *amanuensis* (or male secretary) may have been employed to "flesh out" a general outline provided by Paul. This would explain the unique vocabulary and sentence structure and the similarity between the two works.

B. External Evidence

The early church fathers do not question the authenticity of this epistle.[195] Origin, Irenaeus, and Tertullian all quote from Ephesians as if it is written by the Apostle Paul. The "Canon of Muratori" (AD 140) lists Ephesians as Pauline.

II. DATE

Since Ignatius and Polycarp quote Ephesians as if it were Pauline, then it certainly was written prior to AD 110.[196] Also, Ephesians 3:1, 4:1 and 6:20 indicate that Paul is in prison, either in Caesarea (AD 58-60) or Rome (AD 61-63).[197] Since the church appears to be well developed, Ephesians was probably written during Paul's Roman imprisonment in about AD 62.

---

[192] T.K. Abbott, *The Epistle to the Ephesians*, (Edinburgh, T&T Clark, 1979) xiv-xv.

[193] John A. Allen, *The Epistle to the Ephesians*, (London: SCM Press, LTD, 1959) 15.

[194] Charles Hodge, *A Commentary on the Epistle of the Ephesians*, (Grand Rapids: Baker, 1980) xv.

[195] Abbott, *Ephesians*, v.

[196] Ibid., xii.

[197] Charles R. Eerdman, *The Epistle to the Ephesians*, (Grand Rapids: Baker, 1931) 12.

III. PURPOSE

Tychicus is the bearer of both Ephesians and Colossians (Ephesians 6:21; Colossians 4:7-9) and it is reasonable to conclude that Paul has received a report from these churches concerning their problems. Therefore, both Ephesians and Colossians were written to address theological and doctrinal errors which have crept into the church. Paul is writing *polemically* to fight heresy and undermine false teachings.[198]

In Ephesians and Colossians, false teachers have undermined the pre-eminence of Christ. Perhaps the worship of angels played a role here.[199] A highly developed angelology was part of 1st century Judaism. Often these angels were viewed as intermediaries communicating message between God and man. This would tend to displace Christ as the sole mediator between God and humankind.

---

[198] F.F. Bruce, *The Epistle to the Ephesians*, (Old Tappan, NJ: Fleming H. Revell Co., 1961) 13-15.

[199] Bruce, *Ephesians*, 14.

PART 2—CENTRAL THEMES

The two major themes of Ephesians are *Christology* (or the study of Christ) and *ecclesiology* (or the study of the church).

I. CHRISTOLOGY

"Christology" is a Greek compound word consisting of *christos* which means Christ, and *logos* which means a word or study of. Therefore, the word Christology means a study of Christ. In that the heresy in Ephesus was undermining the supremacy of Christ, a major theme in Ephesus is the development of a very high and lofty Christology.

In battling the heresies in Ephesus, Paul stresses that the grace of God and the benefits of salvation only come through Jesus Christ. There is no other human nor spiritual entity which can mediate the benefits of salvation.[200]

Paul states that grace and peace come from God the Father *and* the Lord Jesus Christ (1:2). Paul represents Jesus and the Father as coequal in power and glory, as copartners in dispensing grace and peace to the heirs of life.

Paul continues to explain that all spiritual blessings (predestination, election, and adoption) come only through Jesus Christ (1:3-6, 11-12). The grace of the atonement can be found only in the blood of Jesus Christ (1:7). Jesus Christ is the sole source of revelation and understanding of the divine mysteries (1:8-10). These words indicate that there was Gnostic heretics who taught that secret wisdom could be obtained through angelic revelations.[201] The core of Paul's Christology is presented in 1:20-23. Here Paul states:

> *Which he exerted in Christ when He raised Him from the dead and seated Him at the right hand in the heavenly realms far above all rule and authority power and dominion and every title that can be given not only in the present age but also in the age to come and God placed all things under His feet and appointed Him to be head over everything for the church which is His body the fullness of Him who fills everything in every way.*

The word that Paul uses for "fullness" here is the Greek word *pleroma*.[202] This was a favorite Greek term to communicate the idea of complete fullness allowing absolutely no other additions of any kind. It follows that all powers, dominions, titles and entities, including the church, have been subjected to the Lord Jesus Christ.

II. ECCLESIOLOGY

"Ecclesiology" is a Greek compound word consisting of the verb *ekkaleo* which means "to call out." As in the previous instance, the second word is *logos*. Ecclesiology means a study or

---

[200] Francis Foulkes, *The Epistle of Paul to the Ephesians*, (Grand Rapids: Eerdmans, 1956) 13.

[201] Bruce, *Ephesians*, 14.

[202] Kenneth S. Wuest, *Ephesians and Colossians in the Greek New Testament*, (Grand Rapids: Eerdmans, 1953) 45.

discussion of those who have been called out. In other words, the word ecclesiology refers to a study of the church.

The exalted nature of Christ has profound implications for his church. Throughout Ephesians, Paul continually focuses upon the glorious nature of the church. He divides his ecclesiology into four major sections. They are:

A. Metaphors or Images Describing the Church

1. The Body of Christ (1:23)[203]

The image of the church as Christ's body is uniquely Pauline. Paul uses an anatomical image because the church is not an institution, it is an organism. Just as the body is controlled by its vital connection with the head, so too the church is controlled by its vital connection with Christ.

2. The Building of Christ (2:20-22)

Paul employs an architectural image in which Christ is the chief cornerstone. The Greek word for "cornerstone" is *akrogonios*, meaning either "keystone" or "cornerstone."[204] A keystone was the central stone of a Roman archway. The stability of the archway was completely dependent upon the keystone which held it all together. The entire weight, integrity, and function of the church rests upon the person and work of Jesus Christ.

The cornerstone was a finely crafted stone which determined the alignment of the rest of the foundation. All of the various stones of the church must come into perfect alignment with the chief cornerstone, who is Christ. The cornerstone often contained an inscription dedicating the building to a particular person. The church is completely dedicated to Christ.

3. The Bride of Christ (5:25-32)

Paul describes the relationship between Christ and the church in terms of a good marriage.[205] He represents Christ as the husband of the church and the church as the bride of Christ.

These three images of the church in Ephesians yield forth the following definition. For Paul, the church was a single functioning body, nonracial, possessing its own standards, and engaged in spiritual conflict on a universal scale (1:22-23).

---

[203] E.K. Simpson and F.F. Bruce, *Commentary on the Epistles to the Ephesians and the Colossians*, (Grand Rapids: Eerdmans, 1957) 201.

[204] Abbott, *Ephesians*, 71.

[205] Bruce, *Ephesians*, 115.

B. The Conduct of the Leaders

The exalted nature of the church carries with it weighty, moral obligations. If the church is the body of Christ, then it must live like the body of Christ. Paul employs the Greek word *peripateo*, meaning "I walk about" to describe the entire lifestyle of the Christian. Paul commands the Ephesians not to walk in sin (2:2). On the contrary, the Ephesians are exhorted to walk in good works (2:10), in unity (4:1-3), in newness of life (4:17 ff.), in love (5:2), in light (5:8), and in wisdom (5:15).

C. The Theme of "In the Heavenlies"

This phrase is only found in Ephesians and is used to communicate that the Christian's experience is not limited to this world.[206] The faith union with Christ means that the experience of Christ becomes the experience of the believer. Paul teaches that "in Christ" the believers are presently in heavenly places (1:3, 2:6). Since we are in Christ, our struggle takes place in heavenly realms (6:12).

D. The Importance of the Holy Spirit

The role and function of the Holy Spirit is an important theme in Ephesians. Christians are sealed with the Spirit (1:13). The Holy Spirit grants complete access to the Father (2:18). The Spirit is the strength of the believer (3:16). Finally, the Holy Spirit unifies the church as one body of Christ (4:3).

---

[206] Foulkes, *Ephesians*, 45.

PART 3—OUTLINE AND CONTENT

I. THE CONSTITUTION OF THE CHURCH (1:3-14)

When describing the constitution of the church, Paul is very Trinitarian. The church owes its existence to the eternal plan of the Father (1:3-6). Yet saving grace is mediated through God the Son (1:6-12). The application of God's grace comes through the empowering of the Holy Spirit (1:13, 14).

II. PAUL'S PRAYER FOR THE CHURCH (1:15-23)

Paul's ecclesiology is revealed in his prayer for the church. For example, he prays that the church be full of all wisdom, knowledge, and enlightenment (1:17-18). Paul understands the church to be the sole channel of God's special revelation in the world. Furthermore, Paul prays that the church be full of God's power (1:19). The church is God's agent of change in the world. Finally, Paul prays that the church might come to experience Christ as its supreme head (1:22-23). For Paul, the church is subordinate to the authority of Christ.

III. THE 2-FOLD NATURE OF THE CHURCH

Paul's understanding of the church in Ephesians reflects a two-fold nature: a vertical dimension and a horizontal dimension.

A. The Vertical Dimension of the Church (2:1-10)

The vertical dimension of the church speaks of the church's relationship with God. The church is to contrast its former life in sin with their present life in Christ (2:1-8). In this way the church will regain a renewed appreciation of its special relationship to God. Also, the church is to reaffirm that salvation comes only through the atonement of Christ (2:8-10).

B. The Horizontal Dimension of the Church (2:11-22)

This aspect describes the relationship of the believer to life in the world. They are to recall that they were Gentiles by nature and thus enemies of God (2:11-12). Yet now they have been reconciled in Jesus Christ (2:13-18), and incorporated into the family of God. They now constitute the building of God (2:19-22).

IV. THE CALLING OF THE CHURCH (3:1-21)

Paul sets forth the unique calling or vocation of the body of Christ. Here he claims that the church has been called to reveal the wisdom of God in the world (3:1-13). Paul teaches that the church has been called to strength, love, faith, knowledge and fullness (3:14-21).

V. THE UNITY OF THE CHURCH (4:1-32, 5:1-20)

Paul develops the theme of one, unified body of Christ[207] in three ways:

---

[207] Tenney, *New Testament*, 321.

A. There is Unity in the Midst of Diversity (4:1-17)

Paul teaches that diversity in the church does not undermine the unity of the body of Christ. He states that there is one Lord, one faith, one baptism, and one Father (4:1-6). Yet in the midst of this solidarity, there is variety. Thus, Paul claims that there are many different members which comprise the sole body of Christ (4:7-16).

B. True Morality Preserves the Unity (4:17-32, 5:1-20)

There is a single ethical norm applicable to all parts of the body of Christ. Paul communicates this ethical norm through the imagery of putting off old clothes and putting on new clothes.[208]

C. Domestic Harmony Preserves Unity (5:22-23, 6:1-4)

Divine order in interpersonal relationships also promotes the integrity of the church. For these reasons, Paul says that wives should submit to their husbands (5:22). Husbands are to love their wives as Christ loved the church (5:23-33). Also, children are to be in subjection to their parents (6:1-3), but fathers are not to provoke their children to wrath (6:4).

VI. THE CONFLICT OF THE CHURCH (6:10-20)

The church exists in a hostile environment and must put on the whole armor of God to resist the hostile forces coming against it.

VII. CONCLUSION (6:21-24)

Paul's concluding words clarify the role of Tychicus. Tychicus was the bearer of Ephesians and Colossians and communicated the present status of Paul to the Ephesians. The final verse of this epistle is a simple *doxology*, or "words of praise."

True/False:

1. T or F   Paul usually writes in long, unbroken sentences as in Ephesians 1:3-10 and 1:15-23.
2. T or F   Paul's name does not appear anywhere in the epistle to the Ephesians.
3. T or F   The Muratorian Canon lists Ephesians under the category of "Pauline."
4. T or F   The worship of angels plays no role in Paul's letter to the Ephesians.

----

1. There are _____ (number) unique words in Ephesians not found in any other Pauline epistles.
2. _____ means "words of praise."
3. Since Ephesians is one of Paul's "Prison Epistles" is could have been written while he was imprisoned at _____ or _____.

4. Ephesians has a close affinity to Paul's epistle to the _____.

---

[208] Wuest, *Ephesians and Colossians*, 109-10.

5. The two Greek words which comprise the word "Christology" are
_____ and _____.

6. The term for the "church" is _____ and literally means "the called-
out ones."

7. The Greek word *akrogonios* means _____ or _____.

8. Paul's image for describing one's lifestyle or conduct is expressed in the Greek word *peripateo*,
meaning "_____."

----

1. List the images or metaphors Paul uses to describe the church in Ephesians:

a. _____

b. _____

c. _____

SELF TEST:

1. With regard to authorship, it was noted that:
    a. Paul usually writes in long, unbroken sentences (cf. 1:3-10)
    b. the name of Paul doesn't appear in the text
    c. there are no unique words in Ephesians
    d. all of these
    e. none of these

2. With regard to background information, it was noted that:
    a. the worship of angels was a part of the Ephesian heresy
    b. Ephesians is not one of the "Prison Epistles"
    c. Ephesians and Colossians were probably written at the same time
    d. A & B
    e. A & C

3. A study of the content of Ephesians reveals that:
    a. the theme of "in the heavenlies" is common in Paul
    b. there can be unity in the midst of diversity
    c. Paul describes the church in two dimensions: depth and width
    d. A & B
    e. B & C

4. It was also noted that:
    a. the mediatorship of Christ was threatened in Ephesus
    b. Paul uses the imagery of walking to describe the lifestyle of the believer
    c. Paul uses the imagery of putting on and taking off clothes to communicate the moral transformation of the believer
    d. all of these
    e. none of these

5. The epistle to the Ephesians reveals that:
    a. Paul is "trinitarian" in his understanding of the church
    b. true morality preserves the unity of the church
    c. Christ is the "cornerstone" or "keystone" of the church
    d. all of these
    e. none of these

LESSON 16—THE EPISTLE TO THE PHILIPPIANS

Part 1	Background Information
Part 2	The Nature of the Church
Part 3	Central Themes
Part 4	Special Contributions

OVERVIEW

Our study, thus far, has revealed that Paul had many trials and burdens in his ministry. Fortunately, not all of his churches were like Corinth! The church at Philippi no doubt held a special place in the apostle's heart. The Philippian church was a very generous church. It was a church full of the joy of the Lord. A quick survey of the epistle reveals that no major doctrinal problems existed there which is so unlike the situation at Ephesus and Colossae. Even when the apostle addresses doctrinal issues, it is in the form of what might be called "preventive medicine." In other words, Paul did not deal with actual problems in Philippi, but he warned the Philippians to be on their guard. The Judaizers, which we studied when discussing Galatians, attempted to spread their heresy in the church at Philippi. Paul did not wait for them to arrive. Rather, he took the initiative to attack them before they could establish their stronghold in Philippi. For all these reasons, Paul felt the liberty to "let his hair down" in Philippians. We gain much insight into the emotions and feelings of Paul for Philippians. Not having to undermine heresies and moral problems, Paul felt the freedom to describe the deeper things of the Lord. A significant example is the Christian state of mind as set forth in Philippians 2:5-11.

All in all, Philippians presents us with what might be called the "model church" of the first century. The state of the church at Philippi is how it should be throughout the body of Christ.

OBJECTIVES

- Explain the background information for this epistle.
- Describe the nature of the church at Philippi.
- List and briefly discuss the central themes of Philippians.
- List and describe the special contributions of Philippians.

HELPS FOR LEARNING AND REMEBERING

1. Study Acts 16 to review Paul's experience in Philippi, to contextualize Paul's words in Philippians.

2. Pay careful attention to the structured presentation of this lesson. The inherent organization of the material will help you master the subject at hand.

3. Philippians is the perfect book for use in small groups. For example, the theme of the Christian state of mind is tailor made for overcoming the stress and anxiety of contemporary life. Attempting to make such connections once again will help you to remember the unique contributions of Philippians.

4. The historical context is helpful in explaining military analogies and terminology that Paul uses.

5. Outline Paul's presentation in Philippians and survey the themes represented therein. Such an exercise will help you get a quick overview of the central points of this great epistle.

6. Seek ways to apply your learning to the contemporary church. If you can "put a face" on your studies, what you have learned will remain with you throughout your ministry.

KEY WORDS

Composite document   katatome   manuscript fragments
Peritome   *pneuma puthoma*   kenao
Kenosis

PART 1—BACKGROUND INFORMATION

I. INTRODUCTION

A. Authorship
1. Internal Evidence

The opening verse identifies Paul as the author. Paul is in prison, and there are references to Timothy and to Epaphroditus.[209] Theologically and linguistically, Philippians is thoroughly Pauline.[210] The sentence structure is Paul's as well. Theologically and conceptually, the epistle is Pauline.[211]

The only objection to the integrity of the epistle concerns the difference in tone found in various parts of the epistle. Chapters 1, 2, and four are very positive, but chapter 3 contains a harsh rebuke of the Judaizers. For this reason, some have suggested that Philippians is a composite document (composed of several literary fragments).[212] Yet it is only logical that Paul would warn the Philippians concerning this doctrinal heresy.[213]

2. External Evidence

There is no external evidence which questions Pauline authorship.[214]

B. Date

Paul was definitely in prison, witnessing to the entire palace, even to Caesar's household (1:7, 12-13, 4:22). Paul indicated that he may soon be executed (1:20, 21, 2:17). Yet he still hoped to be released (1:23-26, 2:24).

All of these factors seem to indicate a Roman imprisonment rather than a Caesarean one, dating about AD 61-64.[215] In that Paul expected execution, Philippians may have been written in the latter part of this time span.[216]

II. THE RELATIONSHIP OF PHILIPPIANS TO ACTS

From Acts, we learned of the dramatic events that characterized Paul's ministry in Philippi.

---

[209] Ralph P. Martin, *The Epistle of Paul to the Philippians*, (Grand Rapids: Eerdmans, 1959) 36.

[210] Ibid., 16.

[211] Martin, *Philippians*, 36.

[212] F.W. Beare, *The Epistle to the Philippians*, (London: Adam & Charles Black, 1959) 3.

[213] William Hendriksen, *Philippians, Colossians and Philemon*, (Grand Rapids: Baker, 1962) 147-48.

[214] Muller, *Philippians and Philemon*, 14-15.

[215] Muller, *Philippians and Philemon*, 28.

[216] Ibid.

1. The "Macedonian Vision," the beginning of the "We Sections," and the gospel enters Europe, changing the course of western history (Acts 16:9-10).[217]

2. Lydia, the first European convert (Acts 16:14-15) and her hospitality characterized the Philippian church and is evidence that the membership was predominantly female.[218]

3. The exorcism of the *pneuma puthoma*, the 'spirit of Pytho" (Acts 16:16-18).[219] Greek mythology taught that the spirit of Pytho served as the mouthpiece of the god.[220]

4. The conversion of the Philippian jailer and his household (Acts 16:25-34).

---

[217] Ibid., 13.
[218] Tenney, *New Testament*, 324.
[219] Bruce, *Acts*, 312.
[220] Ibid.

PART 2—THE NATURE OF THE CHURCH

I. PHILIPPI WAS A ROMAN COLONY

The city was named after Philip of Macedon, father of Alexander the Great.[221] The Greek culture was firmly established in Philippi. The Romans made Philippi a city-state, granting it due process and exemption from taxes.[222] The citizens of Philippi were proud of their heritage, particularly of their Roman citizenship (Acts 10:21, 16:37, 38).

II. PHILIPPI WAS PREDOMINANTLY A GENTILE CITY

Since there was no synagogue in Philippi, the Jewish population was extremely small (Acts 16:13). Paul's warning about circumcision (3:1 ff.) and use of athletic and military imagery suited a Gentile congregation (3:12-13, 4:7).[223]

III. PHILIPPI WAS A GENEROUS AND LOVING CHURCH

After Paul left Macedonia, only the Philippians sent aid to him in Thessalonica and Corinth (4:15-16, 2 Cor. 11:9).[224] Epaphrodites risked his life to minister to the needs of Paul in Rome (2:25-30).

Because of their generosity and love, Paul spoke personally to them, using the personal pronoun "I" more than 100 times.

IV. PHILIPPI POSSESSED A SIGNIFICANT NUMBER OF WOMEN IN THE CHURCH[225]

Paul mentioned women who worked with him (4:3), and exhorted two women to be reconciled (4:2). Recall the role of Lydia as well.

---

[221] Martin, *Philippians*, 15.
[222] Ibid., 15-16.
[223] Bruce, *Philippians and Philemon*, 148-49.
[224] Muller, *Philippians and Philemon*, 148-49.
[225] Tenney, *New Testament*, 324.

PART 3—CENTRAL THEMES OF PHILIPPIANS

The following are four major themes in Philippians:[226]

I. THE GOSPEL

Paul spoke of the fellowship, progress, defense, and labor of the gospel (1:5, 12, 17, 4:3).

II. JOY

Regardless of trials, Paul continually rejoiced and encouraged others to rejoice. He thanked God for the Philippians and for their help (1:3, 4:10). He rejoiced in the sacrifice of Christ, and the ability to sacrifice for Christ (2:17, 18). He commanded the Philippians to rejoice (4:4, 3:1).

III. TOTAL COMMITMENT TO CHRIST AND A WILLINGNESS TO GROW

Paul desired to:

- win Christ at any cost (3:8)
- be found in Christ (3:9)
- know Christ in glory and suffering (3:10-11)
- continue to strive for growth in the Lord (3:12-14)

IV. THE CHRISTIAN STATE OF MIND

Paul spoke to their spiritual development, exhorting them to:

- have a humble state of mind, a willingness to serve regardless of the cost (2:5-8)
- have freedom from anxiety (4:6, 7)
- have pure thoughts (4:8)
- be content, not dependent upon external circumstances for happiness (4:12, 13)

---

[226] Ibid., 326.

PART 4—SPECIAL CONTRIBUTIONS

I. PAUL'S WARNING CONCERNING THE JUDAIZERS

The Judaizing heresy was not actually present, but Paul warns them to be "safe" (3:1 ff.). He called these heretics "dogs," and employed a word-play, telling them to beware of the *katatome* ("mutilators of the flesh") rather than the *peritome* ("the circumcision").[227] Paul said that his Jewish heritage and education is dung compared to the righteousness of Christ.

II. THE "KENOSIS" PASSAGE (2:5-11)

Because this section contains much rhyming, parallelism and vocabulary which is not typically Pauline, Paul was probably using an early Christian hymn to describe the spirit of sacrifice so evident in Christ. Paul used the word *kenao* meaning "to empty" or "humble" to speak of Jesus' identification with humankind in the incarnation. Those who believe Jesus "emptied" himself argued that Christ gave up his divine attributes in the incarnation.[228] But since the scriptures establish the full deity of Christ during the incarnation, "humbled" is the preferred translation.

III. PAUL'S DETERMINATION TO FULFILL HIS CALLING (3:8-15)

This portion of Philippians reveals that Paul is obsessed with doing the will of God, regardless of the cost.

True/False:

1. T or F   The Judaizing heresy had fully infiltrated the church at Philippi.
2. T or F   When Paul preached in Philippi, the gospel entered Europe for the first time.
3. T or F   The church at Philippi was predominantly a Jewish church.
4. T or F   Paul uses a lot of Roman military terms and images in this epistle.
5. T or F   Paul calls the Judaizers "mutilators of the flesh" in 3:1 ff.

----

1. The term *pneuma puthoma* means _____.
2. The personal pronoun "I" is used more than _____ times in Philippians.
3. "Kenosis" means _____.

----

1. List the central themes of Philippians:

a. _____

b. _____

c. _____

d. _____

---

[227] Martin, *Philippians*, 136.
[228] Hendriksen, *Philippians, Colossians and Philemon*, 102-18.

2. What three special contributions has this epistle made?

a. _____

b. _____

c. _____

SELF TEST:

1. From the background information, it was noted that:
   a. the Acts account helps contextualize Philippians
   b. the Judaizers were present in Philippi
   c. there was a large Jewish population in Philippi
   d. all of these
   e. none of these

2. The lesson indicates that:
   a. when Paul preached in Philippi, the gospel entered Europe
   b. Philippi was a Roman city-state
   c. Paul uses athletic and military images in Philippians
   d. all of these
   e. none of these

3. It was noted that:
   a. *pneuma puthoma* means "the spirit of the panther"
   b. *kenao* probably means "humbled" rather than "emptied"
   c. Paul never used early Christian hymns to teach doctrine
   d. A & B
   e. A & C

4. In Philippians, Paul:
   a. told the Philippians to beware of dogs
   b. told them to look out for those who shred the flesh
   c. rarely uses the personal pronoun "I" in Philippians
   d. A & B
   e. A & C

LESSON 17—COLOSSIANS

Part 1	Introduction
Part 2	Purpose
Part 3	The Nature of the Heresy at Colossae
Part 4	Ethical Instructions

OVERVIEW

We will study Paul's epistle to the Colossians at this point because of its similarity to Ephesians. As noted previously, Colossians no doubt was written at the same time as Ephesians. Some of the themes and expressions in Colossians closely parallel those set forth in Paul's letter to the Ephesians. Finally, it appears that the historical context or *Sitz im Leben* is similar to Ephesus. That is to say, some type of early Christian heresy has invaded the church in Colossae. Although the nature of this heresy will be studied in more detail below, the following points should be noted here. It appears that angel worship is once again involved. Also, there are some Gnostic tendencies. Perhaps most importantly, there appears to be a Jewish connection. This peculiar blend of Jewish and Gnostic thought threatens to pollute the theological foundation of the church at Colossae. For these reasons Paul pens the epistle to the Colossians in an effort to stem the tide of false teaching in the church.

We will discuss the background information in an effort to contextualize Paul's letter to the Colossians. Then we will reiterate Paul's purpose for writing Colossians. This will be followed by a more detailed analysis of the heresy in Colossae. Finally, Paul's ethical instructions will be studied.

OBJECTIVES

- Discuss the background information of Colossians.
- List the two-fold purpose of Colossians.
- Discuss the nature of the Colossian heresy.
- Describe the ethical instructions found in Colossians.
- Briefly summarize the major portions of the epistle.

HELPS FOR LEARNING AND REMEMBERING

1. The similarities between Ephesians and Colossians can present difficulties. Develop note cards accentuating the differences between these epistles to avoid confusion.

2. Have a good Bible dictionary nearby. Any terms, places, or names about which you wish to gain additional information can be found in such a work.

3. Search extra biblical sources (resources outside of the Bible, which may give you additional information on Colossae). The biblical information on Colossae is rather limited. However, atlases, encyclopedias and biblical commentaries on Colossians may provide valuable date for a more substantial understanding of Paul's epistle to the Colossians.

4. Make contact with the research librarian in your area. This person is trained to locate sources relevant to particular topics and subjects. A research librarian can put you in touch with many sources, particularly journal articles, which can give you additional information on Paul's epistle to the Colossians. Often just reading the title of these literary works gives you some idea of the issues at stake with regard to Colossians.

KEY WORDS

Paranaesis	pre-eminent	*stoicheia*
Asceticism	monolithic	*Haustafeln*

PART 1—INTRODUCTION

I. BACKGROUND INFORMATION

Our extensive studies of the Pauline epistles, and our recent study of Ephesians permits a more abbreviated survey of this material. With regard to authorship, place, and date the following should be noted.

A. Authorship

1. Internal Evidence

Our study of Ephesians permits a more abbreviated survey here. Colossians 1:1 and 1:23 state that Paul is the author.

In 4:7, we see that Tychicus is with the Apostle Paul again, just as in Ephesians. Additional evidence can be found in 4:9. Here we read that Onesimus, the runaway slave dealt with in Paul's epistle to Philemon, is also present with the Apostle Paul. From this scripture we also understand that Tychicus is the bearer of the Colossian epistle. As previously studied, this holds true for Paul's epistle to the Ephesians as well. Finally, the content of Colossians and Ephesians are very similar.

2. External Evidence

Pauline authorship of Colossians was not disputed by any of the early church fathers. In that the authenticity of Colossians is essentially connected with that of Ephesians, the external data supporting Pauline authorship of Ephesians also applies to that of Colossians.

B. Place and Date

If Paul was imprisoned in Rome rather than in Caesarea, then both Ephesians and Colossians were written somewhere between AD 61-63.[229]

II. THE ORIGIN OF THE CHURCH AT COLOSSAE

The origin of the church at Colossae is a mystery. We know for sure that just as in the case of the Roman church, Paul did not found the church in Colossae. This is true because in 2:1 Paul clearly states that the Colossians have never seen his face. This must mean that Paul has never yet visited the Colossian church, much less founded the church there.

The question remains, "Who started the church at Colossae?" Perhaps Colossians 1:7 gives us a clue. In this verse, Paul says that Epaphras is their faithful teacher and minister. From 1:8 we can see that Epaphras has brought a message from the Colossian church to the Apostle Paul in Rome. Furthermore, Epaphras is mentioned in 4:12, 13. This frequent mentioning of Epaphras may

---

[229] John Eadie, *Commentary on the Epistle of Paul to the Colossians*, (Minneapolis: James and Klock Christian Publishing Co., reprint 1977) xiv.

indicate that he in fact was the one who started the church in Colossae and was pasturing that church at the time of Paul's writing.[230] A careful study of these verses indicates that Epaphras was also a Colossian. It may be that Epaphras was a convert of the Apostle Paul, perhaps converted during Paul's ministry in Ephesus. This would explain why Epaphras sought out the Apostle Paul for help. At any rate, we can conclude that Epaphras had some type of leadership position in Colossae and that the Apostle Paul held an important place in his life. After all, he was willing to travel all the way from Colossae on the behalf of the local church to reach the Apostle Paul in Rome.

In the final analysis, we can be certain, as in the case of his Epistle to the Romans, Paul was writing a letter to a church which he had not personally founded.

Briefly give the argument for Pauline authorship of Colossians:

---

[230] Simpson and Bruce, *Ephesians and Colossians*, 164.

PART 2—PURPOSE

The purpose of Paul's writing to the Colossians concerns some type of doctrinal heresy that had arisen in the church at Colossae. In turn, this false teaching had influenced (in a negative sense) the ethical behavior of the Colossians. Once again, we see the interrelationship between sound doctrine and moral conduct. Theological orientation dictates or determines moral behavior.

For all of these reasons, Paul's purpose in writing to the Colossians appears to be two-fold:[231]

> 1. To correct doctrinal error in the church
> 2. To impart sound ethical principles

Discuss how the church at Colossae may have been founded:

---

[231] Edward Lohse, *A Commentary on the Epistles to the Colossians and to Philemon,* (Philadelphia: Fortress, 1971) 2.

PART 3—THE NATURE OF THE HERESY AT COLOSSAE

The false teaching which had invaded the church appears to contain the following characteristics:

I. IT DETRACTED FROM THE PREEMINENCE OF CHRIST[232]

The Colossian heresy perverted the nature of Christ and his provision for the church. As in Ephesians, Paul's response was to present a very high Christology, encapsulated in 1:18, "That in all things he might have preeminence" (cf. also 1:14-22). Paul's Christology established the preeminence of Christ over the entire cosmos:[233]
> 1. Creation (1:16-17)
> 2. Redemption (1:20)
> 3. The Church (1:21)
> 4. Personal Ethics (1:22)

Thus, Paul's Christology addressed the subject of ecclesiology (Jesus is Lord over the church). Redemption only comes through Christ Jesus.[234] Paul's Christology established Jesus as Lord over the individual believer. One's personal conduct is defined solely on the basis of Christ Jesus himself.[235]

II. IT HAD A PHILOSOPHICAL CHARACTER[236]

Paul warns the Colossians not to allow anyone to spoil them with philosophy and vain deceit (2:8). The word "philosophy" is derived from a Greek compound word *philosophos*. The first component *philo* menas "to love." The latter component *sophos* means "wisdom"; so the word "philosophy" means "to love wisdom." Paul's words do not constitute some type of anti-intellectualism or a rejection of wisdom. Paul was fighting "false wisdom." He was attacking those who thought they possessed secret wisdom open only to a 'spiritual elite."[237] The phrase "the rudiments of this world" or *stoichea* supports this interpretation.[238] The Gnostics used this word to refer to the elemental principles of knowledge. Thus, an embryonic or beginning Gnosticism may have been infiltrating the Colossian church. This philosophy was being presented as superior to the revelation of Jesus Christ and his death on the cross.

III. IT HAD A JEWISH CONNECTION[239]

First century Judaism was not *monolithic* (consisting of only one body of beliefs and traditions). Like contemporary Protestantism, there were different factions within Judaism, both orthodox and unorthodox. The problem at Colossae sprang from a combination of Judaism and pagan philosophies, beliefs and practices. It appears to have involved circumcision, the "traditions of

---

[232] Ibid., 3.
[233] Simpson and Bruce, *Ephesians and Colossians*, 169.
[234] Wuest, *Ephesians and Colossians*, 167.
[235] Eadie, *Colossians*, xlii-xliii.
[236] Simpson and Bruce, *Ephesians and Colossians*, 165-69.
[237] Wuest, *Ephesians and Colossians*, 167.
[238] Lohse, *Colossians and Philemon*, 2-3.
[239] Wuest, *Ephesians and Colossians*, 163.

men" and excessive ceremonialism (2:8, 11, 3:11). The "false humility" of 2:18 may refer to a counterfeit form of Jewish piety. This verse also speaks of a worshiping of angels. As in Ephesus, angel worship undermined the unique mediatorship of Jesus Christ. Finally, extreme *asceticism*, or the denying of bodily appetites (food, clothing, sleep, etc.) was part of the heresy (2:22-23). Such deprivations were thought to bring one closer to God, but in actuality rejected the all-sufficiency of the cross. Paul clearly teaches that Jesus alone grants us forgiveness of sins (1:14) and provides reconciliation (1:20-22).

PART 4—ETHICAL INSTRUCTIONS

Colossians 3:5 begins with the word "therefore." This word forms a link with the previously discussed material in Colossians.[240] The "therefore" serves as a transition element which carries the reader from the doctrinal portion of the epistle into the ethical exhortations of the 2nd half of the letter. In this way, Paul makes a connection between theological and doctrinal knowledge and personal practical Christian living.

In Colossians 3:5, Paul commands his readers to execute or slay the flesh. The word flesh in the Greek is *sarx*. In this particular context, *sarx* refers to the fallen human nature which has a tendency to resist the will and way of the Lord. With regard to ethical conduct, Paul tells the Colossians that they must execute or kill the fallen human nature. One of the interesting points of this particular verse is that Paul equates covetousness with idolatry. In Paul's theology, an inordinate desire for something supplants or replaces the place of God in our lives. This is the essence of idolatry.[241]

Paul employed a familiar image (3:8-10) to describe the life of sanctification. Here, as was the case in Ephesians, Paul uses the imagery of putting off old clothes and putting on new clothes.[242] An interesting contrast, however, with Ephesians is that in Ephesians Paul commands them to put off the old man and put on the new man. However, in Colossians, Paul expresses himself in a somewhat different manner. Here Paul says that the Colossians *have* put off the old man and *have* put on the new man. This may indicate that the moral corruption in Ephesus was more advanced or problematic than what Paul had to face in Colossae.

Colossians 3:18-4:1 deals with the domestic aspect of our existence. The word domestic deals with special interpersonal relationships such as husbands, wives, children and the relationship that exists between masters and slaves. The German word *Haustafeln* is often used to describe these domestic directives of the Apostle Paul.[243] This German word literally means "household codes." In Colossians, as in Ephesians, Paul says that our life in Christ must have a direct bearing upon the special interpersonal relationships that we experience in this world.

Colossians 4:16 contains some interesting information. In this verse, Paul tells the Colossians that they should share or exchange their letter with them.[244] This may indicate that Paul has in fact written an epistle to the Laodiceans. However, since we have absolutely no knowledge of such an epistle, we can only conclude that it has been lost. If you will recall, a careful analysis of Paul's Corinthian correspondence indicates that at least two of Paul's epistles to the Corinthians have been lost as well.

---

[240] Edward Schweizer, *The Letter to the Colossians*, (Minneapolis: Augsburg, 1976) 181.
[241] Simpson and Bruce, *Ephesians and Colossians*, 270.
[242] Ibid., 267.
[243] Lohse, *Colossians and Philemon*, 154.
[244] Eadie, *Colossians*, 299.

Discuss the two-fold purpose for writing the epistle to the Colossians:

True/False:

1. T or F   Paul started the church at Colossae.

2. T or F   Epaphras may be the pastor at Colossae.

----

1. The word "philosophy" consists of two Greek words, _____ meaning "love" and _____ meaning "wisdom."

2. The German word _____ means "household codes."

---

1. Paul's Christology establishes the preeminence of Christ over the entire cosmos, emphasizing four areas. List them:

a. _____

b. _____

c. _____

d. _____

2. List the three major characteristics of the heresy at Colossae:

a. _____

b. _____

c. _____

SELF TEST:

1. The heresy in Colossae:
    a. detracted from the preeminence of Christ
    b. was a form of Jewish Gnosticism
    c. was of a philosophical nature
    d. all of these
    e. none of these

2. It was noted in this lesson that:
    a. in Colossians Paul spoke against philosophy in general
    b. first century Judaism was a monolithic system of beliefs
    c. Epaphras probably started the church in Colossae
    d. A & B
    e. A & C

3. It was noted that:
    a. asceticism played no part in the problems at Colossae
    b. the *Haustafeln* were important for actualizing faith
    c. Paul tells the Colossians that they must put off the old man *just as he does in Ephesians*
    d. all of these
    e. none of these

4. It was observed that:
    a. Paul equates covetousness with idolatry
    b. Paul wrote a letter to the Laodiceans
    c. there was no problem with angel worship in Colossae
    d. A & C
    e. A & B

5. It was noted that:
    a. the *stoichea* refers to Paul's preaching at Colossae
    b. Paul started the church at Colossae
    c. Tychicus carried both Ephesians and Colossians to the churches
    d. A & B
    e. B & C

LESSON 18—1 THESSALONIANS

Part 1	Background Information
Part 2	Central Themes
Part 3	Expanded Outline

OVERVIEW

The operative word for both 1 and 2 Thessalonians is *eschatology* or "a study of the last things." The Thessalonians were thoroughly confused about the nature of the Second Coming.[245] Some were worried about why the Lord had delayed his coming. Would those who died in Christ be left at his coming?

For these reasons, Paul's task in 1 Thessalonians is three-fold:

1. He must comfort the Thessalonians.
Paul must assure them that Jesus is indeed coming again, and that the dead in Christ will be resurrected at that time.

2. He must teach them of the nature of the Second Coming.
1 Thessalonians sets forth central doctrines of Christian eschatology.

3. He must show that ethics and eschatology are inseparable.
The soon return of the Lord should motivate them to live holy lives.

OBJECTIVES

- Give the background information for 1 Thessalonians.
- Briefly discuss the central themes of 1 Thessalonians.
- Give an expanded outline of 1 Thessalonians.
- Summarize the central truths of 1 Thessalonians.

HELPS FOR LEARNING AND REMEMBERING

1. Realize that Paul is addressing a new topic in 1 Thessalonians, for the Second Coming was not a theme in letters studied thus far. This will help you focus on the unique contribution of 1 Thessalonians.

2. Totally immerse yourself in the material. Remove yourself from all distractions, and have a set time for studying 1 Thessalonians. Approaching the subject in an intentional and intense way will certainly help in memorizing the major contributions of 1 Thessalonians.

3. Continually think of how the message of Thessalonians can be applied to contemporary life in the church. You may want to develop several Bible studies or sermons from the material that you

---

[245] Leon Morris, *The First and Second Epistles to the Thessalonians*, (Grand Rapids: Eerdmans, 1959) 22.

study. In making contemporary applications of the ancient text, its meaning and message become part of our life and work.

4. Do not be afraid to write in this book. Underline, highlight, and jot down notes in the margin. This book is a learning tool and should be used accordingly.

KEY WORDS

Parousia   Marcion   Muratorian Canon

PART 1—BACKGROUND INFORMATION

I. AUTHORSHIP

A. Internal Evidence

The internal evidence will consist of data gleaned from 1 Thessalonians concerning Paul's authorship. The very first verse states that the Apostle Paul is the author of this epistle (1:1). We discover that Paul's name is also mentioned in 2:18. Therefore, the internal evidence indicates that Paul is indeed the author of 1 Thessalonians.[246] Also, there are numerous references to Paul visiting the Thessalonians and sending Timothy to Thessalonica (3:1-6). This evidence from 1 Thessalonians coincides with Luke's record in the Book of Acts. Acts 17:1-10 records Paul's second missionary journey. Paul had just recently been released from prison in Philippi and began evangelizing in the city of Thessalonica (Acts 17:1-4). As was so often the case, the Jews began to stir up the people and to cause a riot (Acts 17:5-9). Under cover of darkness, Paul and Silas continue on to Berea (Acts 17:10). When the Jews from Thessalonica discover his location, they force him to travel even further south to Athens (Acts 17:13-14). It will be noticed that Silas and Timothy stayed behind at Berea. All of these facts coincide with Paul's words in 1 Thessalonians 2:17.

B. External Evidence

Once again, the Gnostic Marcion (AD 140) comes to our aid.[247] Even though Marcion was a heretic, he clearly acknowledges that Paul was the author of 1 Thessalonians. The Muratorian Canon (AD 170) affirms Paul's authorship of this epistle. The Muratorian Canon was discovered by Cardinal Muratori in the early 19th century.[248] This early Christian document was written in an attempt to counter the negative influence of Marcion. The Muratorian Canon gave an authoritative list of the early Christian writings. In this list, 1 Thessalonians is placed in the category of Pauline epistles. Finally, the early church father Irenaeus (AD 180) quotes 1 Thessalonians by name, and states that it was written by the Apostle Paul.[249]

II. DATE

1 Thessalonians 3:1 ff. states that Paul has sent Timothy from Athens, Greece to Thessalonica. However, 1 Thessalonians 1:1 and 3:6 indicate that Timothy and Silas are now present with the Apostle Paul. Timothy has already gone to Thessalonica from Athens and has returned to be with the Apostle Paul at the time of the writing. All things considered, Paul must have written this epistle during his second missionary journey, probably in the region of Corinth, Greece. This would date 1 Thessalonians somewhere in the area of AD 51.[250]

---

[246] F.F. Bruce, *1 & 2 Thessalonians*, Word Biblical Commentary, vol. 45 (Waco: Word Books, 1982) xxxii.

[247] William Hendriksen, *Exposition of 1 and 2 Thessalonians*, (Grand Rapids: Baker, 1955) 23.

[248] Tenney, *New Testament*, 189, 408.

[249] Hendriksen, *1 & 2 Thessalonians*, 23.

[250] Morris, *Thessalonians*, 26.

PART 2—THE CENTRAL THEMES OF 1 THESSALONIANS

In 1 Thessalonians, Paul develops the following 3 themes:

I. SECOND COMING (PAROUSIA)

The word *parousia* literally means "the presence." The Thessalonians were wondering when will the real presence of the Lord be experienced on the earth again. The Thessalonians thought that Jesus should have already returned to earth. What had delayed his coming? What about those who had already died in the Lord? When he returned, would they be left behind?[251]

The importance of the parousia can be seen in that it is mentioned near the end of every chapter in 1 Thessalonians. Without a doubt, 1 Thessalonians is one of the most eschatological epistles of Paul.

II. COMFORT IN PERSECUTION

Unbelieving Jews are persecuting the Thessalonians because of their faith in Jesus (1 Thessalonians 2:14-15, 3:3-4). Paul desires to comfort them in the midst of their persecution and earnestly prays to that end (1 Thessalonians 3:4-13). Despite their suffering, Paul prays that their hearts by established in purity and holiness even unto the Second Coming (3:13).

III. PAUL'S DEFENSE OF HIS APOSTLESHIP

As in 1 & 2 Corinthians and Galatians, Paul must affirm his apostolic calling and authority. His enemies claim he is conceited, greedy for money, and immoral (2:3-9). Throughout 1 Thessalonians, Paul must defend himself against these slanderous accusations.[252]

---

[251] James Everett Frame, *The Epistles of Paul to the Thessalonians*, (Edinburgh: T&T Clark, 1970) 11.

[252] Bruce, *1 & 2 Thessalonians*, 23-39.

PART 3—AN EXPANDED OUTLINE OF 1 THESSALONIANS

The content of 1 Thessalonians can be divided into the following six major parts:

I. THE GREETING AND PRAYER OF THANKSGIVING (1:1-10)

Paul adopts the Greco-Roman form of letter writing, identifying himself and his recipients, followed with an expression of thanks and a prayer that they be blessed and prosper.

II. PAUL'S DEFENSE OF HIS MINISTRY IN THESSALONICA (2:1-16)

Throughout the second chapter, Paul reiterates that he had pure motives while ministering in Thessalonica and gives his personal character as proof. He encourages them to stand fast in the Lord and not yield to those who seek to undermine the gospel of grace (2:14-16).

III. PAUL'S PRESENT RELATIONSHIP TO THE THESSALONIANS (2:17-3:13)

Paul explains that his long absence from them is not because he does not love them (2:17-20). Satan has hindered Paul from returning to Thessalonica (2:18). His only joy in this life is the souls he has won for the Lord, and he will visit them soon (2:19-20, 3:10).

It is clear from 3:4 that Paul experienced considerable anxiety over the status of the Thessalonians. He feared that they would collapse under persecution and that his ministry there would have been in vain.[253]

IV. PRACTICAL EXHORTATIONS (4:1-12)

Paul roughly divided his epistles into two parts: the first half concerns doctrinal matters and the second half contains short pithy exhortations governing personal behavior. In this way, Paul demonstrates that theology and ethics are inseparable.

In this section, Paul commands the Thessalonians to live a holy life (4:1-8). "Holiness" means increasing in brotherly love one for another (4:9-10). It also means living right before the world. They were to avoid being idle and continually gossiping (4:11-12).[254] They were to work hard with their own hands, pay their bills, and as much as possible, live a debt-free life.

V. THE PAROUSIA (4:13-18, 5:1-11)

Paul makes three major points:

A. The Dead in Christ will Rise First (4:13-16)

Paul comforts the Thessalonians by stating that the dead in Christ will rise first, and then the living saints will be transformed and "raptured" or caught up to be with the Lord forever.

---

[253] Morris, *Thessalonians*, 161-62.
[254] Frame, *Thessalonians*, 161-62.

B. The Precise Time of the Parousia is Unknown (5:1-3)

The time of the Lord's return is unknown, but it is sure and will be sudden, like a thief, like birth pains.[255]

C. They must live circumspect lives (5:4-11)

The suddenness of the Second Coming requires holiness. The Second Coming is a day of accountability. Paul demonstrates that personal ethics and Christian eschatology are inseparable.

VI. FURHTER EXHORTATIONS AND CONCLUSIONS (5:12-28)

Paul addresses three major areas:

A. Social Responsibilities (5:12-15)

Paul teaches that hard work is to be respected, peace is to be sought, and vengeance is to be avoided.[256]

B. The Spiritual Attitude of the Believer (5:16-17)

The individual Christian is to possess a spirit of joy, prayerfulness, and thankfulness in all circumstances.

C. The Order of Christian Worship Services (5:19-22)

There were some who resisted the spontaneous move of the Holy Spirit in church.[257] Paul warns them not to quench the Spirit, nor despise charismatic gifts of prophecy. Yet, they were to test all spiritual manifestations to see if they be of God. They were to hold to the good and reject the evil.

The conclusion and doxology are set forth in 5:23-28. It is Paul's clear intention that this letter be read to all the brethren in the church (5:27).

True/False:

1. T or F In an ironic way, the Gnostic heretic Marcion helps in establishing the authorship of 1 Thessalonians.
2. T or F It appears that the Thessalonians are being persecuted for their faith.
3. T or F The Thessalonians were worried about the destiny of those who died prior to the Second Coming of the Lord.
4. T or F *Parousia* means "the presence."

---

[255] Charles John Ellicott, *Commentary on the Epistles of Paul to the Thessalonians*, vol. 1 (Grand Rapids: Zondervan, 1957) 69.

[256] Morris, *Thessalonians*, 22-23.

[257] Frame, *Thessalonians*, 205-06.

1. The central concern of 1 Thessalonians can be encapsulated in one word: _____
----

1. List the three major themes of 1 Thessalonians:

a. _____

b. _____

c. _____

Explain how Paul interrelates Christian eschatology with Christian ethics in 1 Thessalonians:

Explain how Paul comforts the Thessalonians concerning the Second Coming:

SELF TEST:

1. The Thessalonians were:
      a. concerned about the parousia
      b. experiencing persecution
      c. having problems in their worship services
      d. all of these
      e. none of these

2. In 1 Thessalonians:
      a. the Gnostic Marcion helps establish Pauline authorship
      b. *paranesis* means "the Second Coming"
      c. eschatology and ethics are inseparable
      d. B & C
      e. A & C

3. The lesson notes that:
      a. some were trying to quench the Spirit
      b. the exact time of the parousia is known
      c. the imminence of the parousia is unrelated to personal ethics
      d. all of these
      e. none of these

LESSON 19—2 THESSALONIANS

Part 1	Background Information
Part 2	Central Themes
Part 3	Eschatological Issues
Part 4	Additional Problems

OVERVIEW

It appears that some in Thessalonica have overreacted to Paul's first epistle and are teaching that the Lord *has come already*.[258] There will be no literal, physical, return of Christ, for the Lord has already returned in a spiritual sense. This misunderstanding of the parousia has affected the social interrelationships at Thessalonica. Some were simply dropping out of society, no longer working or carrying about their daily routines.

Paul must now argue that although the Lord is coming, his coming is yet in the future. In 2 Thessalonians, Paul gives certain signs which must come to pass before the Lord returns.[259] Finally, Paul must address the problem of forgeries in the church. Apparently, some were writing letters in the name of Paul.[260] This may explain how certain heresies got started in Paul's churches.

OBJECTIVES

- Give the background information for 2 Thessalonians.
- Discuss how 2 Thessalonians differs from 1 Thessalonians.
- Describe the 2 main problems in 2 Thessalonians.
- Describe six interpretations of the "Restrainer."
- Discuss the issue of forgeries in the early church.
- Be able to summarize the major points in 2 Thessalonians.

HELPS FOR LEARNING AND REMEMBERING

1. A real challenge in this lesson is to clearly differentiate the issue of 1 Thessalonians from 2 Thessalonians. You might want to make some note cards which clearly delineate the issues of 1 Thessalonians from those presented in 2 Thessalonians.

2. Don't forget to block out special times to study this material. Often if we do not clearly establish times for study it will not get done. Again, be very protective and jealous of the times you have scheduled to study New Testament Survey. Do not permit any interruptions or displacement of this time of study.

---

[258] Bruce, *Thessalonians*, 24.
[259] Tenney, *New Testament*, 284.
[260] Frame, *Thessalonians*, 311.

3. Attempt to correlate what you study in this lesson with the contemporary life in the church. What are some present concerns about the Second Coming? How can some of the errors of the Thessalonians relate to the modern church today? In making a contemporary application, the material "comes alive" and is more easily remembered.

4. Continue to write up a list of questions which address the central points of 2 Thessalonians. In developing these questions, you help clarify the central issues of the epistle. Also, by the end of your study, you will have a list of excellent questions which can help you master the materials of this lesson.

KEY WORDS

Apostasy	apocalyptic	parallelism
Restrainer	providence	

PART 1—BACKGROUND INFORMATION

I. AUTHORSHIP

A. Internal Evidence

The internal evidence for 2 Thessalonians is very similar to that of 1 Thessalonians. For example, the author of 2 Thessalonians clearly refers to himself as Paul in 1:1 and in 3:17. Also a careful study of Paul's travels in 2 Thessalonians coincides with what we find in Acts (cf. 2 Thess. 1:10, 3:7-10, Acts 17:1-9). Finally, the themes, theology, and writing style in 2 Thessalonians are typically Pauline.

B. External Evidence

The external evidence is even stronger than that for 1 Thessalonians. Ignatius of Antioch (ca. AD 125), Polycarp (ca. AD 100), and Justin Marytr (ca. AD 150) all clearly endorse Pauline authorship.[261]

The only objection to Pauline authorship is of a subjective nature. The question is, why would Paul write such a similar letter to the same church? The answer is simply that a new situation required another letter. Paul needed to re-emphasize truths stated in his first letter, but addressed new problems in his second letter.

II. DATE

2 Thessalonians 1:1 indicates that Silas and Timothy were present with Paul. The only place where both were present with Paul was in Corinth (cf. Acts 18:5). 2 Thessalonians was written soon after 1 Thessalonians from Corinth. This would mean that 2 Thessalonians was written on Paul's second visit to Thessalonica recorded in Acts 20:1-4. Considering these facts, a date of about AD 51—52 seems reasonable.

---

[261] Morris, *Thessalonians*, 29.

PART 2—CENTRAL THEMES

A careful study of 2 Thessalonians reveals that the problems addressed in Paul's first epistle to the Thessalonians still exist. That is, the Thessalonians continue to misunderstand the nature of the Second Coming of the Lord. Nevertheless, the confusion on their part has taken a different form in 2 Thessalonians. It is clear that some in Thessalonica had overreacted to Paul's epistle to them. If you will recall, Paul emphasized that even though the Lord appears to have delayed his coming from our perspective, Jesus will most assuredly come again. Paul's emphasis on the certainty of the Second Coming has led some to believe that Jesus has in fact returned already.[262] Some of the believers in Thessalonica were evidently teaching that there will be no physical Second Coming of the Lord but there already has been a spiritual Second Coming of the Lord. On the other hand, some believed that the Lord would return momentarily. For this reason, they lost interest in this present life and were virtually dropping out of society.

In summary, the central themes of 2 Thessalonians are as follows. First, Paul must correct the error of those who believed that the Lord has already come. Secondly, he must in some way convince others that the Lord's return is soon, yet not imminent. We are to live as if the Lord will return at any moment. However, we are to be prepared to occupy our present calling and station in life until Jesus comes again.

These central themes have given rise to several eschatological issues in 2 Thessalonians. Such issues will be the discussion of the next section.

---

[262] Frame, *Thessalonians*, 18.

PART 3—ESCHATOLOGICAL ISSUES

The 3 major eschatological issues are:

I. THE SECOND COMING IS NOT IMMINENT

Some in Thessalonica believed that the Second Coming was imminent, had dropped out of society, and were milling around waiting for the Lord to return.[263] Paul's response to such an interesting dilemma can be found in 2 Thessalonians 3:10-12. Paul's apostolic rebuke in this regard is very pragmatic (cf. 3:10-12). If someone refuses to work, then they are not to be given food to eat. Apparently, those who had dropped out of society were receiving handouts from other believers. Paul commands such persons to keep quiet, mind their own business, and to go back to work.

II. THE SECOND COMING IS YET FUTURE

As noted, there were some who "spiritualized" the Second Coming and believed that the day of the Lord had occurred already (2:2-3). Paul teaches that 3 great events must take place before the end will come. They are:[264]

A. There will be a Great Apostasy (2:3)

Paul communicates the biblical principle that just prior to the end there will be an increase of evil and many will abandon the faith. Paul may be making reference to the words of Jesus in Mark 13:11-37.

B. The "Man of Sin" must be Revealed (2:3-5)

Before the end will come, "the man of sin" or "the son of perdition" must be revealed (cf. Mark 13:14). Paul makes it clear that he taught these principles to them when he was with them in Thessalonica (2:5). The phrase "the man of sin" may come from Jewish apocalyptic literature, and usually referred to false messiahs. The "man of sin" may refer to some false messianic figure (the antichrist).[265]

C. The "Restrainer" must be Taken Away (2:6-8)

The wicked one will not be revealed until the Restrainer is removed. But who is the Restrainer? There are six major theories. They are:[266]

1. The Restrainer is simply a human personality.
For example, Seneca, the tutor of Nero, was known to "restrain" the ruthless oppression of Nero. When the influence of Seneca was removed, then Nero would begin his persecution of the church.

---

[263] Bruce, *Thessalonians*, 175.
[264] Morris, *Thessalonians*, 218-20.
[265] For a thorough treatment of "The Antichrist," see Bruce, *Thessalonians*, pp. 179-88.
[266] Ibid.

2. The Restrainer is simply a political system.
The Romans enforced the *Pax Romana*, ("Roman peace" cf. Romans 13:1-7). When the Roman political system is removed, this will permit the "man of sin" to rise to power.

3. The Restrainer is Gentile domination of the world.
When the time of the Gentiles is fulfilled, then the "man of sin" will be revealed and the end time will come (Luke 21:24).

4. The Restrainer is God's providential care of the world.
In some way the controlling influence of God will be removed from the world, and this will permit the "man of sin" to rise to power. Nevertheless, it is difficult to understand how God could be taken out of the way.

5. The Restrainer is the activity of the Holy Spirit in the church.
Just prior to the flood, God said that his Spirit would not always strive with humankind (Gen. 6:3). Likewise, when the restraining influence of the Spirit is removed, then the "man of sin" will be revealed.

6. The Restrainer is the church.
When the presence of the church is removed from the world, this will allow wickedness to increase in an unprecedented way. In the midst of this wicked environment the "wicked one" will be revealed.

The first two options can be dismissed out of hand. Seneca and Nero have come and gone, yet the world continues. The Roman Empire has passed away, yet the end has not yet come. The New Testament does not view Gentile domination as a restraining influence. It is difficult to imagine how God could be taken out of the world. The Greek text definitely has the masculine article ("he" before "Restrainer"). Paul never refers to the church as "he," but rather as 'she' (the bride of Christ) or "it" (the body or building of Christ). So, the Restrainer is not the church. Many contend the phrase "the Restrainer" more than likely refers to the restraining activity of the Holy Spirit in the church. There will come a time *when the dynamic activity* of the Holy Spirit will be removed. Not that the Holy Spirit will be removed, but the manner in which he works will be altered. This will permit the "man of sin" or that "wicked one" to come to power. The end will not come prior to these events.

PART 4—ADDITIONAL PROBLEMS

In the introductory portion of this course, we discussed the issue of false writings in the church. Under the section entitled "The Canon" we spoke of the existence of pseudepigrapha or "false writings." You might recall that very early in the church false gospels, epistles, and even false books of Acts were circulated among the churches. 2 Thessalonians 2:2 may indicate that some of the confusion in Thessalonica was caused by false letters which were written in the name of the Apostle Paul. Here Paul tells the Thessalonians not to be disturbed by any spirit or word or even by some letter supposedly from him. These words may indicate that someone had forged the Apostle Paul's name to a letter to the Thessalonians.[267] Some false teacher may have wanted to spread his understanding of the Second Coming within the churches of Thessalonica. He may have used Paul's name in order to lend authority to his perception concerning the end time. 2 Thessalonians 3:17 lends support to this theory of false writings in the name of Paul. At this point, Paul takes the pen from the hand of the amanuensis (male secretary) and writes the salutation in his own hand. The very fact that Paul signed his epistles in this way indicates that forgeries may have been present in the church, especially at Thessalonica.

True/False:

1. T or F   It appears that some of the Thessalonians had overreacted to Paul's instruction in I Thessalonians.
2. T or F   Some in Thessalonica taught that the Lord had come already in a spiritual sense.
3. T or F   In 2 Thessalonians, Paul teaches that things will get better and that more people will come to the Lord just prior to the Second Coming.
4. T or F   Paul frequently uses the word "Antichrist" throughout 2 Thessalonians.
5. T or F   Paul often refers to the church as "he."
6. T or F   2 Thessalonians 2:2 indicates that some may have been forging Paul's name to false epistles.

----

1. Paul says that the _____ must be taken out of the way before the end comes (2:6-8).
2. "Pax Romana" means _____.
3. The technical term for "false writings" is _____.

----

1. List the six options given for the meaning of "the Restrainer":
a. _____

b. _____

c. _____

d. _____

e. _____

f. _____

---

[267] Elliot, *Thessalonians*, 106-08.

SELF TEST:

1. In 2 Thessalonians, it was learned that some:
   a. have overreacted to Paul's first epistle to them
   b. believe that the Second Coming is imminent
   c. have 'spiritualized" the Second Coming
   d. all of these
   e. none of these

2. It was also noted that:
   a. the heresy in 2 Thessalonians had no societal effects
   b. forgeries were a problem in Thessalonica
   c. Paul wants them to support those who quit work
   d. A & B
   e. A & C

3. Paul, the author of 2 Thessalonians,
   a. frequently refers to the church as "he"
   b. saw the *Pax Romana* (Romans 13:1-7) as keeping law and order throughout the empire
   c. may be referring to the apocalyptic words of Jesus in Mark 13
   d. A & B
   e. B & C

4. The "Restrainer" has been referred to as:
   a. God
   b. the Roman Empire
   c. the activity of the Holy Spirit in the church
   d. all of these
   e. none of these

5. With regard to forgeries, it was noted that:
   a. Paul personally signed all of his letters
   b. forgeries did not serve as a vehicle to spread heresy in the church
   c. *pseudepigrapha* were not a problem at Thessalonica
   d. B & C
   e. A & B

LESSON 20—1 TIMOTHY AND TITUS

Part 1	Background Information
Part 2	Central Themes
Part 3	Major Concerns
Part 4	Qualifications for Church Leadership
Part 5	Guidelines for Interpersonal Relationships

OVERVIEW

Apart from Philemon, these are the first Pauline epistles addressed to individuals. More specifically, these letters are the first to be explicitly addressed to pastors of local churches. For this reason, the Pastorals are particularly relevant to the clergy. In these letters, Paul addresses such issues as pastoral leadership in the face of opposition. He also instructs Timothy and Titus on the qualifications for church leadership. Various people-groups such as widows, elders, slaves, etc. are discussed in the Pastorals. Finally, the Pastorals represent Paul as a master pastor who mentors other pastors in the Lord. He continually encourages and challenges Timothy and Titus to be diligent and honest in their ministries.

These epistles are relevant to contemporary ministry. The complexity of the ministry today requires highly qualified and proficient persons. In another vein, the many moral scandals prevalent in the ministry today call for a redefining or clarification of what it means to be a true minister of God.

OBJECTIVES

- Explain the background information for 1 Timothy and Titus.
- Articulate the central themes of 1 Timothy and Titus.
- Discuss Paul's major concerns in these epistles.
- List the major qualifications for church leadership.
- Outline Paul's guidelines for interpersonal relationships.

HELPS FOR LEARNING AND REMEMBERING

1. Take special note of the change in *literary genre* (literary "type" or "category"). Paul is no longer writing to churches, but to individuals who are charged with leading the church.

2. Note of the similarities between 1 Timothy and Titus. They are so similar in content that they will be considered together.

3. Quickly read through 1 Timothy and Titus. Notice any areas of similarity or repetition. Take note of these areas and watch for the discussion of these areas in this lesson.

4. While rapidly reading through 1 Timothy and Titus, briefly outline these two epistles. Constructing a rough outline of each epistle will not only give you a grasp of the central

principles set forth in each epistle, but can reveal the similarities and contrasts that exist between the epistles.

5. Take out a sheet of paper and write the following title across the top: "What I see in Timothy and Titus." Every time you notice a contemporary model for ministry, church difficulty or area of ministerial development which parallels Paul's presentation in the Pastorals, jot this down. By making what we study relevant to our daily life and experience, the material comes alive.

KEY WORDS

Ecclesiastical	bishops	gnosis
Neophutos	presbuteros	*hapax*
Literary genre	overseer	kosmios
Deacon	elders	sophron
Episcopae	presbyter	plektes
Diakonos	amanuensis	tetuphotai

PART 1—BACKGROUND INFORMATION

Of all the epistles, the background information for the Pastorals is the most important because they are the most contested.

I. AUTHORSHIP

Pauline authorship of the Pastorals is disputed on the following grounds:[268]

A. Historical

Historical information in the Pastorals does not coincide with what we know from Acts. For example:
1. Timothy had been left behind at Ephesus and Paul was in Macedonia (1 Tim. 1:3).
2. Titus had been left at Crete (Titus 1:5).
3. Paul was a prisoner in Rome (2 Tim. 1:16, 17, 4:16).

There is nothing in Acts indicating that Paul left Timothy in Ephesus while in Macedonia. There is nothing about leaving Titus in Crete, or even that Paul ever visited Crete. If he were a prisoner in Rome, how can we explain him leaving Timothy in Ephesus and Titus in Crete?

A possible solution is that Paul may have been released from his first Roman imprisonment, and this would have permitted him to continue missionary activity before being arrested for a second time.[269] Since Acts is not a comprehensive record of Paul's life, and all Christians are acquitted by Roman judges, it is possible that Paul was released by Caesar, and continued westward to Spain. Paul could have worked in the east to some extent (in Ephesus and Crete).

B. Ecclesiastical

The Pastorals speak of various church offices, such as, bishops, presbyters, or elders and deacons.[270] It is argued that such church offices are too advanced for the apostolic period and are more indicative of the 2nd and 3rd centuries. It is further argued that the bishop in the Pastorals is the "monarchical bishop" of the early Catholic church, ruling over vast territories (1 Tim. 3:6).[271]

In response, it must be admitted that Paul gave more attention to church offices in the Pastorals than in any other epistle. Yet Paul did appoint elders in the churches (Acts 14:23). In Acts 20:17 ff., Paul sent for the elders and bishops (*episcopoi*, literally "overseers") of Ephesus. Thus, Paul spoke of elders and bishops at least a decade prior to the Pastorals.

---

[268] Guthrie, *New Testament*, 589.
[269] Ibid., 596.
[270] Donald A. Ward., *Commentary on 1 & 2 Timothy and Titus*, (Waco: Waco Books, 1974) 10.
[271] Ibid., 11.

C. Doctrinal

The content of the Pastorals is different from what we find in his other epistles.[272] Little is mentioned of the fatherhood of God, the spiritual union between the believer and Christ, the church as the body of Christ, and the person and work of the Holy Spirit.

Yet Paul was writing to pastors and assumes that they knew the rudimentary doctrines of the faith.[273] He was not writing to correct doctrinal errors but to strengthen and inform young pastors on how to lead the church.

D. Linguistic

The vocabulary and writing style of the Pastorals differs greatly from other Pauline epistles.[274] There are 175 *hapaxes*, or words "only mentioned once."

It should be noted that all of the *hapaxes* were in use at the time of Paul and have been found in extra-biblical literature of the 1st century. Additionally, half of these new words occur in the *LXX* (Septuagint). The different occasion called for new expressions and vocabulary. Paul would have used an amanuensis, or "male secretary," who may have been given quite a bit of latitude in producing the epistles. This may account for some of the unique vocabulary we find in the Pastorals.

II. DATE

If one accepts Pauline authorship and assumes a second Roman imprisonment, then a possible time line would be as follows:[275]

- Paul's release from first Roman imprisonment in about AD 63.

- He continues missionary activity westward to Spain (Romans 15:23-29), and the assigning of Timothy to Ephesus, and Titus to Crete (1 Tim. 1:3; Titus 1:5, 3:12; 2 Tim. 1:17, 4:13, 20).

- Paul's second Roman imprisonment and death in AD 67.

If this time line is correct, then the Pastorals were written between the release from his first Roman imprisonment (AD 63) and his second Roman imprisonment and execution (AD 67).

---

[272] Guthrie, *New Testament*, 593.
[273] Donald Guthrie, *The Pastoral Epistles*, (Grand Rapids: Eerdmans, 1957) 12.
[274] Guthrie, *New Testament*, 594.
[275] French L. Arrington, *Maintaining the Foundations*, (Grand Rapids: Baker Book House) 18.

PART 2—CENTRAL THEMES

Paul's major focus in these two epistles is self-evident: a master pastor was giving his disciples instructions concerning how to minister and to administer in their churches. With respect to 1 Timothy, Paul felt it necessary to encourage Timothy. Throughout this epistle, Paul challenged Timothy to stand firm in the gospel. From this we can surmise that this young pastor had come under considerable pressure and Paul needed to support him and encourage him in the ministry. A central theme of both 1 Timothy and Titus is the mentoring and development of young pastors in the ministry.[276]

Secondly, Paul was very concerned about doctrinal heresy in 1 Timothy and Titus.[277] Indeed, doctrinal heresy had made inroads into their churches (1 Timothy 1:3; Titus 1:5). But as noted in the introduction, Paul was not primarily concerned with refuting the heresies in 1 Timothy and Titus. Rather, he was concerned with how Timothy and Titus would handle the heretics in their churches. This may explain why Paul did not fill the Pastorals with doctrinal content as in his other epistles. Rather, the Pastorals are full of apostolic instruction on how to handle troublemakers in the church. At any rate, a central theme of 1 Timothy and Titus is that they "maintain the foundations" of the faith.[278]

In summary, the central themes of 1 Timothy and Titus are pastoral development and church administration. The latter theme is especially focused on how to handle the false teachers and their teachings in the churches. This last point addresses the major concerns of the Apostle Paul in 1 Timothy and Titus.

---

[276] Guthrie, *New Testament*, 622.
[277] Arrington, *Maintaining*, 25.
[278] Ibid., 26.

PART 3—MAJOR CONCERNS

The major concerns are:

I. GNOSTICISM

A. Full-blown Gnosticism

Those who reject Pauline authorship believe that the major concern is full blown Gnosticism of the 2nd century.[279]   1 Timothy 6:20 warns against ideas which are "falsely called knowledge" or *gnosis* (cf. also 1 Timothy 6:4; 2 Timothy 2:23; Titus 3:9).

B. Embryonic Gnosticism

Paul did focus on some type of false knowledge, which indicates the presence of "embryonic Gnosticism" of the first, but not the 2nd century.[280]

II. THE HYPERSPIRITUALISTS

The "hyperspiritualists" claimed that the resurrection had already occurred (2 Timothy 2:18). If one possessed the *gnosis*, then he/she had already experienced the resurrection.

III. ASCETICISM[281]

1 Timothy 4:3 speaks of abstaining from food and marriage. Since the Gnostics believed that the things of this world were evil, they may be the cause of asceticism here.

IV. LEGALISM[282]

False teachers were claiming that "nothing was pure" (Titus 1:14, 15), and may indicate Hellenistic Jewish Gnostics were emphasizing asceticism and legalism in the churches.[283]   The presence of Old Testament themes lends support to this theory (1 Timothy 1:6-10; Titus 1:14-16, 3:9).

---

[279] Ibid., 21.

[280] Gordon D. Fee, *1 and 2 Timothy, Titus* (Peabody, MA: Hendrickson, 1984) 9.

[281] French L. Arrington, *Paul's Aeon Theology in 1 Corinthians*, (Washington, D.C.: University Press of America, 1977) 181-87.

[282] Arrington, *Maintaining*, 21.

[283] Fee, *1 and 2 Timothy, Titus*, 8.

PART 4—QUALIFICATIONS FOR CHURCH LEADERSHIP

If Timothy and Titus were overseeing house churches, they might have been grappling with faulty leadership in several congregations. Unlike Galatians and Corinth, the troublemakers in Timothy and Titus seem to have arisen *from within* the congregation.

Paul's extraordinary emphasis on qualifications for leadership is understandable. He gave detailed descriptions of the ecclesiastical criteria required of anyone seeking the office of bishop or deacon (1 Timothy 3:1-13; Titus 1:5-9).

I. BISHOP

The Greek word for bishop is *episcope*, literally meaning "overseer."[284] Again, this is not the monarchical episcopate of the 2nd century, for the church at Philippi had several "bishops." More than likely the word bishop here simply means pastor.

Paul only listed the *qualities* of a bishop and did not go into the *duties* of the overseer (1Timothy 3:2 ff). The immoral background of early Christian converts may explain why Paul focused on the character rather than on task. The overseer must:

A. Be above Reproach

"Above reproach" literally means "not to be taken hold of."[285] There must not be anything in the life of the overseer that could be seized upon by those who wanted to undermine the ministry.

B. Be a "One-Woman Man"

Is this forbidding polygamy, which was practiced throughout the Roman Empire? Or does he mean that the overseer can only have been married once, forbidding divorce or remarriage? How would being single place the overseer beyond reproach?

C. Be Temperate

The Greek word here refers to the pursuit of pleasure.[286] The church leader must not be motivated by the pursuit of pleasure.

D. Be Sensible, Respectable, Hospitable

The overseer must be *sophron* (sensible or dignified, cf. 1 Timothy 1:7; Titus 1:8, 2:2, and 5). He must be *kosmios* (respectable).[287] He must be "hospitable" (concerned about the social programs of the church, especially with regard to the widows, 1Timothy 5:10; Titus 1:8).

---

[284] Ward, *1 & 2 Timothy and Titus*, 54.
[285] Arrington, *Maintaining*, 77.
[286] Ibid., 79-80.
[287] Ibid., 80.

E. Be able to Teach

The Christian leader must not only know the word of God but be able to communicate the word of God to others. This is a gift of the Spirit (Romans 12:6 ff.).

F. Not be Given too much Wine[288]

Literally he should not "sit long at wine" (not be overindulgent in alcohol, 1Timothy 3:3). Although total abstinence is not explicitly taught in the Pastorals, in our particular culture this is the best practice.

G. Not be Violent or Quarrelsome

The church leader must not be *plektes* (not a "giver of blows").[289] He must be *amacos*, literally "not a fighter." The minister must not be given to fist fights or tongue lashings. No doubt the false teachers in Ephesus were given to violent arguments concerning myths and genealogies (1Timothy 1:4). Church leaders should not become entangled with such nonsense.

H. Not be a Lover of Money

The Christian leader must not be a thorough-going materialist who loves the riches of this world (recall Demus, I1Timothy 4:10).[290]

I. Manage His Household

The state of a person's private life (especially family relationships) reflects upon one's ability to lead the church (1Timothy 3:4,5).[291]

J. Not be a Recent Convert

"Recent convert" is *neophutos*, literally "newly planted" (1Timothy 3:6).[292] The emphasis is on experience in the Lord and not necessarily upon one's age. A new convert lacks the experience and spiritual development needed to lead the church.

K. Have a Good Standing

Lack of personal integrity before the community would undermine the work of the church (cf. 1Thess. 4:12; Colossians 4:5).[293]

---

[288] Ibid., 82.

[289] Ibid., 81.

[290] Fee, *1 and 2 Timothy and Titus*, 82.

[291] M. Dibelius and H. Conzelmann, *The Pastoral Epistles*. Hermeneia, (Philadelphia: Fortress, 1972) 53.

[292] Arrington, *Maintaining*, 84.

[293] Arland J. Hultgren, *1 and 2 Timothy and Titus*, (Minneapolis: Augsburg, 1984) 73.

II. DEACONS (1Timothy 3:8 ff.)

The word for "deacon," *diakonos*, having both masculine and feminine forms in the New Testament, indicates that there were both male and female deacons in the church (cf. Romans 16:1).[294] It literally means "to serve, wait upon, or care for," denoting one who helps rather than one who supervises.[295]

The requirements for the deacon parallel those of a bishop, with the addition that they be "tested." The word "tested" originally referred to testing the value of metal coins (1Timothy 3:10).[296] So, "the metal" of a deacon's life must prove worthy of the office.

1Timothy 3:11 begins to address the qualifications of wives. Was Paul simply addressing the wives of the deacons, or was he setting forth the criteria to be a deaconess?[297] Since the qualifications of wives parallel those of the bishop and deacon, Paul may be referring here to female leadership in the church.

---

[294] Ward, *1 & 2 Timothy and Titus*, 59.
[295] Ibid.
[296] Arrington, *Maintaining*, 87.
[297] Ward, *1 & 2 Timothy and Titus*, 59.

PART 5—GUIDELINES FOR INTERPERSONAL RELATIONSHIPS

Paul instructed Timothy on how to relate to various people groups, such as, widows, elders, backsliders, slaves, and heretics.

I. WIDOWS (1Timothy 5:3-16)

Paul eliminated anyone who did not qualify as a true widow (5:11-16).[298] If persons seeking aid were self-indulgent (5:6) or had family members to help them, they could not be supported by the church (1Timothy 5:9, 10). If they qualified, they should reciprocate and minister to the church (1Timothy 5:10). Younger widows should remarry and establish new families (1Timothy 5:11-16).

II. ELDERS (1Timothy 5:1-2, 17-19; Titus 2:1-3)

The word for "elder" is *presbuteros* and can refer to an old person or a leadership position which is financially supported by the church (cf. 1Timothy 5:18-19).[299] Because of their youth, Paul carefully instructed Timothy and Titus on how to relate to senior members of the church and the leading elders. In each case, all must be done with respect and tact.[300] The task of the elders cannot be determined, but they may have functioned like a pastor's counsel.

III. BACKSLIDERS (1Timothy 5:19-25)

Since Paul had been dealing with church leadership, he may have been addressing backsliding clergy.[301] To prevent malicious slander, no accusations against the leadership should be accepted unless substantiated by two or three witnesses (cf. Deut. 19:15). Once the charge has been established, discipline should be firm and public (1Timothy 5:20). If Timothy had not disciplined the leadership of the church, he would have been accountable in the final judgment (1Timothy 5:21).

The best way to avoid the unpleasant task of disciplining church leaders is to place the right persons in office in the beginning. Thus, Paul told Timothy he should not be in a hurry to ordain just anybody, because ordination is a public identification with the ones being ordained (1Timothy 5:22).[302] If they failed in ministry, Timothy would be implicated as well.

IV. SLAVES (1Timothy 6:1-2; Titus 2:1-3, 9)

We may be disappointed that Paul did not directly attack slavery. However, slavery was a deep-rooted evil in Paul's day, and to address the issue of slavery may well have undermined the establishment of the gospel. Ultimately, the Christian message certainly led to the abolishment of slavery in the world. Even so, Paul was not concerned with maintaining the status quo. The slave

---

[298] Dibelius and Conzelmann, *The Pastorals*, 74.
[299] Ibid., 89.
[300] Arrington, *Maintaining*, 108.
[301] Ward, *1 and 2 Timothy and Titus*, 88.
[302] Ibid., 89.

was to view his service as a type of ministry.[303] Thus, Paul elevated the master/slave relationship to the level of Christian worship. Let everything be done unto the Lord.

V. HERETICS (1 Timothy 6:3-8)

The heretics were not only flawed in doctrine, but in character as well. They were *tetuphotai*, (literally "puffed up with smoke)",[304] arrogant egotists, full of hot air, who love senseless arguments about words (1 Timothy 6:4-5). Chrysostom likened such to mangy sheep who spread infection throughout the flock by rubbing against those who are healthy.[305]

Paul set forth the true character of Christian ministry in 1 Timothy 6:6-7. Godly gain is being content with food and clothing, and to experience the inner peace of the Holy Spirit.

True/False:

1. T or F   The record of Paul's activities in the Pastorals completely coincides with Acts.
2. T or F   The Pastorals reflect a fairly well developed church structure (the mention of bishops, presbyters, and deacons).
3. T or F   There are 175 hapaxes in the Pastorals.
4. T or F   Hyperspiritualists who value Gnosis caused trouble for Timothy and Titus.
5. T or F   Paul was concerned with teaching doctrine in the Pastorals.
6. T or F   Both the masculine and feminine forms of *diakonos* (deacon) are used in the scriptures (Romans 16:1).

----

1. The term "monarchical bishop" refers to a:
    a. king who is in the church
    b. type of butterfly
    c. powerful church official who ruled over vast areas during the Middle Ages

2. The heretics in the Pastorals:
    a. promoted asceticism
    b. were very legalistic
    c. were probably Hellenistic Jewish Christians
    d. all of these
    e. none of these

----

1. The word *episcope* literally means _____.
2. Paul's major task was to _____ Timothy and Titus not to give up the ministry and to fight _____ _____ being spread by heretics in the church.

---

[303] Arrington, *Maintaining*, 108.
[304] Ibid., 89.
[305] Ward, *1 and 2 Timothy*, 95.

SELF TEST:

1. With regard to background information, it was noted that:
    a. Paul's activities in the Pastorals completely coincides with Acts
    b. the "bishop" of the Pastorals is the "monarchical bishop" of the 2nd century
    c. there are 175 *hapaxes* in the Pastorals
    d. A & B
    e. A & C

2. From the Pastoral Epistles it can be seen that:
    a. Paul's main purpose in the Pastorals is to teach doctrine
    b. the word *episcope* literally means "to serve"
    c. the word *presbuteros* can mean either an old person or the office of an elder
    d. all of these
    e. none of these

3. The heretics in the Pastorals:
    a. promote asceticism
    b. are very legalistic
    c. are probably Hellenistic Jewish Christians
    d. all of these
    e. none of these

4. It was observed that:
    a. Paul directly attacks the institution of slavery
    b. a single accusation against a church leader is sufficient to initiate discipline
    c. if one hastily ordains an unfit minister, then one partakes in his failures
    d. A & C
    e. B & C

5. Also noted in the Pastorals was that:
    a. if a widow has family, she is not to be supported by the church
    b. only the masculine form of *diakonos* is used in the New Testament
    c. "backsliders" can even refer to wayward ministers
    d. A & B
    e. A & C

LESSON 21—PAUL'S EPISTLE OF 2 TIMOTHY

Part 1	Background Information
Part 2	Courage to Lead
Part 3	Pauline Exhortations
Part 4	How to Handle Heretics

OVERVIEW

The pastoral spirit evidenced in 1Timothy and Titus is continued in 2 Timothy. Paul was vitally concerned with mentoring, developing and strengthening this young pastor in the ministry. As will be noted below, Paul focused attention on Timothy rather than addressing the various problems in the church. For these reasons, Paul addressed such issues as having the courage to actualize one's spiritual gifts, self-discipline in the face of hardship, and demonstration of one's competence and consistency in conduct. It is to these subjects that we now turn.

OBJECTIVES

- Note the difference in tone among 1& 2 Timothy and Titus.
- Discuss the 3-word pictures used to encourage Timothy in 2 Timothy.
- Identify the ways Paul tells Timothy to handle heretics in the church.

HELPS FOR LEARNING AND REMEMBERING

1. Compare and contrast 2 Timothy with 1 Timothy and Titus.

2. Concentrate on word pictures used in 2 Timothy.

3. Quickly review the various parts of this lesson and read the introductory words. Realize that the more similar material is, the more easily it can be confused. Therefore, the similarities between 1 Timothy and Titus and your study here on 2 Timothy should be noted. As you study through 2 Timothy, you should take note of and record any similarities and differences that exist between the Pastorals. This will help you to differentiate the data of 2 Timothy with that of 1 Timothy and Titus.

4. Finally, a rapid reading of all of 2 Timothy will help you gain an overview of the entire epistle. Once you understand the "lay of the land" mastering the individual portions of the epistle will be easier.

KEY WORDS

Sugkakopatheo   *dokimazo*   *logomachiai*
Gangrene

PART 1—BACKGROUND INFORMATION

The issues of authorship and date have already been dealt with in our study of 1 Timothy and Titus, and therefore need not be repeated here. It may serve you well to review that material now. The only additional information at this point concerns the <u>tone</u> of 2 Timothy. Paul was writing from prison and he clearly believed that he would be executed soon. For this reason, the apostle was in a very reflective mood.[306] He recalled how God had blessed him throughout his life and ministry and yet he looked forward to the reward he would receive from Jesus Christ. In this sense, 2 Timothy marks the transition from the apostolic period to the post-apostolic period. The letter is filled with a sense of urgency. Paul wanted to ensure that Timothy was prepared to carry on and expand upon the ministry.

---

[306] Dibelius and Conzelmann, *The Pastorals*, 98.

PART 2—COURAGE TO LEAD

In preparing Timothy to take on the new leadership role, Paul encouraged him to actualize his spiritual gifts (1:6-12). Timothy appears to have been a man of a gentle spirit. Paul exhorted him to appropriate the charismatic gifts which the Lord had placed in him (1:6-7). Paul was careful to note that leadership involves suffering (1:8), and he used an interesting word here to describe this aspect of the ministry. The word is *sugkakopatheo*[307] and literally means "to experience pain together." Paul was telling Timothy that he must be prepared to experience pain together with him in the ministry if he was going to actualize his spiritual gifts to the greatest extent possible.

In conclusion, Paul stated that since God had not given Timothy a spirit of fear (1:7) he could actualize the charismatic ministry of the Lord. However, Paul was careful to note that in actualizing his spiritual gifts, Timothy would also experience intense suffering (1:8). Nevertheless, Timothy was exhorted to experience pain together with the Apostle Paul in carrying on the ministry. In verses 11 and 12, Paul set himself forth as a prime example of one who had suffered and faithfully witnessed for the gospel. Paul was not asking Timothy to do anything that he himself had not done throughout his life and ministry.

---

[307] Zerwick and Grosvenor, *A Grammatical Analysis of the Greek New Testament*, (Rome: Biblical Institute Press, 1981) 639.

PART 3—PAULINE EXHORTATIONS

Paul realized that Timothy would face many difficulties and must be self-disciplined in the midst of suffering (2:3-13). In this section, Paul used 3-word pictures, or images, in preparing Timothy for a difficult trial ahead.

I. A SOLDIER (2:3-4)

The first image is that of a soldier. Just as a soldier was not to become entangled in equipment during battle, Timothy was not to become entangled in the affairs of this world.[308] As a soldier cannot be preoccupied with civilian affairs, so too, allegiance to God must take top priority in the life of a minister.

II. AN ATHLETE (2:5)

The principle of self-discipline and purpose are continued here.[309] Paul is referring to those athletes who partook in the Olympic Games. Such persons trained up to 1 year prior to competing. Dedication, singleness of purpose, and careful observance of the rules are necessary to be successful in the ministry.

III. A FARMER (2:6)

The third image is taken from the agricultural world. Paul's point here is that the hard-working farmer will eventually reap rewards for his labor.[310]

In conclusion, the life of self-discipline is essential to be successful in the ministry. As a soldier, Timothy was to have no distractions in executing his ministerial duties. As an athlete, he must demonstrate extraordinary discipline and self-sacrifice in order to be successful in the work of the Lord. And as a hard-working farmer, Timothy could be assured that his labor for the Lord would ultimately receive a reward.

---

[308] Guthrie, *Pastorals*, 139.
[309] Dibelius and Conzelmann, *The Pastorals*, 108.
[310] Ibid.

PART 4—HOW TO HANDLE HERETICS

Paul explains that the best way to handle heretics is to demonstrate your confidence, consistency in conduct, and consecration in service.

I. CONFIDENCE (2:14-19)

Paul commanded Timothy to spare no effort in demonstrating his competency in the Lord (2:15). He borrows the term *dokimazo* from metallurgy to describe Christian character.[311] It was used to prove the value of metal coins. The surest way Timothy could demonstrate his "metal" was to correctly interpret the Word of God. The word used for "interpret" literally means "to cut a straight line."[312] The best way to handle heretics is to show one's ability to cut a straight line (properly discern the word of God). He was not to become embroiled in senseless chatter and human speculation (2:16). These false prophets were like gangrene, spreading error throughout the church (2:17).[313]

II. CONSISTENCY (2:20-26)

His words here parallel Romans 9:22, 23. Paul argued that the pluralism in the church explained the existence of heretics; he used the image of a large house to illustrate his point.[314] Just as a large house contains many different vessels, some honorable and some dishonorable, the church also consists of orthodox Christians and persons of questionable integrity and doctrine. The latter promote ignorant debates and enjoy becoming involved in *logomachiai* or "word battles" (2:23, cf. also 1 Timothy 6:4; 2 Timothy 2:14).[315]

III. CONSECRATION (4:1-5)

Rather than become involved in such controversies, Paul commanded Timothy to steadfastly preach the Word. The phrase "in season and out of season" probably does not refer to the subjective feelings of Timothy.[316] More than likely Paul was commanding Timothy to preach the Word whether the people want to hear it or not. Regardless of the spiritual status of the congregation, Timothy was to steadfastly preach the Word.

True/False:

1. T or F   Paul exhorted Timothy to "experience pain together" with him.
2. T or F   Paul used images from athletic competition to encourage Timothy to be self-disciplined.

\-

---

[311] Fee, *1 and 2 Timothy and Titus*, 205.

[312] Ibid.

[313] J.N.D. Kelly, *A Commentary on the Pastoral Epistles*, (Peabody, MA: Hendrickson, 1987) 184.

[314] A.T. Hanson, *The Pastoral Epistles*, (Grand Rapids: Eerdmans, 1982) 137.

[315] Kelly, *Pastorals*, 189.

[316] Hanson, *Pastorals*, 152.

1. *Dokimazo* is derived from metallurgy and means the testing of the _____ of a coin.

2. Paul encourages Timothy to actualize his _____

   _____.

----

1. The phrase "in season and out of season" (4:1ff) probably refers to when:
   a. Timothy feels like preaching or when he does not feel like preaching the Word
   b. people feel like hearing or when the people do not feel like hearing the Word
   c. a particular kind of food can be found in the marketplace and when it cannot be found in the marketplace
   d. all of these
   e. none of these

2. Paul exhorts Timothy, using the imagery of:
   a. a soldier, a shepherd, and a deacon
   b. an athlete, a shepherd, and a merchant
   c. a soldier, an athlete, and a farmer
   d. none of the above

How does the tone of 2 Timothy differ from that in 1 Timothy and Titus?

SELF TEST:

1. It was noted that:
     a. 2 Timothy may mark a transitional phase from the apostolic period to the post-apostolic period
     b. the tone of 2 Timothy is the same as in the other Pastorals
     c. Timothy is urged to actualize his gifts
     d. A & C
     e. A & B

2. Paul exhorts Timothy:
     a. "to experience pain together" with him
     b. " to cut a straight line" in interpreting the word
     c. to get in there and "mix it up" with the gangrenous heretics
     d. A & C
     e. A & B

3. It was noted that Timothy:
     a. must "prove his metal" (recall *dokimazo*)
     b. is told to preach the Word whether *he* feels like it or not
     c. should get involved in *logomachiai*
     d. all of these
     e. none of these

4. Paul teaches that:
     a. plurality in the church explains the presence of heretics
     b. farmers have something to teach Timothy about the ministry
     c. athletics have something to teach Timothy about the ministry
     d. A & C
     e. B & C

5. Timothy is to be:
     a. confident
     b. consistent
     c. consecrated
     d. all of these
     e. none of these

LESSON 22—PAUL'S EPISTLE TO PHILEMON

Part 1	Background Information
Part 2	Central Themes
Part 3	The Spiritual Significance of Philemon

OVERVIEW

Our reasons for going on to Philemon at this point are as follows: our study of Colossians and Ephesians revealed that the epistle to Philemon is integrally connected to these epistles. Colossians 4:10-14 mentions that Mark, Demas, Luke and Aristarchus are present with the Apostle Paul. These same persons are mentioned in Philemon 24. This indicates that Colossians and Philemon were written at the same time. Additionally, in Colossians 4:9, Paul mentions that Onesimus was in fact a Colossian. This data seems to indicate that Philemon, Colossians and Ephesians were written at the same time and sent from Paul in Rome.

Another reason for studying Philemon at this point relates to the introductory material presented at the beginning of the course. It will be recalled that Paul's epistle to Philemon had a difficult time getting into the canon. After all, Philemon seems to address a completely secular issue; a runaway slave. The early church naturally had questions concerning its lasting spiritual significance. It is important to evaluate Philemon in this light. What exactly does this short epistle have to offer to the church?

Finally, the epistle to Philemon reveals an interesting aspect of Paul's ministry. It shows that the Apostle Paul was not simply involved in evangelizing and mission work. Rather, he was infinitely involved in the daily affairs of his converts. In the case of Philemon, we ca see that Paul marshaled all of his pastoral gifts in presenting us with a beautiful example of conflict resolution. In Philemon, a domestic conflict had arisen, which could have had life threatening implications. Paul did not hesitate to apply the spiritual principles of the gospel in bringing a satisfactory conclusion to this issue.

OBJECTIVES

- Explain the relationship between Philemon and Colossians.
- List and briefly describe the central themes of Philemon.
- Outline the spiritual significance of Philemon.
- Describe Paul's character as revealed in Philemon.

HELPS FOR LEARNING AND REMEMBERING

1. Philemon is one of the shortest epistles in the New Testament, consisting of one chapter. Do not let its length mislead you, for it is full of spiritual and theological significance.

2. Continually ask yourself, "What does the epistle to Philemon mean for ministry today?" The more we can anchor the situation in Philemon in our present ministerial context, the more memorable and useful the work becomes.

3. You might also want to ask yourself, "What can I learn about the Apostle Paul from this epistle?" Insight into the personality of the Apostle Paul may help us evaluate ourselves as ministering persons. Finally, you may want to ask the question, "To what extent should a minister of the gospel become involved in social issues?" After all, Paul is addressing a master/slave relationship. Even during Paul's day, this was a highly controversial issue. To what extent can we apply the gospel to contemporary social issues?

4. These guidelines and suggested questions will help provide a framework for your study of Philemon. Continually look for creative ways which will help you master the material.

KEY WORDS

Pseudopigrapha	vicarious	autocratic
Sitz im Leben	agape	

PART 1—BACKGROUND INFORMATION

I. AUTHORSHIP

Our introductory remarks to this epistle have already addressed the subject of authorship. Also, our discussion of the canon in the introductory portion of this course has addressed the authenticity of Philemon. As you might recall, the epistle to Philemon was listed among the antilegomena. That is to say, the epistle to Philemon had a difficult time being accepted into the Canon. It was not thought to be a pseudepigraphal work, or a "false writing." Pauline authorship was not the issue. Rather, the lasting spiritual significance of the epistle was a concern of the early church council. Exactly what did the problem of a runaway slave have to do with the gospel?

Apart from these concerns, the internal evidence of the epistle is thoroughly in favor of Pauline authorship.[317] In fact, verses 1, 9, 19 explicitly mention Paul as the author. It is also clear from verses 1, 19, 22, 23 that the author of this epistle is a prisoner. Finally, the theological motifs are thoroughly Pauline in nature. The idea of intercession, atonement, and reconciliation are plainly set forth in Paul's epistle to Philemon.

In conclusion, Pauline authorship of Philemon was never seriously doubted in the church. The internal evidence of the epistle clearly substantiates Paul as the author.

II. DATE

Since Paul was in prison and referred to himself as the "aged," he wrote this epistle in the latter stages of his ministry;[318] this points to imprisonment in Rome rather than a Caesarean imprisonment. Colossians 4:9-14 indicates that Philemon was probably written at the same time as Colossians and Ephesians (in about AD 62).[319]

III. DESTINATION

The destination of the epistle cannot be determined with any certainty. However, since Colossians 4:9 mentions that Onesimus was a Colossian, it is very likely that his owner, Philemon, was also from that city.[320] If this be true, then the destination of the epistle to Philemon would have been Colossae. It would mean that at the time of writing Colossians, Paul could have also penned Philemon and sent it by the same hand to the city of Colossae.

---

[317] Jacobus J. Muller, *The Epistle of Paul to the Philippians and to Philemon*, (Grand Rapids: Eerdmans, 1955) 161.

[318] F.F. Bruce, *The Epistle to the Colossians to Philemon and to the Ephesians*, (Grand Rapids: Eerdmans, 1984)   211-12.

[319] Muller, *Philippians and Philemon*, 164-65.

[320] H.C.G. Moule, *The Epistles to the Colossians and to Philemon*, (London: C.J. Clay and Sons, 1893) 152-54.

PART 2—CENTRAL THEMES OF Philemon

Sitz im Leben is a technical term borrowed from German and meaning "situation in life." It is important for discovering the central themes of Philemon. The two central themes are:

I. PAUL'S INTERVENTION INTO A DOMESTIC/SECULAR MATTER

Paul personally intervened on behalf of a slave named Onesimus who had escaped from his owner Philemon and taken some of his master's property. In a sense, Onesimus was a thief on two counts: he stole himself and his master's property.

It is clear that Paul knew Philemon and may have led him to the Lord (v. 19). Also, Philemon had a church in his house (v. 2).

II. THE STORY OF SALVATION

Paul had won Onesimus to the Lord (v. 10). He then sought a reconciliation between Philemon and Onesimus. Paul did not desire that the relationship continue as usual. Rather, Paul requested that Philemon receive Onesimus as a brother in the Lord (v. 16). Finally, Paul promised to repay anything that Onesimus had stolen (vs. 18-19).

As will be studied in more detail below, every major aspect of the gospel is portrayed in this real-life situation.[321] Paul can be viewed as a "Christ figure" who interceded and atoned for the transgression of Onesimus.

---

[321] Eerdman, *Colossians and Philemon*, 133.

PART 3—THE SPIRITUAL SIGNIFICANCE OF PHILEMON

During Paul's time, the penalty for a runaway slave was death.[322] Paul was aware of the critical issues at stake and acted decisively in the Lord to bring redemption. He must not only save Onesimus" soul, but his life as well. With regard to the story of salvation, observe the following:

I. A SERIOUS OFFENSE (V. 11, 18)

Onesimus was a thief on two counts. By running away from Philemon, he had literally stolen himself. In the Roman world, slaves were viewed as the rightful property of their owners.[323] Secondly, as noted above, Onesimus had taken some of the property of his master. In this sense, Onesimus" actions represent transgression.

II. AN EXPRESSION OF DIVINE LOVE (V. 10)

Just as God did not punish our transgressions as we deserved, so too Paul expressed *agape* love for Onesimus.

III. INTERCESSORY PRAYER (V. 17)

As Christ intercedes to the Father on our behalf, so Paul interceded with Philemon on behalf of Onesimus. As Christ asks the Father to receive us, Paul requested that Philemon receive Onesimus.

IV. SUBSTITUTIONARY SACRIFICE (VS. 18-19)

We know that the cross death of Christ paid the debt for all of our sins, including those of Onesimus. In an analogous way, Paul told Philemon that he would pay any debt which Onesimus may have incurred. In this sense, the principle of "vicarious sacrifice" came into play. As Jesus is our substitutionary atonement, so Paul desired to take Onesimus" place and pay his debt to Philemon.

V. THE PRINCIPLE OF RESTORATION (VS. 15-16)

In these verses, Paul acknowledged that Onesimus had been temporarily separated from Philemon. But he urged that Philemon receive him again and restore Onesimus to a new relationship with him. Similarly, our transgression temporarily separated us from fellowship with God, but now Christ brings about an eternal restoration and an uninterrupted fellowship with the Father.

VI. ELEVATION TO A NEW RELATIONSHIP (V. 16)

This principle of the gospel has been mentioned several times already. We are no longer enemies of God. On the contrary, we are brethren in Christ and are now incorporated into the family of God. We have an essentially new relationship with the Father, which far surpasses any previous

---

[322] Bruce, *Colossians, Philemon and Ephesians*, (196.
[323] Moule, *Colossians and Philemon*, 154-55.

relationship we may have had with Him. In the same way, Paul requested that Philemon harbor no animosity towards Onesimus. On the contrary, Paul fully expected that Philemon would not only forego retribution, but that he would grant full emancipation to Onesimus. In this way, Philemon and Onesimus would enjoy a relationship which far transcends the master/slave relationship that they previously experienced. They would now be brothers in Christ.

The extreme care by which Paul addressed this very serious, yet delicate, situation has already become apparent to some degree. In the next part, what we can learn about the personality and character of Paul will be studied.

Discuss the two central themes which can be derived from the *Sitz im Leben* of Philemon:

PART 4—A PERSONALITY PROFILE OF PAUL

Paul was dealing with a very delicate and serious issue: the reinstatement of a runaway slave. In the epistle to Philemon, Paul used all of the tact and diplomacy at his disposal in addressing this situation. In the process, he revealed major aspects of his personality and character. Furthermore, we gain insight into the procedures of the Apostle Paul in dealing with conflict management. With regard to these points the following should be observed:

I. HIS USE OF APOSTOLIC AUTHORITY (VS. 8-9)

Because of Paul's special relationship to Philemon, he could have used his apostolic authority in this situation.[324] He could have simply demanded that Philemon receive Onesimus. But he did not do that. Rather than availing himself of his ecclesiastical authority, for the sake of divine love, he requested that Philemon receive Onesimus (vs. 8, 9).

II. USE OF WIT (VS. 9-10)

Paul used humor to defuse a potentially explosive situation.[325] In that Onesimus means "profitable," Paul employed a word play for the sake of humor.[326] He says that profitable had become unprofitable but was now profitable both to Philemon and to himself. At last Onesimus was living up to his name.

III. USE OF RESPECT (VS. 13-14)

Paul had a right to retain Onesimus for the furtherance of the gospel, but he desired that Philemon willingly release Onesimus.

IV. USE OF TACT (V. 19)

Paul tactfully reminded Philemon of his debt to him.[327] In that Paul was instrumental in Philemon's conversation, Paul requested that Philemon release Onesimus.

V. USE OF DIPLOMACY (V. 21)

Diplomatically, Paul expressed confidence in the character and integrity of Philemon.[328] In verse 21, Paul stated that he not only expected Philemon to grant his request concerning Onesimus but that he was confident that Philemon will do above and beyond what he has asked.

In conclusion, the tactfulness and diplomacy of the Apostle Paul are supremely evident in this short epistle. Paul resisted the temptation to be autocratic. Rather, through the love of God he requested of a fellow brother help in resolving a very serious and, indeed, a life-threatening

---

[324] Lewis B. Radford, *The Epistle to the Colossians and the Epistle to Philemon*, (London: Metheun & Co. Ltd., 1931) 354.

[325] Bruce, *Colossians, Philemon and Ephesians*, 213.

[326] Ibid.

[327] Ibid., 220.

[328] Moule, *Colossians and Philemon*, 12.

situation. He used humor, some friendly cajoling and expression of good faith in Philemon to accomplish his purposes in this epistle.

True/False:

1. T or F   The Book of Philemon was immediately accepted into the canon by the early church.
2. T or F   Philemon was listed among the "antilegoumena."
3. T or F   Colossians 4:9 gives us some insight into the destination of Philemon.
4. T or F   Paul serves as a "Christ figure" in Philemon.
5. T or F   Even though Paul uses diplomacy he tells Philemon that he "owes him one."
----
1. The *Sitz im Leben* of Philemon involves:

a. false teachers in the church
b. gross immorality in the church
c. a runaway slave by the name of Onesimus

2. The name "Onesimus" means:

a. "a loser"
b. "a winner"
c. "profitable"

SELF TEST:

1. The Book of Philemon:
    a. was one of the *antilegoumena*
    b. was written at the same time as Ephesians and Colossians
    c. is one of the "Prison Epistles"
    d. all of these
    e. none of these

2. It was noted that:
    a. Philemon was a Colossian
    b. Paul used his apostolic authority in requesting Onesimus" release
    c. "Onesimus" means "unprofitable"
    d. A & C
    e. B & C

3. In Philemon:
    a. Paul is a Christ figure
    b. Paul uses humor to resolve a conflict
    c. all the major aspects of salvation are revealed
    d. all of these
    e. none of these

4. The *Sitz im Leben* of Philemon involves:
    a. false teacher in the church
    b. gross immorality in the church
    c. a runaway slave
    d. all of these
    e. none of these

5. In Philemon, it was noted that:
    a. Paul never got involved in domestic/secular affairs
    b. Onesimus stole himself and his master's property
    c. the penalty for a runaway slave was death
    d. A & C
    e. B & C

SECTION 5:

THE GENERAL EPISTLES AND REVELATION

Lesson 23	The Epistle to the Hebrews
Lesson 24	The Epistle of James
Lesson 25	The Epistle of 1 Peter
Lesson 26	The Epistle of 2 Peter
Lesson 27	The Epistles of John
Lesson 28	The Epistle of Jude
Lesson 29	The Book of Revelation

OVERVIEW

Congratulations! You have completed a study covering over two-thirds of the New Testament. Before launching into the final third, it is important to take note of what you have accomplished thus far.

You have studied the "Background of the New Testament" which included material on "The World of the New Testament" as well as "The Canon." The "Synoptic Gospels" (Matthew, Mark, and Luke) have also been covered. The unique contributions of the Gospel of John have been noted as well. The importance of the Book of Acts and its central themes were studied in detail. Finally, the entire Pauline corpus has been reviewed. Each of the 13 epistles has been studied individually.

This final third consists of the "General Epistles." They are so named because most of them were "encyclicals." That is, they were intended to be read by the churches in an entire general area rather than being used in a denominational sense, but rather in the sense of its true meaning "universal." In other words, these epistles are universally applicable. They were not addressed to any one congregation.

The General Epistles consist of the following: Hebrews, James, 1 and 2 Peter, 1, 2, and 3 John and Jude. Upon completing these epistles, all that remains is the Book of Revelation.

BLANK PAGE

LESSON 23—THE EPISTLE TO THE HEBREWS

Part 1	Background Information
Part 2	The "Christ is Better" Motif
Part 3	Additional Characteristics

OVERVIEW

Since this epistle is addressed to Jewish Christians in general and not to any specific Christian congregation, it is the first to be studied among the General Epistles. Also, it is the first anonymous epistle to be studied. Although traditionally the Apostle Paul has been accepted as the author of this epistle, there is no name attached to this letter. In this sense, one could say that this is the first non-Pauline epistle to be studied thus far.

Nevertheless, the epistle to the Hebrews is one of the most important letters of the New Testament. What Matthew is to the gospel material, Hebrews is to the epistles. Just as Matthew was concerned with winning Jews to Christ, the author of Hebrews is also highly concerned with evangelizing the Jews. As Matthew pointed to the fulfillment of prophecy as proof that Jesus was the Messiah, Hebrews also demonstrates that Christ is the fulfillment of the entire Old Testament revelation. Furthermore, Hebrews clearly states that, as far as Christianity is concerned, Judaism has come to an end. For the Christian, salvation is only in Jesus Christ. The synagogue can no longer serve as a religious sanctuary for the believer in Christ.

OBJECTIVES

- Discuss the background material of Hebrews.
- List the various components of the "Christ is Better" motif.
- List the three major additional characteristics of Hebrews.

HELPS FOR LEARNING AND REMEMBERING

1. Take full note that a new type of epistle is being addressed.

2. Carefully focus on the section discussing the purpose of this epistle. Once the historical context of this epistle is understood, its meaning becomes more apparent.

3. The concept of "divide and conquer" may be helpful in mastering the material on Hebrews. Yet, if one clearly divides each subject into various components such as introductory material, central motifs and final evaluations, mastering the subject matter will become easier.

4. Once again, not only should the content of this lesson be subdivided, but the time devoted should be portioned out as well. Several clearly established periods of study will prove more beneficial in learning Hebrews than simply devoting one or two marathon study sessions to the subject.
5. Finally, any supplemental materials will aid in your understanding of the message of Hebrews. As noted earlier, a good evangelical commentary on Hebrews as well as a Bible dictionary will

facilitate your studies here. The more you understand about the background of this particular epistle, the more comprehensible its message becomes.

KEY WORDS

Codex Vaticanus	Codex Sinaiticus
Yom Kippur	

PART 1—BACKGROUND INFORMATION

I. AUTHORSHIP

Unlike the Pauline epistles, there is no name attached to this epistle. Therefore, establishing the authorship of Hebrews has been a thorny problem throughout the history of the church.

A. Internal Evidence

The traditional theory is that Paul wrote Hebrews.[329] There is some internal evidence to support this view. Hebrews 13:23 makes reference to Timothy and it appears that the author is in prison. Both Hebrews and Paul recognize the elemental nature of the law (cf. Galatians 3:24; Hebrews 7:19). Finally, both Hebrews and Paul have a very high Christology (cf. Ephesians 1:20-23; Hebrews 1:2-3).

However, there is much internal evidence which argues against the traditional view.[330] For example, since Paul attaches his name to every one of his epistles, why is no name attached to Hebrews? Also, the Greek of Hebrews is very polished, resembling classical Greek (as was the case with Luke). They style of Hebrews varies greatly from Paul. One example is that Paul often says, "It is written," but Hebrews says, "Thus sayeth the Lord" (8:8) or "the Holy Spirit says" (3:7). Finally, although both note the elemental nature of the law, Paul insists that the law is essentially holy, just, and good (Romans 7:12). The law was made weak because of the flesh (Romans 8:3). But Hebrews says that the law in inherently deficient (Hebrews 8:7, 13, 10:3-4).

B. External Evidence

Some external evidence supports Pauline authorship.[331] Clement of Alexandria records that Paul originally wrote this epistle in the Hebrew and that Luke subsequently translated it into Greek. This would explain the polished Greek and the difference in writing style. Yet the Greek of Hebrews does not appear to be "translation Greek." Origin suggested that the thoughts contained in Hebrews are Pauline, but someone else actually wrote the letter. Clement of Rome (AD 96) quoted from Hebrews as if it were Pauline. The earliest complete manuscripts of the Bible, Codex Vaticanus and Codex Sinaiticus, both place Hebrews in the Pauline corpus.

Yet, there is external evidence which rejects Pauline authorship.[332] Tertullian (AD 150-222) maintained that Hebrews was written by Barnabas. The Muratorian Canon rejected Pauline authorship and the canonicity of Hebrews. Finally, Hebrews evidences allegorical, Platonic interpretation that was popular in Alexendria (cf. 8:2-5 and the extensive use of "type").[333]

---

[329] F.F. Bruce, *The Epistle to the Hebrews,* (Grand Rapids: Eerdmans, 1964) xxxvi.

[330] Harold W. Attridge, *A Commentary on the Epistle to the Hebrews,* Hermeneia (Philadelphia: Fortress, 1989) 2-3.

[331] Ibid., 1-2.

[332] Bruce, *Hebrews,* xxxvi-xxxvii.

[333] Ibid., xvii.

Both of the great reformers, Martin Luther and John Calvin, rejected Pauline authorship.[334] Luther believed Apollos wrote Hebrews, while Calvin opted for Luke.

In the final analysis, perhaps Origen (AD 180-250) was most correct, when he said, "God only knows who wrote the epistle of Hebrews."[335]

II. DATE

Since Clement of Rome (AD 96) quotes from Hebrews, the epistle must have been written during the first century. The author heard the gospel from those who witnessed Jesus Christ, so he lived during the apostolic period (2:3). No mention is made of the destruction of the temple in Hebrews in AD 70. Hebrews 10:1 ff. indicates that sacrifices are still being offered.[336] Hebrews 10:32 and 12:4 indicate that the recipients of the epistle have not yet resisted unto death. Since the martyrdom of Christians began under Nero in AD 64, Hebrews was written prior to this time.

For these reasons, it appears that Hebrews was written in the early to mid 60's AD.[337]

III. DESTINATION

Theories concerning the destination of Hebrews range from Jerusalem in the east to Spain in the west.[338] The epistle was either written from Rome to Jewish Christians residing in Jerusalem, or was written from Jerusalem to Jews of the Diaspora. Since Hebrews 13:24 states, "they of Italy salute you," this may indicate that Italian Jews were sending greetings back to their home church in Rome.[339]

IV. RECIPIENTS

The title of the earliest manuscript is "To the Hebrews." The epistle is replete with references to the Old Testament, the Law, and the tabernacle. No explanation is given for any of these Jewish practices and beliefs. This may indicate that the recipients do not need an explanation because they were Hebrews.[340]

V. THE PURPOSE

The writer to the Hebrews clearly desired that the recipients make a clean break with Judaism (13:7-14).[341] They must not give in to persecution and return to the synagogue; those who did would forfeit salvation (6:4-6). To keep them from apostasy, the author presents the superiority of Christianity over Judaism.[342]

---

[334] Attridge, *Hebrews,* 2-6.

[335] Bruce, *Hebrews,* xlii.

[336] A.B. Bruce, *The Epistle to the Hebrews,* (Minneapolis: Klock & Klock Christian Publishers, reprint 1980) 25.

[337] Bruce, *Hebrews,* xliii.

[338] Guthrie, *New Testament,* 711-12.

[339] Bruce, *Hebrews,* xxxiv.

[340] Attridge, *Hebrews,* 10.

[341] Guthrie, *New Testament,* 703.

[342] Harris, *New Testament,* 261.

PART 2—THE "CHRIST IS BETTER" MOTIF

The author must demonstrate that Christ is better than anything that Judaism has to offer. He does so by arguing that:[343]

I. CHRIST IS A BETTER MESSENGER (1:1-2:18)

The dramatic opening of Hebrews argues that although God occasionally and progressively revealed himself in the Old Testament, in these last days the Father has definitively revealed himself in his own Son, Jesus Christ. The angels and all of the prophets are simply creations of God, but Jesus, as the Son of God, is the Creator. The Creator is superior to the creation.

II. CHRIST IS A BETTER SPIRITUAL LEADER (3:1-4:13)

The writer argues that Jesus is a better spiritual leader, even better than Moses. Moses was a servant in God's household, but Jesus built the house. Moses offered the Promised Land, but Jesus offers the ultimate rest (heaven).

III. CHRIST IS A BETTER HIGH PRIEST (4:14-7:28)

Aaron was merely human, had sin, and ultimately died. Jesus has an eternal priesthood after the order of Melchizedek. That is, Jesus was directly appointed by God, has no sin, and lives eternally to intercede for believers. Aaron ministered in an earthly tabernacle, but Jesus ministers in the very presence of God.

IV. CHRIST MINISTERS A BETTER COVENANT (8:1-9:28)

The blood of animals could make one ceremonially pure, but could not effect one's conscience. Jesus offered his pure humanity as a sacrifice which thoroughly effected the human conscience. The old covenant was written on tables of stone, but the new covenant is written on human hearts and minds.

V. CHRIST OFFERED A BETTER SACRIFICE (10:1-31)

The repeated offerings in the Old Testament proved that they were inadequate. Throughout the Old Testament, there was limited access to the throne of God. Only on the Day of Atonement [*Yom Kippur* ("The Day of Covering")] did the high priest come before God on behalf of the people.

But the sacrifice of Jesus was of ultimate atoning value. There is no need for repetition because the sacrifice of Christ is fully effective, providing continuous access to the throne of God.

---

[343] Guthrie, *New Testament,* 728-31.

VI. CHRIST PROVIDES A BETTER WAY: FAITH (10:32-12:29)

In Christ, salvation is not dependent on a slavish obedience to carnal commandments, but rather on faith in the Son of God. God has provided many examples of faith, but the greatest example is embodied in the Lord Jesus Christ. All those who have faith in the sacrifice of Christ are the sons of God and will inherit eternal life.

PART 3—ADDITIONAL CHARACTERISTICS

There are three major additional characteristics of Hebrews:

I. HEBREWS IS AN EPISTLE OF WARNING[344]

After each section in Hebrews the author gives a very strong warning to his readers not to apostatize. In 2:1-4, he tells them not to neglect the salvation of Christ. In 3:7-19, he warns them not to doubt the revelation they have received. In 4:11-13, he exhorts them not to disobey. In 5:11-6:12, he commands them to forsake immaturity. Finally, in 10:5-18 and 12:25-29, the author warns them not to reject the gospel. If they violated any of these warnings, they would lose their salvation.

II. HEBREWS IS FULL OF CHALLENGES[345]

The recipients seemed to be weakening in their faith. For this reason, the author presented 13 challenges intended to stimulate them to spiritual growth, frequently using the exhortation, "let us" (4:1, 11, 14, 16; 10:22, 23, 24; 12:1, 28). The final exhortations are found in Hebrews 13:13, 15.

III. HEBREWS EMPHASIZES THE FINALITY OF JESUS CHRIST[346]

Jesus is the final and ultimate revelation of God (1:1,2), and the priesthood of Jesus Christ is final as well (7:24). There will be no subsequent covenant apart from Jesus Christ (8:6). This means that the sacrifice of Christ is complete and all encompassing (9:26, 10:10).

True/False:

1. T or F The Apostle Paul is definitely the author of Hebrews.

2. T or F The Greek of Hebrews seems to be "translation Greek" (translated from an original Hebrew or Aramaic original).

3. T or F The author says that the recipients have resisted unto death (cf. 10:32, 12:4).

----

1. With regard to the "Christ is Better" motif:
   a. Christ is just "one among many" as far as the messengers of God are concerned
   b. the Holy Land is a type of heaven
   c. just as the High Priest must atone for his own sins first, Jesus had to offer sacrifice for his sins as well
   d. all of these
   e. none of these

---

[344] Tenney, *New Testament,* 361-62.
[345] Guthrie, *New Testament,* 707.
[346] William Lane, *Hebrews: A Call to Commitment,* (Peabody, MA: Hendrickson, 1985) 26.

2. Hebrews is:
    a. an epistle of warning
    b. full of warnings
    c. an epistle that emphasizes the finality of Christ
    d. all of these
    e. none of these

Explain the "Christ is Better" motif, incorporating in your discussion the ways in which Christ is better than the Old Covenant.

SELF TEST:

1. With regard to authorship, it was noted that:
   a. Paul definitely wrote Hebrews
   b. Hebrews is "translation Greek"
   c. Luther and Calvin accepted Pauline authorship
   d. all of these
   e. none of these

2. In Hebrews, the author:
   a. employs a Platonic, allegorical method of interpretation
   b. taught that the law is inherently good
   c. taught that one could believe in Jesus and still attend the synagogue
   d. A & B
   e. A & C

3. With regard to the purpose of Hebrews, the readers:
   a. are exhorted to make a clean break with Judaism
   b. are being persecuted, but not yet martyred
   c. have already apostatized
   d. A & B
   e. B & C

4. With regard to the "Christ is Better" motif, it was noted that:
   a. the Holy Land was a "type" of heaven
   b. Jesus built "the house" that Moses ministered in
   c. the words "Yom Kippur" refer to Israeli salted fish
   d. A & C
   e. A & B

5. The epistle to the Hebrews is:
   a. an epistle of warning
   b. an epistle that emphasizes the finality of Christ
   c. full of challenges
   d. all of these
   e. none of these

LESSON 24—THE EPISTLE OF JAMES

Part 1	Background Information
Part 2	Central Characteristics
Part 3	Central Themes

OVERVIEW

The Epistle of James is the most practical letter of the New Testament. True faith is not simply a matter of confession but profession. Genuine faith in God will be evidenced in everyday life. It is not enough to simply wish a brother or sister well, but one must take concrete steps to alleviate the suffering of those about him. It is not enough just to hear the Word, one must do the Word. The purest form of religion is to look after the fatherless and to relieve the suffering of the widowed. Faith without works is dead. After all, even the demons believe that there is one God, yet they do nothing to help establish the kingdom. In James, the wealthy are severely criticized. They are not to place trust in material things, for the riches of this world are fleeting, but the treasures of the kingdom are eternal. Favoritism is strictly forbidden in the body of Christ. He who cannot control his tongue is seriously flawed spiritually. All must acknowledge their limitations and mortality, and trust the Lord for tomorrow. The true believer will submit to the sovereignty of God.

OBJECTIVES

- Briefly discuss the background information for James.
- List and briefly describe the major characteristics of James.
- Outline the central themes of James.

HELPS FOR LEARNING AND REMEMBERING

1. Although James is the most practical of all epistles, it is one of the most disorganized. A rapid reading of the entire epistle will provide an overview of the themes.

2. James is picturesque and his speech parabolic. Visualize the images and word pictures of James to help memorization.

3. One of the literary characteristics of James is repetition. James frequently repeats a theme in a slightly different form throughout his epistle. He does this so that his readers might remember the principles set forth in his epistle. Similarly, as you study through the material on James, frequent repetition and review will help you to master the subject at hand.

4. Make all of the contemporary applications you can. Perhaps you can use James as a "diagnostic tool" to identify problems and solutions for the church today. Such exercises will help you incorporate the theological principles and doctrine of James.

5. Finally, realize that learning the basic content of each of the New Testament books is a formidable task in itself. Therefore, reward yourself at the end of each lesson for a job well done. This will help motivate you to take on the next block of study.

PART 1—BACKGROUND INFORMATION

I. AUTHORSHIP

The author identifies himself as "James" in the first word of the epistle. Yet there are at least four men in the New Testament called "James." They are:

- James, the father of Judas, not Iscariot (Luke 6:16)
- James, the son of Zebedee, the brother of John. He was one of the original 12 disciples (Matthew 4:21, Luke 9:54, Acts 1:13)
- James, the son of Alphaeus, also a disciple of Jesus (Matt. 10:3, Luke 24:10, Mark 6:3).
- James, the half-brother of our Lord (Galatians 1:19, Matt. 13:15)

The author cannot be James the son of Zebedee. Herod Agrippa I had this James beheaded shortly after the resurrection (Acts 12:1-2). Also, James, the father of Judas, is only mentioned in Luke 6:16, and is otherwise completely unknown. It is not impossible that the author was James, the son of Alphaeus, who was also a disciple of Jesus, yet he is an obscure figure in the gospel and is not mentioned again in the New Testament.

More than likely, James, the half-brother of the Lord, penned the Epistle of James. In Galatians 1:18-19, Paul explicitly refers to this James as "the Lord's brother" (Galatians 1:18-19). He is also one of the leaders of the early church (Galatians 2:9, Acts 15:13-21). By Acts 15, this James had superseded Peter as the head of the Jerusalem church, presiding over the Jerusalem Council. Finally, the writing style of James is very similar to the words of Jesus. James speaks in common images from life and agriculture, similar to the parabolic speech of the Lord. All things considered, James, the half-brother of the Lord, is the most likely candidate.

II. DATE

There is evidence that James was written at a very early date. It lacks well-developed Christian terminology. For example, the word *sunagoge* ('synagogue") is used for the place of worship, not *ecclesia* or "church." It is possible that the recipients of the epistle of James were still meeting in the synagogue for worship services. This would mean that these Jewish Christians had not yet realized their full Christian identity at this stage of their development. Also, there is no reference to a strong Gentile element in the church, indicating that a Gentile mission was not yet in full swing. Finally, the letter is addressed to "the 12 tribes which are scattered abroad." Some type of dispersion has taken place among the Jewish believers. Could they have been scattered by the persecution Saul of Tarsus in about AD 35? Since there is no mention of problems with Gentile converts, the letter was probably written before the Jerusalem Council of AD 49 or 50. Thus, James was penned somewhere between AD 35 and 50, probably in the latter 40s AD.

III. DESTINATION

James speaks of salvation and of being born again (1:18, 21; 5:8). He calls the recipients "brethren" and tells them to have faith in Jesus, and to look forward to His Second Coming (2:1, 5:7). But James 2:2, 19 makes reference to Jewish oaths, which may reflect the liturgy of the Jewish synagogue; therefore, he may have been addressing Hellenistic Greek-speaking Jews as "the 12 tribes of a dispersion" (cf. Acts 11:19). This would mean that James was writing an encyclical letter to Christian Jews living outside of Israel.

IV. OCCASION

The moral fiber of the Jewish Christian church was rapidly deteriorating. They were worldly, corrupt and were showing special favors to the rich and powerful. They were despising the poor and ignoring the needs of the weak and powerless. They had abused the doctrine of justification by faith, rejecting all rules and regulations. They had become *antinomians* (literally "against law") adhering to no laws or principles. Consequently, their faith had no practical application for life.

For these reasons, James spoke out against the social injustices of the rich and the carnal lives of the Jewish Christians.

PART 2—CENTRAL CHARACTERISTICS

James railed forth in the spirit of an Old Testament prophet.[347] He exposed injustice, corruption and moral degradation without hesitation. He used biting sarcasm and irony to drive forth his message (2:19; 5:5, 6). He spoke parabolically concerning the evil of the tongue (3:1-12). He wrote repetitiously, stating a theme and then periodically returning to that theme. His work contains many Jewish elements or 'semitisms."[348] Although the epistle of James is thoroughly Jewish in character and content, his Greek is excellent. The author had a good command of the Greek language and knew how to use it well.

James pled for reality in religion. He called for action and works, not simply confessions of faith. The extreme practicality of James led Martin Luther to describe it as "an epistle of straw," seeing in the epistle a conflict with Paul's concept of justification by faith.[349] James did believe in justification by faith but claimed that faith without some real manifestation is empty, powerless, and dead. Thus, as the prophets of old, James exhorted his readers to faith; he went further to say that faith is evidenced by action and Christian works.

---

[347] Alexander Robs, *The Epistles of James and John,* (Grand Rapids: Wm. B. Eerdmans, 1954) 20.
[348] Ralph P. Martin, *James,* (Waco: Word Books, 1988) lxviii.
[349] William Barclay, *The Letters of James and Peter,* (Philadelphia: The Westminster Press, 1976) 6.

PART 3—CENTRAL THEMES

The central themes of James are:

I. THE TRUE NATURE OF FAITH

A. True Faith is Stable (1:6-8)

Halting between two opinions is not indicative of genuine faith in God.[350]

B. True Faith is Active (2:14-26)[351]

Genuine faith is automatically realized in life and experience. James used Abraham to show that he was justified by works; yet, 2:24 states, "and not by faith only." James acknowledged the necessity of faith, but true faith is manifested in works. James is actually complementing Paul's doctrine of justification by faith.[352] One is truly justified by faith when that faith alleviates suffering in the world and promoted God's kingdom.

II. THE NATURE OF WISDOM

James argued that all true wisdom comes from God and divine wisdom is antithetical to the wisdom of this world (1:5, 3:13-17).[353]

III. THE NATURE OF RICHES[354]

The riches of this world are temporary (1:10-11), can lead to favoritism (2:1-7), and oppression of the poor (5:1-6).

IV. THE NATURE OF TEMPTATION[355]

Temptation does not destroy true faith but strengthens it (1:2-4). Temptation does not originate with God (1:13). Even though God is sovereign, he is not the source of temptation. The source of temptation comes from the fallen human nature (1:13-15). James graphically represented the process of temptation in terms of birth.[356] First, there is an attraction, followed by a conception. This conception leads to the birth of sin and ultimately culminates in death (4:1-5).

V. THE NATURE OF THE TONGUE (1:26, 3:1-12)[357]

---

[350] Alec Motyer, *The Message of James,* (Downers Grove: Inter-Varsity, 1985) 36 f.

[351] R.V.G. Tasker, *The General Epistle of James,* (Grand Rapids: Eerdmans, 1971) 63 f.

[352] Robs, *James,* 22.

[353] Sophie Laws, *The Epistles of James,* (San Francisco: Harper & Row, 1980) 158 ff.

[354] Martin, *James,* 22ff., 172 ff.

[355] Tasker, *James,* 40.

[356] Ibid., 47.

[357] Robs, *James,* 57 ff.

James used many word pictures (a horse's bit, a ship's rudder, and a small spark) to describe the evil nature of the tongue (3:3-6). In all cases, a small element controls the destiny of a much larger object. Similarly, the tongue is a small member of the body, but can determine the destiny of our total existence. The tongue is as poisonous as a snake (3:8), hypocritical, and contradictory in nature (3:9-12).

VI. THE POWER OF PRAYER (5:13-18)[358]

The proper response to suffering and temptation is sincere prayer. The writer spoke of prayer, praise, anointing with oil, and mutual confession. In true prophetic fashion, James spoke of Elijah when discussing the power of fervent prayer (3:17, 18).

True/False:

1. T or F   The epistle of James seems to have been written at a late date in the early church.
2. T or F   Galatians 1:18-19 and Acts 15:13-21 give insight into the authorship of James.
3. T or F   The recipients of James" letter seem to be still meeting in the synagogue.
4. T or F   The heresy of "antinomianism" had infiltrated the churches addressed by James.

----

1. When studying the central characteristics of James, it was noted that:
    a. James wrote as a prophet, similar in style to the Old Testament prophets
    b. the writing style is very similar to the words of Jesus in the Gospels
    c. James did not believe in justification by faith
    d. A & B
    e. B & C

2. James teaches that:
    a. there are two types of "wisdom" in this life
    b. temptation does not come from God, but God can use the effects of temptation to develop the believer.
    c. materialism can lead to favoritism
    d. all of these
    e. none of these

---

[358] Motyer, *James,* 186 ff.

SELF TEST:

1. The background information concerning the epistle of James noted that:
    a. Galatians 1:18-19, 29 and Acts 15:13-21 give us insight into the authorship of James
    b. James was written at a very late date
    c. the recipients were still meeting in the synagogue
    d. A & B
    e. A & C

2. James:
    a. was writing to unbelieving Jews of the Diaspora
    b. wrote very similarly to Old Testament prophets
    c. wrote parabolically, similar to Jesus
    d. A & B
    e. B & C

3. It was noted that:
    a. James said that Abraham was justified by works only
    b. James did not believe in justification by faith
    c. James was fighting antinomianism
    d. all of these
    e. none of these

4. James teaches that:
    a. there are two types of wisdom
    b. temptation comes from God
    c. materialism can lead to favoritism
    d. B & C
    e. A & C

5. It was noted that James:
    a. was probably writing to Hellenistic Greek-speaking Jewish Christians of the Diaspora
    b. pointed to Elijah as an example of how to pray
    c. is "an epistle of straw"
    d. A & B
    e. B & C

LESSON 25—THE EPISTLE OF 1 PETER

Part 1	Background Information
Part 2	The Writing Style of 1 Peter
Part 3	Central Themes
Part 4	Additional Characteristics

OVERVIEW

These are the first epistles studied which were written by a disciple of the historical Jesus. You will recall that Paul was not a follower of Jesus during his ministry on earth. Even James, the brother of the Lord, was not a disciple of Jesus until after the resurrection. It is interesting to note the parallels that exist between the epistles of Peter and the gospel records.

1 Peter is an extremely relevant work for the contemporary church. Peter spoke about how to live one's faith in the midst of a hostile world. Although the church in America is not experiencing open or physical persecution, it still exists in the midst of a fallen world. The epistle of 1 Peter helps us to interpret our faith in the context of an unbelieving and ungodly environment. It is safe to say that such coping skills will become increasingly important as the day of the Lord draws near.

OBJECTIVES

- Discuss the background information for 1 Peter.
- Describe the writing style of Peter.
- List the central themes contained in 1 Peter.
- List and briefly discuss unique characteristics of 1 Peter.

HELPS FOR LEARNING AND REMEMBERING

1. It is important to realize that you are studying the work of a new author. In this sense, comparing and contrasting the content and style of Peter with that of Paul and James may be beneficial.

2. Remember that there are two epistles attributed to Peter in the New Testament. This creates a tendency to confuse the content of both of these epistles. Special effort will have to be made to distinguish the contribution of 1 Peter from that of 2 Peter.

3. Any parallels that you can draw between 1 Peter and the gospel record will help anchor this material in your mind.

4. The theme of how to cope with suffering is a major contribution of 1 Peter. It may be helpful to look for ways in which this particular theme can apply to specific persons and situations in your life.

5. The problem of evil has been a perennial difficulty for those who trust in God. If God is good and has all power, why does he permit suffering in this world? Moreover, why does he permit his people, the special object of his love, to experience pain and trials? Seeking answers to questions like these will help you process the material contained in 1 Peter.

KEY WORDS

Christological   eschatological   imperative

PART 1—BACKGROUND INFORMATION

I. AUTHORSHIP

A. Internal Evidence

The first words of the epistle identify Peter as the author and claim that he was an eyewitness of Jesus (1:1,3). The language of Peter in Acts coincides with what we find in 1 Peter (cf. Acts 10:34; 1 Peter 1:17).[359] In both Acts and 1 Peter (Acts 3:6, 16; 1 Peter 4:14, 16), Peter teaches that God revealed to the prophets that Jesus would suffer and die. In both cases, Peter associated persecution with "the name" (his abbreviation for "Christianity").[360]

B. External Evidence

The early church fathers unanimously accepted Petrine authorship.[361] Polycarp (AD 96) quotes 1 Peter with authority. Eusebius, perhaps the first church historian, included 1 Peter in the canon. Irenaeus (AD 185) states that Peter was the author of this first epistle.

Modern theologians such as B.F. Streeter and Adolph Holtzmann rejected Petrine authorship on the following grounds:[362]

1. Language and Style

> Acts 4:13 describes Peter as "unlearned and ignorant." Since the Greek of 1 Peter is good and he frequently quotes the *LXX*, how could an unlearned Galilean fisherman have produced such a fine document?

> In response, it should be noted that Acts 4:13 does not indicate that Peter was uneducated and ignorant. It simply means that he was not formally trained as a rabbi and that he was not involved in public life.[363]

2. Persecution

> 1 Peter 1:6, 2:12 and 4:12-16 indicate that the church was being persecuted because of "the name." Pliny, governor of Pontus and Bithynia under Trajan (AD 112) wrote that Christians were being persecuted because of "the name."[364] For this reason, some conclude that 1 Peter was written after the apostolic period.

> However, nothing in 1 Peter indicates an official Roman persecution.[365] 1 Peter 2:13-17 instructs those persecuted to submit to the authority of the Roman state. More than likely

---

[359] Guthrie, *New Testament,* 779-80.

[360] Alan M. Stibbs, *The First Epistle General of Peter,* (Grand Rapids: Eerdmans, 1971) 160-61.

[361] Guthrie, *New Testament,* 771 ff.

[362] Ibid., 776.

[363] Bruce, *Acts,* 94-95.

[364] Harris, *New Testament,* 267.

[365] Tenney, *New Testament,* 344-45.

the persecution referred to in 1 Peter was regional rather than empire wide. Acts notes that Paul was persecuting Christians and was in turn persecuted by Jewish opponents.

In conclusion, there is nothing in the internal or external evidence which compels one to reject Petrine authorship.

II. DESTINATION

Peter addressed the elect scattered abroad in the areas of Pontus, Galatia, Cappadocia, Asia, and Bithynia (1:1). Therefore, the destination of 1 Peter was the area situated between the Black Sea and the Mediterranean Sea (Asia Minor).[366] 1 Peter was an encyclical letter to be read by the churches throughout Asia Minor.

III. RECIPIENTS

1 Peter seems to have been written to a mixed group.[367] He addressed slaves and free citizens, Jews and Gentiles (2:11-25). The opening verse contains the phrases "strangers in the world" and "scattered throughout," sounding very similar to the terminology of the Diaspora. They were to have a good testimony among the Gentiles (2:12). Some of his readers were Jewish, but 2:9-10 states that at one time, they were "no people of God." This may refer to the Gentiles.

IV. PURPOSE

Peter wrote to give the meaning of suffering in the lives of Christians.[368] The believer was to look beyond his or her present suffering and focus on the future glory which will be shared by those who are in Christ Jesus.

---

[366] Stibbs, *Peter,* 63.
[367] Guthrie, *New Testament,* 795.
[368] Tenney, *New Testament,* 353.

PART 2—THE WRITING STYLE OF 1 PETER

The following are four major aspects of Peter's writing style.

I. HIGHLY THEOLOGICAL[369]

Peter wrote of God as the "Holy One" (1:15), "the Creator" (4:19), and "the Judge" (4:5). God created all things, yet is distinct from his creation and separated from sin. Peter affirmed the sovereignty of God as Judge, stating that all things are subject to his divine disposition.

II. CHRISTOLOGICAL[370]

Just as the great prophets of old, Jesus is described as the "Servant of Yahweh" (2:22). Jesus is the "Passover Lamb" (1:19). Peter reflected on the first Passover and saw Jesus as the fulfillment of the entire Jewish sacrificial system.

III. ESCHATOLOGICAL[371]

1 Peter 1:7, 13; 4:13; 5:1 all speak about the Second Coming of the Lord. The eschatological judgment of God and the end of the world play an important role in 1 Peter.

IV. ETHICAL[372]

Peter was careful to anchor his theological reflections in real life. He called on all believers to exercise self-control under trying circumstances (1:13). He exhorted them to have patience in the midst of suffering (3:16-18), bidding them to exhibit humility in all things and under all circumstances (3:8, 5:5). They were to have a clean conscience before God and humankind (3:15 ff.).

---

[369] Stibbs, *Peter,* 150, 164.
[370] Barclay, *James and Peter,* 184.
[371] Ibid., 139.
[372] Harris, *New Testament,* 268.

PART 3—CENTRAL THEMES

The foremost theme of 1 Peter is the meaning of Christian suffering. Some form of the word 'suffering" is used 17 times in this short epistle.[373] Seven of these relate to the suffering of the Lord, while the remaining 10 instances refer to Christians. The derivatives of this theme are as follows:

I. A CHRISTIAN RESPONSE TO SUFFERING

A. Patient Endurance

The Christian should patiently endure suffering just as Jesus bore suffering in this world. He reminded them that the Lord suffered severely, exceeding our personal sufferings (2:20-24).[374]

B. Suffering Aids in Spiritual Formation

Peter acknowledged the sovereignty of the Lord in all of our experiences (5:10).[375] Similar to Paul in Romans 8:28, Peter taught that all things work together for the good of those that love God.

C. Hope Fosters Perseverance

The Christian could bear suffering because the Second Coming was close at hand (1:7, 13, 14).[376] The Second Coming is the eschatological hope which makes our present suffering bearable.

II. THE ROLE OF SUFFERING IN THE LIFE OF A CHRISTIAN

A. Suffering gives an Opportunity to Witness

We should be prepared to give a reason for the hope that lies within us in all circumstances and at any time (3:13-16).[377]

B. Suffering Purifies the Soul

Peter taught that suffering in faith has a purifying influence (1:7, 3:17-22).

C. Suffering is Part of Living in a Fallen World

We are still in this world, and the end of all things is yet future (4:1-11). Ironically, present sufferings are sure signs that our heavenly redemption is at hand.[378]

---

[373] Morris, *New Testament Theology,* 316.
[374] Ernest Best, *1 Peter,* (Grand Rapids: Eerdmans, 1971) 119 ff.
[375] Stibbs, *Peter,* 173-74.
[376] Barclay, *James and Peter,* 177 ff.
[377] Ibid., 230-31.
[378] Stibbs, *Peter,* 145-50.

PART 4—ADDITIONAL CHARACTERISTICS

The following are three additional characteristics of 1 Peter.

I. THE USE OF IMPERATIVES[379]

1 Peter is full of imperatives (commands) and reads more like a sermon than a doctrinal treatise. Beginning with 1:13, the author used a steady stream of imperatives to the end of the epistle; 34 in all (cf. 1:13, 2:17, 3:15, 4:13, 5:8). This demonstrates the passion and concern that Peter had for the recipients.

II. PERSONAL REFERENCES[380]

There is evidence in 1 Peter of Peter's personal experience with the Lord. There are frequent references to the suffering of Christ, no doubt reflecting Peter's eyewitness of the crucifixion. 1 Peter 5:2 exhorts, "tend the flock of God," which recalls John 21:15-17, where Jesus tells Peter to feed the flock of God. 1 Peter 5:5 commands, "gird yourselves with humility" and may refer to Jesus washing the feet of the disciples (John 13:4).

III. THE IMPORTANCE OF GRACE

Peter's experience of grace seems to be reflected in the vocabulary of 1 Peter. The word "grace" appears ten times; five of which directly relate to the grace of God. Grace is the central aspect of God's character (5:10), and only God gives grace to the believer (4:10, 5:5, 12). Peter stressed that God gives special grace to those who suffer for his sake (2:19-20). Finally, the grace of God takes many different forms to meet a variety of needs (4:10).

True/False:
1. T or F   The Greek language and writing style of 1 Peter is so poor that Peter appears to be truly "unlearned and ignorant" as noted in Acts 4:13.
2. T or F   The recipients of 1 Peter were not experiencing persecution.
3. T or F   As was the case with Galatians and Colossians, 1 Peter appears to be an encyclical letter.
4. T or F   The membership of the churches addressed by Peter seems to be mixed (comprised of Jews and Gentiles).
5. T or F   The major purpose of 1 Peter is to explain the meaning of suffering in the life of the Christian.
6. T or F   The Christological emphasis of 1 Peter is sometimes expressed in terms reminiscent of the Old Testament prophets (cf. 2:22).
7. T or F   Peter argues that suffering can have very positive results in the life of a Christian believer.
8. T or F   The frequent use of imperatives in 1 Peter makes this epistle more like a sermon than a doctrinal treatise.

---

[379] Tenney, *New Testament,* 352-53.
[380] Stibbs, *Peter,* 41.

9. T or F   Despite the fact that Peter was a disciple of the historical Jesus, there are no personal references in 1 Peter to this time in his life.

10. T or F   1 Peter's emphasis on <u>grace</u> can be seen in his frequent use of the word (ten times) in this epistle.

SELF TEST:

1. Our study of 1 Peter revealed that:
   a. the Greek and writing style is so poor that Peter appears to be truly "unlearned and ignorant" (Acts 4:13)
   b. the recipients of 1 Peter were not experiencing persecution
   c. 1 Peter is an encyclical
   d. all of these
   e. none of these

2. It was also noted that:
   a. Peter was writing to a "mixed group" of Jews and Gentiles
   b. the purpose of 1 Peter was to explain suffering in the life of a Christian
   c. Peter's Christological emphasis is often expressed in terms similar to Old Testament prophets (cf. 222)
   d. all of these
   e. none of these

3. In this epistle:
   a. Peter explained suffering in terms similar to Romans 8:28
   b. the believers were being persecuted by the Roman state
   c. believers were being persecuted because of "the name"
   d. B & C
   e. A & C

4. It was noted that:
   a. Peter taught that suffering can aid spiritual formation
   b. there are no personal references to the historical Jesus in 1 Peter
   c. Peter used a lot of imperatives in 1 Peter
   d. A & C
   e. A & B

5. It was taught that suffering:
   a. gives an opportunity to witness
   b. purifies the soul
   c. is part of living in this fallen world
   d. all of these
   e. none of these

LESSON 26—THE EPISTLE OF 2 PETER

Part 1	Background Information
Part 2	Central Theme
Part 3	Unique Contributions

OVERVIEW

You might recall from our section on the canon that 2 Peter was listed among the antilegomena, or "disputed works." As our study will reveal, there are some genuine problems concerning the authorship of 2 Peter. As will be discussed under our study of Jude, a good portion of 2 Peter parallels that epistle.

Nevertheless, this brief epistle does make some significant contributions to New Testament doctrine and theology. It speaks of the true knowledge of God. It gives us some interesting insight into the nature of scriptural interpretation and prophecy. In addition, this epistle sheds additional light on the nature of the Second Coming of our Lord.

Despite the problems mentioned at the outset, the theological and doctrinal contributions of 2 Peter make it indispensable to the New Testament canon.

OBJECTIVES

- Discuss the problems related to authorship.
- List the central themes of 2 Peter.
- Briefly discuss the unique contributions of 2 Peter.

HELPS FOR LEARNING AND REMEMBERING

1. Clearly delineate the material learned in 1 Peter from that of 2 Peter. Their similarities create the tendency to confuse the unique contributions of each.

2. Focus on the theological and doctrinal significance of this epistle. By encapsulating the core contribution of 2 Peter, its role in the New Testament canon will become more apparent.

3. You should jot down any questions that might arise as you study 2 Peter. By the end of the epistle, you will have a list of questions which can serve as a guideline for further investigation. Once again, any thoughts or impressions on the value or significance of 2 Peter should be recorded immediately. These spontaneous notes can be referred to in the future as areas of further study. Make a detailed outline of 2 Peter, developing a series of lessons or sermons on this epistle. We learn by teaching. By incorporating the subject matter of 2 Peter, it becomes part of our ministerial repertoire.

KEY WORDS

Idias   *epiluseos*   *pheroumenoi*
Parousia   pseudepigrapha   polemic

PART 1—BACKGROUND INFORMATION

I . AUTHORSHIP

A. Internal Evidence

The author clearly identifies himself as Simon Peter (1:1, 3:1). There is a clear allusion to the transfiguration of the Lord in 2 Peter 1:16, 17, and Peter was one of the eyewitnesses of this event. 2 Peter 3:16-18 indicates that the author knew Paul, which coincides with what we know from Acts and Galatians.

The writing style of 2 Peter is much more complicated than that of 1 Peter.[381] Unlike the first epistle, the Greek and sentence structure of 2 Peter are awkward. Perhaps these differences may be explained by the use of an amanuensis.[382]

B. External Evidence

The external evidence does not present a very favorable view of 2 Peter. None of the early church fathers quote 2 Peter. Origin (AD 180-220) stated that 2 Peter was in doubt even during his day.[383] Nevertheless, the Council of Laodicea (AD 363) and the Council of Carthage (AD 397) both fully acknowledge the canonicity of 2 Peter.[384]

II. DATE

The date of 2 Peter is bound up with the question of authorship. Those who do not accept Petrine authorship conclude that it is a forgery, part of the *pseudepigrapha*, written sometime in the early 2nd century.[385]

On the other hand, the high ethical content of 2 Peter refutes the theory that it is a forgery. The author tells his readers to live holy and Godly lives (3:11) and frequently warns against false teacher (2:1 ff.). If 2 Peter is a forgery, its author would be guilty of gross hypocrisy. The early church would have detected this and discounted 2 Peter from the start. In conclusion, it should be noted that there are no heresies or unique doctrines which contradict other biblical truths. The fanciful biographies so common to the false writings of the New Testament are totally absent from 2 Peter. In the final analysis, both the internal and external evidence do not compel one to reject Petrine authorship of this epistle. It probably was written by Peter shortly after his first epistle to address new problems in the church.

---

[381] Guthrie, *New Testament,* 826.
[382] Michael Green, *2 Peter and Jude,*(Grand Rapids: Eerdmans, 1987) 17.
[383] Guthrie, *New Testament,* 814-16.
[384] Green, *2 Peter and Jude,* 15.
[385] Harris, *New Testament,* 270.

PART 2—CENTRAL THEME

2 Peter addresses false teachers who had infiltrated the church (2:1). The main purpose of 2 Peter, therefore, is to fight doctrinal error and to undermine the influence of those false leaders.[386] The heretics of 2 Peter denied the redemptive power of Jesus (2:1) and lived in open immorality (2:10, 13). They rebelled against all authority (2:10, 12) and were hypocrites and deceivers (2:17-18). They spread doubt concerning the parousia (3:3-4).

To undermine the influence of the false teachers, 2 Peter developed the central theme of "knowledge."[387] Some form of the word "knowledge" appears 16 times in this short epistle. Six references relate to a proper knowledge of Jesus Christ. Peter had to remind his readers 3 times of what they were taught in the beginning (1:12-13, 3:1). Peter also spoke of forgetting (1:9, 3:8). His readers were forgetting some of the fundamental doctrines that they received at their conversion.

Peter divided his epistle into three parts. They are:

I. THE NATURE OF TRUE KNOWLEDGE (1:2-21)

As was the case with James, Peter emphasized that true knowledge only comes from God (1:2-4).

II. WARNING AGAINST FALSE KNOWLEDGE (2:1-22)

In this section, Peter told how God will judge false teachers. This is especially evident in 2:21.

III. PROPER ESCHATOLOGICAL KNOWLEDGE (3:1-18)

A true knowledge of the faith will include an accurate understanding of the parousia (or Second Coming of the Lord). Similar to 1 Peter, a correct knowledge of the Second Coming is our only basis for patience in the midst of a fallen world.

In summary, 2Peter is a *polemic* against heresy in the church. He was battling to tear down and destroy the corrupting influence of heresy in the church.[388] His method was to remind his readers of what they received in the beginning. All true doctrine is based upon an accurate understanding of the Lord and his Second Coming.

---

[386] Tenney, *New Testament,* 368.
[387] Guthrie, *New Testament,* 855.
[388] Green, *2 Peter and Jude,* 42 ff.

PART 3—UNIQUE CONTRIBUTIONS

2 Peter makes two important contributions. They are Peter's thoughts concerning:

I. THE NAUTRE OF THE WORD (1:19-21)

Because the false teachers were claiming a proper understanding of the Word of God, Peter was forced to explain the true nature of the Word.

A. No Private Interpretation

2 Peter 1:20 states that no prophecy is a matter of "one's own" (*idias*) interpretation (*epiluseos*, which means "illumination" or "explanation").[389] The point Peter made here is that no prophecy independently explains itself. A prophecy cannot be understood apart from its context. What they were saying had nothing to do with the Old Testament revelation, and contradicted the inspiration of the Spirit. Peter claimed that a true prophecy is intricately connected to God's entire revelation and is in complete harmony with the person of the Holy Spirit.

B. Divinely Inspired

Peter described the inspiration of the Holy Spirit by using the Greek word *pheroumenoi*, literally meaning "those carried along."[390] This particular word describes how sailing vessels are propelled by the wind. The wind fills the sails and one is able to observe the movement, but the force causing the movement is invisible. Similarly, those anointed by the Spirit must have evidence of the Spirit in their lives, yet that spiritual force behind their prophecies remains invisible.

II. THE NATURE OF THE SECOND COMING (3:1-18)[391]

As previously noted, the false teachers in 2Peter were questioning the validity of the Second Coming or Parousia. This in turn was eroding the eschatological hope of the Christian congregations. Peter battled the negative effects of the heretics by stating the following:

A. It is not an Evolutionary Process

The false teachers argued that the cycles of nature indicate that there will be no interruption of the normal processes of this world. The bottom line is, the Lord is not coming.

The regular cycles of nature, however, are no gauge for the Second Coming (3:4).[392] Peter referred to the days of Noah (3:5-7), noting that, just prior to the flood, life continued as normal. A sudden, catastrophic end interrupted the regular basis cycles of life. So shall it be with the Second Coming of the Lord.

---

[389] Ibid., 100.
[390] Ibid., 101.
[391] Guthrie, *New Testament,* 854.
[392] Barclay, *James and Peter,* 338.

B. It is not a Matter of Human Calculation

The false teachers were arguing that it had been a long time since the Lord left this world. This "delay" was interpreted as a denial of the Second Coming.

Peter stated that a human understanding of time cannot serve as a gauge for the Second Coming (3:8).[393]   God is eternal and therefore exists above the dimension of time. Although God understands our perception of time, He is not limited to time. Thus, a day with the Lord is as a thousand years, and a thousand years is as one day.

C. The Reason for the Delay

God's compassion for the lost explains the delay (3:9).[394]   Yet, when the fullness of the body of Christ has come, the end will be sudden and catastrophic (3:10). Jewish apocalypticism, as with Daniel, Ezekiel, and Joel also influenced Peter here.

State the central theme of 2 Peter. Describe how he uses the word "knowledge" to develop this theme.

---

[393] Ibid.
[394] Green, *2 Peter and Jude,* 148.

True/False:

1. T or F   2 Peter had no difficulty getting into the New Testament canon.
2. T or F   The early church fathers unanimously accepted 2 Peter as inspired.
3. T or F   2 Peter states that some were teaching that Jesus would not come back again.
----
1. With regard to the epistle of 2 Peter, it was noted that:
    a. the word "knowledge" plays an important role in this epistle
    b. Peter teaches that each believer is entitled to his/her own private interpretation of the scriptures (cf. 1:20).
    c. the inspiration of the Spirit is described as a wind filling the sails of a ship and carrying it along (*pheroumenoi*).
    d. A & B
    e. A & C

2. With regard to the Parousia, 2 Peter teaches that:
    a. the cycles of nature are an accurate guide to determine the time of the Second Coming
    b. a human understanding of time can serve as an accurate guide for determining the Second Coming of the Lord
    c. the Lord has "delayed" His coming so that more souls will be saved (cf. 3:9).
    d. all of these
    e. none of these

Peter makes two significant contributions to our understanding of the Christian faith. List them and their subpoints:

1. _____

    a. _____

    b. _____

2. _____

    a. _____

    b. _____

SELF TEST:

1. With regard to authorship, it was noted that:
    a. 2 Peter had no difficulty getting into the canon
    b. the early church fathers unanimously accepted 2 Peter
    c. the Greek of 2 Peter is poor and awkward
    d. all of these
    e. none of these

2. In 2 Peter,:
    a. "knowledge" plays an important role in this epistle
    b. every believer is entitled to his/her own private interpretation
    c. the inspiration of the Spirit is described in terms of wind filling the sails of a ship
    d. A & B
    e. A & C

3. With regard to the Second Coming, Peter taught that:
    a. the cycles of nature are an accurate guide
    b. a human understanding of time is an accurate guide
    c. the Lord has delayed His coming so that more souls can be saved
    d. all of these
    e. none of these

4. It was noted that:
    a. 2Peter duplicates large portions of Jude
    b. Peter's name does not appear any place in the text
    c. 2Peter is a forgery
    d. all of these
    e. none of these

5. It was also noted that:
    a. the high ethical content of 2 Peter argues against a forgery
    b. all of the church councils rejected Petrine authorship
    c. Origen stated there were no doubts concerning the authority of 2 Peter during his day
    d. all of these
    e. none of these

LESSON 27—THE EPISTLES OF JOHN

Part 1	Background Information
Part 2	The Epistle of 1 John
Part 3	The Epistle of 2 John
Part 4	The Epistle of 3 John

OVERVIEW

The Epistles of John truly communicate the heart and soul of a pastor. John penned these epistles as a mature and learned father in the Lord. He often referred to his addresses as "my little children." Indeed, as our study continues, the theme of "the family of God" is central to John's epistles. He continually emphasized the concepts of Christian assurance and comfort. John clearly wanted to affirm the unique and distinct identity of the children of God. As was so evident in the Gospel of John, the author was able to communicate profound spiritual truths by using very simple vocabulary. He wrote of light, darkness, the word (*logos*), love, etc. The simplicity of his vocabulary accentuates the complexity of his thought.

John's intense concern for the welfare of his readers is not unfounded. Dangerous heresies had infiltrated the church and were attacking the very foundations of the faith. John viewed the lies of the heretics as a sign of the end time. He taught that such persons were motivated by the spirit of antichrist. Indeed, John argued that the very presence of the antichrist signals that the end is near. In this sense, the Johannine epistles serve as a prelude to the only New Testament book totally dedicated to prophecy (John's Revelation).

OBJECTIVES

- Discuss the background information for the Johannine epistles.
- Identify what motivated John to write these epistles.
- Identify the heretics present in the Johannine epistles.

HELPS FOR LEARNING AND REMEMBERING

1. These three epistles are very short and should be read in a single setting. Compare and contrast the outline of each epistle, fixing the central contribution of each work in your mind.

2. Compare the themes, vocabulary, and spirit of these epistles with the Gospel of John. This will help you develop a concept of the nature and style of Johannine literature as a whole.

3. As with 2 Peter, you must devise means for differentiating the content of each one of these epistles. Perhaps you might condense your findings for each epistle on a single 5x8 card. Encapsulation of the contents of each epistle on a single card may help you differentiate then when studying.

4. Visualize the original context of these epistles. Imagine that you are the shepherd of various congregations spread throughout a wide geographic area. You have heard that serious heresies

have spread through your churches and are casting many of your members into confusion and despair. This is the situation which John faced, and his pastor's heart pours forth on each and every page. In seeking to grasp the sense of urgency of the author, the spirit of the epistles will become part of your ministering spirit. This will help you learn the true content and relevancy of these letters.

KEY WORDS

| *Teknia* | *ho presbuteros* | *eklekte kuria* | |
| Diotrophes | Gaius | Demetrius | Cerinthus |

PART 1—BACKGROUND INFORMATION

The authorship, occasion, and date of each epistle will be considered collectively.

I. AUTHORSHIP

A. Internal Evidence[395]

All three epistles are anonymous. Yet, the author was an eyewitness of the Lord, and thereby, was one of the 12 apostles (1 John 1:1-3). The vocabulary and writing style of these epistles are very similar to the Gospel of John. John used words such as light, darkness, children, the word, etc., to communicate theological principles and the sentence structure is simple but clear. Additionally, the author of these epistles wrote with an air of authority.

He expected his recipients to obey his instructions (1 John vs. 4, 6) and he firmly condemned the heretics (1 John 2:18). He wrote as a father in the Lord seeking to comfort his children (*teknia* "little children"). Only an apostolic figure and one of extraordinary maturity could refer to his congregation in this way. Indeed, the early Christian tradition records that John lived to be quite old.

B. External Evidence[396]

Polycarp (AD 96) is the earliest reference to the Johannine epistles. Other early church fathers, [Irenaeus (AD 130-202), Tertullian (AD 110-220), and Origen (AD 185-254)] cite John as the author of all 3 epistles.

The only serious alternative to Johannine authorship is the following: Papias, a disciple of John, makes references to a person by the name of "John the Elder." The first verse of both 2 and 3 John begins with the word *ho presbuteros*, "the elder." It is suggested that this person, not John the apostle, wrote the epistles. Perhaps the extreme age and experience of John earned him the title "the Elder."

II. OCCASION

The occasion for writing 1 and 2 John is clear. False teachers had entered the church and were troubling the believers. The nature of the heresy in 1 and 2 John appears to be:[397]

A. The Heretics have no Sin

They claimed that they knew God, had fellowship with God, and that they had no sin (1 John 1:6, 8, 10, 2:4). The phrase "they had no sin" does not refer to holy living, because the heretics were immoral. Rather, they were claiming that *in their spirit* they were completely sinless (1

---

[395] John R. W. Stott, *The Letters of John,* (Grand Rapids: Eerdmans, 1988) 20-28.
[396] I. Howard Marshall, *The Epistles of John,* (Grand Rapids: Eerdmans, 1978) 9 ff.
[397] Tenney, *New Testament,* 374-76.

John 1:8, 10) (they had no sin nature).[398] The heretics separated their physical being from their spiritual being and believed that what they did in their body did not affect their spirit.

B. They Rejected Jesus as the Messiah

The heretics did not accept that God would become human and thus denied that Jesus was the Messiah (1 John 2:22, 5:1, 5).[399]

C. They Rejected the Incarnation

The heretics believed that only pure spirit was acceptable to God and that anything material was evil. They could not accept that God would come in the flesh (1 John 4:2-3; 2John vs. 7; cf. also John 1:14).[400]

D. They Broke the Commandments of Jesus

Since they did not recognize that Jesus was God incarnate, they did not obey the commandments of the historical Jesus (1 John 2:4).[401] Nevertheless, they claimed that they had no sin and were accepted by God.

From these characteristics, the heresy appears to be *quasi-gnosticism* (elementary or undeveloped Gnosticism).[402] It was probably very similar to the teachings of Cerinthus, a church leader and contemporary of John.[403] He had incorporated pre-gnostic or quasi-gnostic philosophy into his theology and denied the Virgin Birth, the incarnation, and the messiahship of Jesus.

Polycarp recorded that John actually met Cerinthus.[404] Upon entering a public bathhouse, John, spotting Cerinthus, ran out warning that all should flee for God would surely destroy the premises!

The occasion for 3 John was not the quasi-gnosticism. Rather, John's third epistle is more personal than theological. 3 John is more concerned with matters of church administration.[405] A local church leader by the name of Diotrephes had abused his ecclesiastical authority. He would not permit John, or persons sent by John, to visit his congregation. Diotrephes had excommunicated some of the members in John's churches. In this brief epistle, John rebuked Diotrephes, but on the other hand, he commended Demetrius.

---

[398] Rudolf Bultmann, *The Johannine Epistles,* (Philadelphia: Fortress, 1973) 20-22.

[399] Marshall, *Epistles of John,* 157.

[400] Stott, *Letters of John,* 158-59.

[401] Morris, *New Testament,* 289.

[402] Harris, *New Testament,* 272.

[403] Stott, *Letters of John,* 48-50.

[404] Ibid., 50.

[405] Tenney, *New Testament,* 379.

III. DESTINATION

A. 1 John: The destination of 1 John is unclear. All we know is that the author knew his readers on a very personal level and in turn his readers were certainly Christians. Church tradition states that 1 John was addressed to several Christian congregations in and around Ephesus.[406]

B. 2 John: is directed to the *eklekte kuria,* or "the elect lady."[407] The word *kuria* is the feminine form of the word "lord." Is 2 John written to an individual or does the phrase "the elect lady" refer to an entire congregation?[408] If the church was being persecuted, perhaps the phrase "the elect lady" is a code for the local congregations in a particular area. The following presents data supporting both interpretations:

1. The Elect Lady Refers to an Individual Person[409]

This is the most literal interpretation of the phrase. In this case, the elect lady would be a woman of considerable standing and authority in the church. 2 John also speaks to her children, mentions her sister and even sends greetings to her sister's children (2 John vs. 1, 13).

2. The Elect Lady Refers to an Entire Christian Community[410]

2 John addressed biblical commandments, specific doctrines and warnings against false teachers. This seems more appropriate for a church than for an individual person. Throughout 2 John, the writer frequently speaks in the second person plural ("you") (2 John vs. 8, 10, 12).

Although no conclusions can be made with certainty, if "the elect lady" is a code name, then churches were experiencing severe persecution, probably under the emperor Nero.

If we accept the literal interpretation, this raises interesting questions concerning female leadership during the apostolic period.

C. 3 John: In 3 John, the apostle was writing to a church leader by the name of Gaius, but his identity is uncertain.

IV. DATE

If the author is John, and the problem he was addressing was quasi-gnosticism, then the epistles were probably written between AD 90 and 95.[411]

---

[406] Guthrie, *New Testament,* 873-75.
[407] Tenney, *New Testament,* 378.
[408] Ibid.
[409] Guthrie, *New Testament,* 389.
[410] Ibid.
[411] Ibid., 883.

PART 2—THE EPISTLE OF 1 JOHN

I. WRITING STYLE AND VOCABULARY

The vocabulary of 1 John is similar to that in the Gospel of John. Words such as "the word," "the beginning," "abiding," and "begotten" are found frequently throughout both. The verb "to witness" is used 33 times in the gospel, and six times in 1 John.[412] The verb "to believe" is used 98 times in the gospel, and nine times in 1 John.[413] Two important words for both the Gospel of John and the epistle of 1 John are "light" and "love." These two words govern a large portion of 1 John.

Light is symbolic of God's truth and characterizes the children of God, defining their social relationship (1 John 1:5-7; 2:7-11).

Love lies at the center of God's person and nature (4:7-12).

II. CENTRAL THEMES

There are three major themes in 1 John. They are:

A. The Johannine Polemic against Heresies

Some form of quasi-gnosticism had infiltrated the church. Throughout 1 John, the author sought to undermine and destroy the influence of this heresy.

B. The Theme of Christian Assurance

The quasi-gnostic heretics were boasting of a superior knowledge. John reassured his readers that they truly were the children of God (1 John 5:13).[414] He emphasized that they have a divine knowledge, by frequently using the phrase "we know" (2:3; 3:14; 4:13; 5:18-20). These verses serve to strengthen the assurance of the believer in Christ Jesus.

C. The Theme of the Family of God

The principle of the family of God is based upon the following relationship between the Father and the Son:

1. The relationship is an eternal relationship (1:2).
This echoes what John says about the Logos in John 1:1-14.

2. It is an equal relationship (1:3; 2:22-24).
The Son is equal to the Father, equal in power and glory. To have fellowship with the Son is to have fellowship with the Father. To reject the Son is also to reject the Father.

---

[412] Morris, *New Testament,* 389.
[413] Ibid., 274.
[414] Stott, *Letters of John,* 58.

3. Jesus is the only advocate (2:1).
The Gnostics were teaching that there were many different advocates and intermediaries between God and man. John teaches that our place in the family of God is secured only through one mediator, Jesus Christ.

4. The Son is divinely commissioned by the Father (4:14).
The will of the Father and the Son are in perfect harmony.

Because of the unique relationship between the Father and the Son, believers have the following relationship with the Father:

    1. It is a relationship of true fellowship (1:3)
    2. It is a relationship based on genuine knowledge (2:13)
    3. It is a relationship based on divine love (3:1)
    4. It is a relationship based on divine nature (3:9-10)

"The seed" in 3:9 ff. is the divine nature spoken of in 2 Peter 1:4.[415] Through regeneration, believers are the children of God by nature. In their essence, those who are born again are not sinners like the world, for the world is diametrically opposed to the Father (2:15-16). To love the world is to hate the Father and to love the Father is to hate this world.

Who is the "Elect Lady"?

---

[415] Marshall, *Epistles of John,* 186.

PART 3—THE EPISTLE OF 2 JOHN

The content of 2 John is very similar to 1 John. Verse 7 speaks about deceivers who deny that Jesus has come in the flesh. Such persons are "the antichrist." Union with the Father automatically constitutes union with the Son and vice versa (vs. 9-10). The theme of assurance continues in vs. 4-6. The exhortation to love one another and to obey the commandments parallel John's first epistle.

True/False:

1. T or F   John the Elder was the author of the Epistles of John, not the Apostle John.
2. T or F   The imagery and word pictures used in the Johannine epistles are very similar to what we find in the Gospel of John.
3. T or F   The phrase "they had no sin" alluded to in 1 John 1:6,8,10; 2:4 means that the heretics claimed that they had no sin nature.
4. T or F   The heresy in 1 John seems to be some variety of early Christian Gnosticism.
5. T or F   In 2 John the writer teaches that "antichrists" have already entered into the world.
6. T or F   It is possible that the *eklekte kuria* of 2 John refers to an entire congregation rather than to a single individual.

----

1. With regard to the heresy addressed in the Johannine epistles,
    a. the false teaching may have been similar to the teachings of Cerinthus
    b. the heretics believed in the physical resurrection of the dead
    c. both of these
    d. none of these

2. The heretics:
    a. denied that Jesus was the Messiah
    b. saw no need for the blood sacrifice of Christ
    c. lived immoral lifestyles, yet claimed to have continual communion with God
    d. all of these
    e. none of these

PART 4—THE EPISTLE OF 3 JOHN

3 John deals with administrative matters rather than doctrinal matters. It is a personal letter addressed to Gaius. The exact identity of Gaius is unknown, but he was probably a pastor of a local church. He was to show hospitality to the believers and to strangers (vs. 5-8). John told him that Diotrephes was to be rebuked and Demetrius was to be commended.

<table>
<tr><td>Discuss the authorship of the Johannine epistles:

</td></tr>
</table>

SELF TEST:

1. Regarding the Johannine epistles:
     a. John the Elder, and not the Apostle John, wrote these epistles
     b. vocabulary and sentence structure of these epistles are very similar to John's gospel
     c. the heresy addressed was probably *quasi-gnosticism*
     d. B & C
     e. A & B

2. It was noted that:
     a. in 2 John, John says that antichrists have come into the world already
     b. 3 John deals with doctrinal rather than administrative matters
     c. the phrase "they had no sin" (1 John 1:6-10, 2:4) means that heretics lived sinless lives
     d. all of these
     e. none of these

3. With regard to the heresy:
     a. it was similar to the teachings of Cerinthus
     b. the heretics accepted the incarnation
     c. the heretics believed that Jesus was the Messiah
     d. all of these
     e. none of these

4. The heretics:
     a. boasted of a special knowledge of God
     b. lived immoral lives, yet claimed that they had fellowship with God
     c. claimed that their spirit was sinless
     d. all of these
     e. none of these

5. When discussing the "Family of God," it was noted that:
     a. the Father and Son are equal in glory and power
     b. the word *teknia* is part of the "Family of God" motif
     c. 'seed" (1 John 3:9-10) refers to the divine nature resident in the regenerated
     d. all of these
     e. none of these

LESSON 28—THE EPISTLE OF JUDE

Part 1	Background Information
Part 2	Peculiar Characteristics of Jude
Part 3	Central Themes

OVERVIEW

As noted under our section on the Canon, Jude was listed among the antilegomena or "disputed works." In fact, Jude is one of the most controversial books in the entire New Testament. As we will see below, a good portion of Jude parallels material in 2 Peter chs. 2, 3. The question is whether Jude has copied from 2 Peter. It will be discovered that Jude quotes from apocryphal works. You will recall that the word apocryphal means "uninspired" or "non-canonical." Nevertheless, in time, the place of this epistle in the New Testament was secured.

OBJECTIVES

- Discuss the background information for the Epistle of Jude.
- List and discuss the peculiar characteristics of Jude.
- List and discuss the three central themes of Jude.

HELPS FOR LEARNING AND REMEMBERING

1. Considering the difficulties encountered in Jude, several good evangelical commentaries will be helpful.

2. The value of this epistle lies in its contemporary application. Continually seek ways in which the burden and message of Jude can be applied to the local church today.

3. Despite the controversies associated with Jude, it should be acknowledged that it has stood the test of time. In other words, the church openly endorsed and continually used the Epistle of Jude for doctrine and edification. Therefore, focusing on the positive contribution of this brief epistle may help you to incorporate, learn and apply its contents to the church of today.

4. Two apocryphal works will be mentioned in our study of Jude. Reading through these works and noting how they influenced the first century religious milieu may help shed some light on your studies of Jude. Jude did not write in a vacuum. Even though these works are non-canonical, they were well known by Jude and his readers. An understanding of the Assumption of Moses and 1 Enoch can facilitate an understanding of Jude.

KEY WORDS

Apocryphal	the Assumption of Moses	doxology
Antilegomena	the Book of Enoch	Latin Vulgate
Muratorian Canon	antinomianism	triads

PART 1—BACKGROUND INFORMATION

I. AUTHORSHIP

The author identifies himself as a servant of the Lord and a brother of James (verse 1). If this James is the one who wrote the Epistle of James, that is the brother of the Lord Jesus Christ (Mark 6:3; Matt. 13:55; Galatians 1:19) then this would mean that Jude is also a half-brother of the Lord.[416]   As with James, Jude was not a believer during the early ministry of Jesus (John 7:5); yet, Acts 1:14 notes that Jude was converted after the ascension of Jesus. At any rate, Jude was not a prominent figure in the early church and verse 17 indicates that Jude did not consider himself to be an apostle.

His writing style is very similar to what we find in James. He too wrote using many word pictures and analogies from nature. He also emphasized personal ethics and some of the vocabulary of Jude is quite similar to what we find in James. All of these points support the theory that indeed Jude is the brother of James.

II. DATE

The close association of Jude with 2 Peter has a bearing on the date. A significant portion of Jude parallels 2 Peter, ch. 2 and 3. If Jude was written after 2 Peter, the date would be somewhere around AD 67 or 68. However, verse 17 indicates that many years may have elapsed since the apostles set forth the doctrines of the faith. Jude, therefore, could have been written perhaps as late as AD 80 to 85.[417]   Both dates still place the book within the apostolic period of the church.

---

[416] Michael Green, *2 Peter and Jude,* (Grand Rapids: Eerdmans, 1987) 48-49.
[417] Guthrie, *New Testament,* 908-12.

PART 2—PECULIAR CHARACTERISTICS OF JUDE

The introductory remarks to this lesson have indicated that Jude was accepted into the canon after great controversy. The two primary reasons for these difficulties were that a good portion of Jude parallels 2 Peter and that Jude quotes from the apocryphal works.

I. THE PARALLELS BETWEEN JUDE AND 2 PETER[418]

The chart below shows the parallel passages of Jude and 2 Peter.

THE PARALLEL PASSAGES

JUDE	2 PETER
4	2:1-3
5,6,7	2:4,6
8,9,10	2:10,11 & 12
11, 12a	2:13,15
12b—13	2:17
17	3:2
18	3:3

What accounts for the nearly verbatim agreement between these two epistles? The following are four explanations:[419]

A. The Two Documents are Totally Unrelated

Peter and Jude were simply addressing similar churches having similar problems. Although this is possible, it does not explain the close verbal similarities.

B. Both Jude and 2 Peter had Access to a Third Document

They both drew from a common source.

C. 2 Peter Borrowed from Jude

2 Peter is longer than Jude, and Peter may have expanded Jude's epistle. Those who do not accept Petrine authorship of 2 Peter choose this option.

D. Jude Wrote his Epistle after Reading 2 Peter

Jude 3 clearly states that he originally planned to write devotional literature. He states that he has changed his original intention, and must write apologetically (to fight for the faith). 2 Peter continually warns that in the last days false teachers will enter into the church. On reading this, Jude realized that this had already occurred in his church; so, he borrowed words and phrases from 2 Peter, yet organized his letter independently from 2 Peter.

---

[418] Simon J. Kistemaker, *Peter and Jude,* (Grand Rapids: Baker, 1987) 357.
[419] Guthrie, *New Testament,* 919-27.

II. JUDE QUOTES FROM THE APOCRYPHAL WORKS[420]

A. The Assumption of Moses

Jude 9 quotes from "The Assumption of Moses" (cf. Origen's *First Principles*). The Assumption of Moses states that after the death of Moses, Michael the archangel and Satan appeared on the scene. Satan claims the body because it is material and because Moses was a murderer during his lifetime. Michael argued that God created everything, even the human body and responds, "The Lord rebuke you." Satan immediately leaves.

Jude 16 speaks of grumblers and complainers, which closely parallels The Assumption of Moses 7:7. He also speaks of high-sounding words (cf. The Assumption of Moses 7:9) and speaks against persons who use flattery to gain favor with others, as does The Assumption of Moses (5:5).

B. 1 Enoch

Jude quotes 1 Enoch 1:9 which speaks of God coming with thousands of his holy ones to cast judgment upon the ungodly who have spoken hard things against the Lord. Also, 1 Enoch 60:8 speaks of "Enoch, the seventh from Adam." 1 Enoch 48:10 speaks of the ungodly as those who "have denied the Lord of spirits and his anointed. 1 Enoch 12:4-13:1 speaks of the rebellion of Satan and his angels. 1 Enoch 2:3 also speaks about clouds without water, and 13:11 speaks of trees that have been plucked up and are withered. All of these references sound very similar to Jude 4-6, 12-13.

Origin noted that many rejected Jude during his lifetime.[421] Jerome, the church father who translated the Latin Vulgate in the 4th century, flatly denied the inspiration of Jude. However, the Muratorian Canon (AD 140) lists Jude as canonical. Origin himself as well as Clement of Alexandria, accepted the authority of the epistle of Jude.

It should be noted that Jude never says his sources are inspired. The Assumption of Moses and 1 Enoch may contain spiritual truths, just as Paul quotes truth from pagan poets (Acts 17:28). In the final analysis, nothing in Jude contradicts the eschatological teachings of the New Testament. It has withstood the test of time and has been beneficial for doctrine and faith.

---

[420] Green, *2 Peter and Jude,* 57-58.
[421] Guthrie, *New Testament,* 905.

PART 3—CENTRAL THEMES

Jude 3-4 tell us the purpose of the letter. Since the very nature of the faith was in danger, Jude changed his mind about writing of "the common salvation." Heretics were "turning the grace of God into lasciviousness, denying the only Lord God and our Lord Jesus Christ" (vs. 4). The problem of *antinomianism* (lawlessness) was present (the kind that Paul warned against in Romans 6:1 ff.). Jude's love for triads (groups of 3) led him to select 3 central themes in fighting the heretics. They are:[422]

I. EXAMPLES OF APOSTATES (VS. 5, 6, 7)

A. Unbelief

Jude 5 warns against the sin of unbelief and gives Israel as an example. God delivered the Israelites from Egypt, but because of unbelief, he later destroyed them in the wilderness. Just because one has experienced the grace of God at one point does not mean that one can stop believing.

B. Disobedience

Jude 6 warns against the sin of disobedience and gives the angels who rebelled as an example. Pure spiritual beings, who were in the very presence of God, lost their state because of disobedience. Mankind should also take heed!

C. Uncleanness

Jude 7 gives a sever warning against uncleanness or sexual immorality, offering Sodom and Gomorrah as examples.

The heretics are guilty of all of these sins and are like Satan who blasphemes, like Cain who was self-willed, like Balaam who loved money, and like Korah who obtained spiritual leadership by force (8-10).

II. EXHORTATIONS TO SPIRITUAL PROGRESS (VS. 17-23)

Once again Jude used a triad to warn his readers.

A. The Example of the Holy Apostles

Jude 17-18 states that one can avoid falling from grace by remembering the words of Christ spoken through the holy apostles. Adherence to orthodox doctrine is a safeguard against apostasy.

---

[422] A.R.C. Leaney, *The Letters of Peter and Jude,* (Cambridge: University Press, 1967) 82-87.

B. Edify One Another

Believers are to build up one another and pray in the Holy Spirit. Some see this verse as a reference to speaking in tongues. They are to continually seek the love and mercy of God (cf. vs. 20-21).

C. Rescue the Perishing

True believers are to rescue those who are in danger of destroying themselves spiritually (vs. 22-23). In other words, the strong are to look after the spiritual welfare of the weak.

III. SAFEGUARDS AGAINST APOSTASY (VS. 24-25)

Here the Book of Jude presents one of the most beautiful doxologies (literally "words of glory") in the New Testament, emphasizing the keeping power of God.[423] Praise and worship are safeguards against apostasy.

True/False:
1. T or F Jude does not quote from apocryphal books.
2. T or F Large portions of Jude parallel 2 Peter, almost word for word.
3. T or F Jude states that he changed his original intention for writing this epistle.
4. T or F Just as Paul found truth in some of the things in which the Greek pagan poets said (cf. Acts 17:28), Jude discovered truth in the books of 1 Enoch and The Assumption of Moses.
5. T or F Antinomianism does not seem to be a problem in the epistle of Jude.
6. T or F Jude contains one of the most beautiful doxologies in all of the New Testament.

---

[423] Green, *2 Peter and Jude,* 206-08.

SELF TEST:

1. Our study of Jude revealed that:
     a. Jude quotes from apocryphal works
     b. large portions of Jude parallel 2 Peter
     c Jude changed his original intention for writing the epistle
     d. all of these
     e. none of these

2. It was noted that:
     a. Paul quotes from pagan Greek poets
     b. antinomianism is not a problem in this epistle
     c. Jerome rejected the authenticity of Jude
     d. A & B
     e. A & C

3. It was discovered that:
     a. Peter definitely borrowed from Jude
     b. Jude is longer than 2 Peter
     c. Jude contains one of the most beautiful doxologies in the New Testament
     d. A & C
     e. B & C

4. It was also noted that:
     a. Jude is fond of triads
     b. Jude uses many examples from the Old Testament to warn against apostasy
     c. Jude is probably the half-brother of Jesus
     d. all of these
     e. none of these

5. We can say that:
     a. Jude emphasizes "eternal security"
     b. praise and worship safeguard against apostasy
     c. unbelief, disobedience and uncleanness lead to apostasy
     d. A & B
     e. B & C

LESSON 29—THE BOOK OF REVELATION

Part 1	Background Information
Part 2	Central Themes
Part 3	The Four Visions

OVERVIEW

Just as with the epistle of Jude, Revelation was not accepted into the canon without controversy. Revelation was also listed among the antilegomena. Of interest here is that the history of the church had a direct bearing upon the evaluation of the Book of Revelation.[424] Heretics began to use the Book of Revelation to support their corrupted form of Christianity. This in turn led orthodox Christians to be skeptical about the value of the Book of Revelation in general.

Nevertheless, Revelation plays an extremely important role in the New Testament canon. It is the only book in the New Testament which is totally dedicated to prophecy.[425] The Book of Revelation is one of the best examples of Jewish apocalyptic in the entire Bible.[426] If there is a beginning, (the Book of Genesis), the biblical story is not complete unless there is a clearly articulated ending (the Book of Revelation). Revelation forms the perfect counterbalance to Genesis. It serves as the period for the entire biblical story. The problem arises in interpreting exactly what that final statement of the Bible really means. The elaborate symbolism and strange images of Revelation have eluded some of the most dedicated biblical scholars throughout centuries. Yet, the prophecies still speak and seize the church with an authority born of divine inspiration.

OBJECTIVES

- Discuss the background information for Revelation.
- List the central themes of Revelation.
- List the four major visions of Revelation.

HELPS FOR LEARNING AND REMEMBERING

1. Congratulations are genuinely in order! Your study of Revelation naturally marks the conclusion of a survey of all 27 New Testament books. Focusing on the magnitude of this accomplishment can motivate you to concentrate on mastering this final book of the Bible.

2. Fully acknowledge the unique literary genre encountered in your study of Revelation. It is apocalyptic literature which speaks in bizarre symbols and images of future events.

---

[424] Robert H. Mounce, *The Book of Revelation,* (Grand Rapids: Eerdmans, 1977) 38.
[425] Tenney, *New Testament,* 381.
[426] Morris, *New Testament,* 292.

3. Although Revelation is difficult to interpret, it is one of the most highly organized books of the Bible. With some effort you should easily be able to delineate the major components of this book.

4. Revelation is one of the most Jewish books of the entire New Testament. Many Jewish symbols, ceremonies and religious holidays are reflected throughout its pages. Frequent references to a good Bible dictionary can be of great help in interpreting the very serious message of the Revelator.

5. Concentrate on the broad scheme of things in this particular work. Do not get caught up in the individual details and symbols. Apocalyptic literature is known for communicating impressions and feelings. In other words, the intense nature of apocalyptic literature often reveals the broad scheme of things and not the significance of each and every detail of the picture.

KEY WORDS

Apocalyptic	encyclical	Dionysius
Hapaxes	Cerinthus	numerology
Montanus	ecstasy	

PART 1—BACKGROUND INFORMATION

I. AUTHORSHIP

A External Evidence[427]

Although Revelation became listed with the antilegomena, it had very early acceptance in the church. It was an encyclical to be read and accepted by the seven churches of Asia Minor (1:11). Each church made a copy of this important book prior to passing it on, therefore, Revelation enjoyed a rapid distribution and acceptance by the church.

Irenaeus (ca. AD 170) accepted Revelation and said that he had copies he considered to be ancient. Ignatius (AD 110-170) also accepted Revelation, and the Muratorian Canon (AD 140) included Revelation as inspired. Tertullian (AD 150-225) quotes from 18 of the 22 chapters of Revelation, and Origen (AD 180) also accepted Revelation as divinely inspired. Therefore, Revelation enjoyed a very wide distribution and acceptance during the first 250 years of the church.

By the middle of the 4th century AD, the authority of Revelation came into question.[428] The primary reason was due to the apocalyptic nature of the work. The church simply could not decipher its meaning. Also, the Gnostic heretics Montanus and Cerinthus were using Revelation to support their false doctrines. For this reason, Dionysius, the bishop of Alexandria, rejected the authenticity of Revelation.

B. Internal Evidence

Dionysius sought to discredit Revelation by rejecting its apostolic authority. Dionysius did not believe that the Apostle John wrote Revelation. He pointed out that:[429]

1. Different Vocabulary

There are 108 *hapaxes*, or "unique words" found only in Revelation. Ninety-eight additional words are mentioned in only one other place, and not necessarily in the gospel of John.

2. Different Grammar

Revelation has the worst sentence structure of the entire New Testament. The Gospel of John and the epistles do not evidence bad grammar.

3. Different Style

---

[427] Guthrie, *New Testament,* 934-40.

[428] R.C.H. Lenski, *St. John's Revelation,* (Minneapolis: Augsburg, 1963) 13.

[429] Leon Morris, *The Revelation of St. John,* (Grand Rapids: Eerdmans, 1983) 28. cf. also Guthrie, *New Testament,* 940.

The Gospel of John emphasizes love and that Christ is the Savior. On the contrary, Revelation represents Christ as a super conqueror and emphasizes the wrath of God.

4. Author Explicitly Stated

You might recall that the author of the Gospel of John and the epistles never explicitly identifies himself as the apostle. Revelation 1:1, 2, 4 clearly state that John is the author. Dionysius felt that the Apostle John would never have done this, and that the repeated use of John in Revelation evidences a forgery.

There is much internal evidence which argues for Johannine authorship.[430] Despite the unique vocabulary, the Gospel of John and Revelation have much vocabulary in common. Both use the words "truth," "light," "life," and "lamb" which have the same special meaning in both books. The *logos doctrine* is also found in Revelation.

With regard to the poor grammar and sentence structure, the following should be noted. Revelation 1:10 says that John was "in the spirit" when writing Revelation. This state of spiritual ecstasy may have affected the way John wrote Revelation. Also, John may have employed an amanuensis in producing the gospel but had no access to one on the Isle of Patmos. Revelation may have been the way John really wrote. With regard to differences in style and tone, it must be acknowledged that the Gospel of John and Revelation are working with totally different themes. The gospel is concerned with Jesus' ministry on earth, but Revelation focuses on the culmination of the ages. The emphasis on the wrath of God is not incongruous with "a son of thunder" (Mark 3:17).

II. DATE

With regard to the date of Revelation, there are two major options. Revelation 13:18 states that the number of the beast is 666. This is the numerical equivalent of the Hebrew letters which spell Caesar Nero.[431] If this is a correct interpretation of 666, then Revelation would have been written around AD 64 or 65. But Irenaeus claims that John wrote Revelation near the end of Domitian's reign (AD 81–96). Tradition holds that John lived to a very old age. It is possible that Revelation was written as late as AD 90–95.[432]

III. DESTINATION

The seven churches of Asia Minor were experiencing severe persecution, probably official Roman persecution. The same empire which protected Paul a few years earlier had turned against the church. Revelation 13:7 states that the enemy of the church had authority over all nations. Revelation 13:16–17 seems to refer to the official Roman seal required on all significant transactions. Also, Revelation 17:9 alludes to the fact that Rome was located on seven hills.

---

[430] Guthrie, *New Testament,* 938-40.

[431] Tenney, *New Testament,* 383.

[432] Philip E. Hughes, *The Book of Revelation,* (Grand Rapids: Eerdmans, 1990) 10. cf. also Tenney, *New Testament,* 384.

In conclusion, the Book of Revelation was an encyclical letter addressed to the churches of central Asia Minor.[433] These churches were experiencing severe persecution, more than likely at the hands of the Roman Empire.

IV. THE OCCASION

John was motivated to pen Revelation for two major reasons.[434] First, he wrote for the purpose of encouraging Christians in the face of extreme persecution. No doubt many Christians were confused why an all-powerful, all good God was not coming to the aid of those dedicated to his Son, Jesus Christ. Perhaps many were being told to publicly renounce Christ and to conform to the norms of Roman society. John wrote to encourage the Christians to hold on because the end is near. He appeals to the sovereignty of God, and that in the end the believers will be vindicated.

Secondly, John wrote to give an overview of God's plan of history. John emphasized that God is in sovereign control of persons, processes, and powers and that all things are working toward a predetermined end.

---

[433] William M. Ramsay, *The Letters to the Seven Churches,* (Grand Rapids: Baker, 1979) 35 f.
[434] Guthrie, *New Testament,* 961-62.

PART 2—CENTRAL THEMES

I. PROPHECY

Revelation is the only book of the New Testament totally devoted to prophecy and the author himself was fully aware of this (22:6-7) fact. Revelation develops the theme of biblical prophecy on each page.[435]

II. THE MEANING OF SUFFERING

Revelation explains the meaning of suffering for the believer.[436] Those who persecute the church are storing wrath unto the Day of Judgment, and even the death of the saints constitutes a great victory for the kingdom.

III. JEWISH APOCALYPTIC

God is sovereign over all aspects of this present existence.[437] Everything is moving toward a predetermined end. At that point, there will be a supernatural, cataclysmic intervention of God into the affairs of this world. The kingdom of God will be fully realized, and the kingdoms of this world will be destroyed.

The apocalypticism of Revelation contains four aspects:[438]

A. Intense Despair Counterbalanced with Future Hope

The apocalyptic sections of Daniel, Ezekiel, and Joel, as well as the Book of Revelation, all communicate that extreme suffering in the present can be endured because of the glorious hope that lies in the future.

B. Symbolic Language, Dreams, and Visions

It is almost as if normal, conventional language is inadequate to relate the extraordinary intervention of God in the last days.

C. Supernatural Powers are in Christ

The major characteristic of all apocalyptic literature is that God and Satan, light and darkness, and truth and falsehood are engaged in mortal conflict to the end. The favorable resolution of this final struggle introduces the forth characteristic of apocalyptic.

---

[435] Morris, *Revelation,* 23.
[436] Tenney, *New Testament,* 383.
[437] Morris, *New Testament,* 294-95.
[438] Harris, *New Testament,* 277-79.

D. Deliverance of the Righteous and Destruction of the Ungodly

The central theme of biblical apocalyptic, and especially Revelation, is that the sovereign Lord will triumph over evil. The church can take comfort in its present struggles because the outcome is certain.

True/False:

1. T or F   Revelation was widely accepted by the early church, but became listed among the antilegomena by the time of the early 4th century.
2. T or F   In general, the vocabulary of Revelation is very similar to the Gospel of John.
3. T or F   The Book of Revelation has the best Greek grammar in the New Testament.
4. T or F   Just as in the Gospel of John, the name "John" does not appear anywhere in the book of Revelation.
5. T or F   Dionysius consistently argued for Johannine authorship of Revelation.
6. T or F   Since Revelation was addressed to several churches in Asia Minor, it should be regarded as encyclical.
7. T or F   The Book of Revelation is the only New Testament book solely devoted to prophecy.

PART 3—THE FOUR VISIONS

Although Revelation is perhaps the most difficult book to interpret, it is one of the most organized. John developed a highly structured presentation of the final hours of this world. All four visions are clearly identified by the phrase *in the spirit*. The visions which form the content of Revelation are:[439]

I. THE FIRST VISION—CHRIST AMONG HIS CHURCHES (1-3)

John employed *numerology* to lend structure to his work.[440] Numerology is the use of special numbers to communicate spiritual concepts and principles. The numbers seven and three are used repeatedly throughout Revelation and may stand for completeness or wholeness. The seven churches of Asia Minor may symbolize the complete, or universal church.

II. THE SECOND VISION—SUPERNATURAL POWERS IN CONFLICT (4-16)

This vision is comprised of five separate visions:

A. The Vision of Heaven (4-5)

B. The Seven Seals (6)

The seven seals encapsulate God's plan for the final days of this world.

C. The Seven Trumpets (7-11)

The trumpets represent the great and terrible plagues that are to come upon the world.

D. The Seven Signs of Persons in Battle (12-14)

These signs represent the horrific conflict which will occur just prior to the end of the world.

E. The Seven Bowls of God's Wrath (15-16)

The final outpouring of God's judgment has come upon all persons, powers and principalities opposed to God and his people.

III. THE THIRD VISION—CONQUEST AND TRIUMPH (17-21)

A. The Fall of Babylon (17-18)

Babylon is symbolic of all that is ungodly and rebellious.

---

[439] Tenney, *New Testament,* 391.
[440] Mounce, *Revelation,* 168-69.

B. The Beast is Defeated at Armageddon (19:11-20)

Although Revelation does not use the word "antichrist," the beast clearly represents such a personage. The beast is the personification of ungodliness and worldliness. He is defeated at the final confrontation at Armageddon.

C. The Judgment of Satan and the Ungodly (20-21)

This is judgment day, the great and terrible Day of the Lord as spoken of throughout the Old Testament. All injustices, wrongs, and evil will be judged and sentenced by God. The books are balanced, and death, hell, and the grave are cast into the lake of fire.

IV. THE FOURTH VISION—THE HOLY JERUSALEM (22)

Jerusalem is symbolic of the very presence of God among men. The kingdom of God is fully realized on earth. The effects of the fall are completely reversed, and the people of God are reinstated into a perfect environment.

SELF TEST:

1. Our study of Revelation showed that:
    a. Revelation enjoyed early acceptance by the church
    b. Dionysius accepted Revelation
    c. Montanus and Cerinthus were using Revelation to spread heresy
    d. A & B
    e. A & C

2. It was noted that:
    a. Revelation has the best grammar in the New Testament
    b. the name "John" is absent from Revelation
    c. Revelation frequently uses the word "antichrist"
    d. all of these
    e. none of these

3. The Book of Revelation is:
    a. the most disorganized book in the New Testament
    b. an encyclical
    c. the only New Testament book totally dedicated to prophecy
    d. A & C
    e. B & C

4. When studying Revelation, it was noted that:
    a. numerology plays an important role in Revelation
    b. the book is a good example of Jewish apocalyptic
    c. Revelation is the perfect counterpart to Genesis
    d. all of these
    e. none of these

5. In the Book of Revelation:
    a. there are no unique words, or *hapaxes*
    b. the writing style is not the same as that in the Gospel of John
    c. being "in the Spirit" may have affected the vocabulary and writing style of the author
    d. A & C
    e. B & C

BIBLIOGRAPHIC REFERENCES

Abbott, T.K. *The Epistle to the Ephesians*. Edinburgh: T & T Clark, 1979.

Allen, John A. *The Epistle to the Ephesians*. London: SCM Press, LTD, 1959.

Arichea, Daniel and Eugene A. Nida. *A Translator's Handbook on Paul's Letter to the Galatians*. Stuttgart: United Bible Societies, 1976.

Arrington, French L. *Maintaining the Foundations*. Grand Rapids: Baker Book House.

_____. *Paul's Aeon Theology in 1 Corinthians*. Washington, D.C.: University Press of America, 1977.

_____. *The Acts of the Apostles*. Peabody, MA: Hendrickson, 1988.

Attridge, Harold W. *A Commentary on the Epistle to the Hebrews*. Philadelphia: Fortress, 1989.

Barclay, William. *The Letters of James and Peter*. Philadelphia: The Westminster Press, 1976.

_____. *The Letters to the Galatians and Ephesians*. Philadelphia: Westminster, 1959.

Beare, F.W. *The Epistle to the Philippians*. London: Adam & Charles Black, 1959.

Best, Ernest. *1 Peter*. Grand Rapids: Eerdmans, 1971.

Betz, Donald S. "The First Epistle of Paul to the Corinthians," *The Beacon Bible Commentary*, vol. 8. Kansas City: Beacon Hill, 1968.

Borg, Marcus J. *Conflict, Holiness and Politics in the Teachings of Jesus*. New York: The Edwin Mellen Press, 1984.

Bruce, F.F. *The Book of Acts*. Grand Rapids: William B. Eerdmans, 1988.

_____. *The Epistle to the Colossians, to Philemon and to the Ephesians*. Grand Rapids: Eerdmans, 1984.

_____. *The Epistle to the Ephesians*. Old Tappan, NJ: Fleming H. Revell, Co., 1961.

_____. *The Epistle to the Hebrews*. Grand Rapids: Eerdmans, 1964.

_____. "1 and 2 Corinthians," *The New Century Bible Commentary*. Grand Rapids: William B. Eerdmans, 1971.

_____. *1 & 2 Thessalonians. Word Biblical Commentary,* vol. 45. Waco: Word Books, 1982.

Buber, Martin. *Two Kinds of Faith.* London: Routledge and Kegan Paul LTD, 1951.

Bultmann, Rudolf. *The Johannine Epistles.* Philadelphia: Fortress, 1973.

Carter, Charles W. and Ralph Earle. *The Acts of the Apostles.* Grand Rapids: Zondervan, 1973.

Cole, R.A. *Mark.* Grand Rapids: Eerdmans, 1983.

_____. *The Epistle of Paul to the Galatians.* Grand Rapids: William B. Eerdmans, 1970.

Davies, W.D. and Dale C. Allison. *A Critical and Exegetical Commentary on the Gospel According to Saint Matthew.* Edinburgh: T & T Clark, 1988.

Dibelius, M. and H. Conzelmann. *The Pastoral Epistles.* Philadelphia: Fortress, 1972.

Eadie, John. *A Commentary on the Greek Text of the Epistle of Paul to the Galatians.* Minneapolis: James and Klock Christian Publishing Co., reprint 1977.

_____. *Commentary on the Epistle of Paul to the Colossians.* Grand Rapids: Zondervan, 1894.

Eerdman, Charles R. *The Epistle to the Ephesians.* Grand Rapids: Baker Book House, 1931.

Ellicott, Charles John. *Commentary on the Epistles of Paul to the Thessalonians,* vol. 1. Grand Rapids: Zondervan, 1957.

Ellis, E. Earle. *Pauline Theology: Ministry and Society.* Grand Rapids: William B. Eerdmans, 1989.

Fee, Gordon. *The First Epistle to the Corinthians.* Grand Rapids: William B. Eerdmans, 1987.

Foulkes, Francis. *The Epistle of Paul to the Ephesians.* Grand Rapids: William B. Eerdmans, 1956.

Frame, James Everett. *The Epistles of Paul to the Thessalonians.* Edinburgh: T & T Clark, 1970.

Green, Michael. *2 Peter and Jude.* Grand Rapids: Eerdmans, 1987.

Guthrie, Donald. *New Testament Introduction.* Downers Grove, IL: Inter-Varsity Press, 1970.

_____. *The Pastoral Epistles.* Grand Rapids: Eerdmans, 1957.

Haenchen, Ernst. *The Acts of the Apostles: A Commentary.* Philadelphia: Westminster Press, 1971.

Hanson, A.T. *The Pastoral Epistles.* Grand Rapids: Eerdmans, 1982.

Harris, Stephen L. *The New Testament: A Student's Introduction.* Mountain View, CA: Mayfield Pub. Co., 1988.

Harvey, A.E. *Jesus and the Constraints of History: The Bampton Lectures, 1980.* London: Gerald Duckworth and Co. Ltd., 1982.

Hastings, James. *A Dictionary of the Bible.* New York: Charles Scribner's Sons, 1911.

Hendriksen, William. *Exposition of 1 and 2 Thessalonians.* Grand Rapids: Baker Book House, 1955.

_____. *Exposition of the Gospel According to Mark.* Grand Rapids: Baker, 1975.

_____. *Philippians, Colossians and Philemon.* Grand Rapids: Baker, 1962.

_____. *The Epistles to the Colossians and Philemon.* NTC. Grand Rapids: Baker, 1965.

Hodge, Charles. *A Commentary on the Epistle of the Ephesians.* Grand Rapids: Baker Book House, 1980.

Hughes, Philip E. *The Book of Revelation.* Grand Rapids: Eerdmans, 1990.

_____. *The Second Epistle to the Corinthians.* Grand Rapids: William B. Eerdmans, 1962.

Hultgren, Arland J. *1 and 2 Timothy and Titus.* Minneapolis: Augsburg, 1984.

Kelly, J.N.D. *A Commentary on the Pastoral Epistles.* Peabody, MA: Hendrickson, 1987.

Kistemaker, Simon J. *Peter and Jude.* Grand Rapids: Baker, 1987.

Lane, William. *Hebrews: A Call to Commitment.* Peabody, MA: Hendrickson, 1985.

Laws, Sophie. *The Epistle of James.* San Francisco: Harper & Row, 1980.

Leaney, A.R.C. *The Letters of Peter and Jude.* Cambridge: University Press, 1967.

Lenski, R.C.H. *St. John's Revelation.* Minneapolis: Augsburg, 1963.

_____. *The Interpretation of Mark's Gospel.* Minneapolis: Augsburg, 1961.

_____. *The Interpretation of Matthew's Gospel.* Minneapolis: Augsburg, 1961.

_____. *The Interpretation of St. Paul's Epistle to the Romans*. Minneapolis: Augsburg, 1936.

Lohse, Edward. *A Commentary on the Epistles to the Colossians and to Philemon*. Philadelphia: Fortress, 1971.

Marshall, I. Howard. *The Epistles of John*. Grand Rapids: Eerdmans, 1978.

_____. *The Gospel of Luke*. Grand Rapids: William B. Eerdmans, 1978.

Martin, Ralph P. *James*. Waco: Word Books, 1988.

_____. *New Testament Foundations: A Guide for Christian Students,* vol. 1. Grand Rapids: Eerdmans, 1975.

_____. *New Testament Foundations: A Guide for Christian Students,* vol. 2. Grand Rapids: Eerdmans, 1978.

_____. *The Epistle of Paul to the Philippians*. Grand Rapids: Eerdmans, 1959.

Meyer, Ben F. *The Aims of Jesus*. London: SCM Press Ltd., 1979.

Morris, Leon. *Luke*. Grand Rapids: William B. Eerdmans, 1983.

_____. *New Testament Theology*. Grand Rapids: Zondervan Publishing House, 1986.

_____. *The Epistle to the Romans*. Grand Rapids: William B. Eerdmans, 1988.

_____. *The First and Second Epistles to the Thessalonians*. Grand Rapids: William B. Eerdmans, 1959.

_____. *The Gospel According to John*. Grand Rapids: William B. Eerdmans, 1971.

Motyer, Alec. *The Message of James*. Downers Grove: Inter-Varsity, 1985.

Moule, C.G. *The Epistle of St. Paul to the Romans*. London: Hodden and Stroughton, 1896.

_____. *The Epistles to the Colossians and to Philemon*. London: C.J. Clay and Sons, 1893.

Mounce, Robert H. *The Book of Revelation*. Grand Rapids: Eerdmans, 1977.

Muller, Jacobus J. *The Epistle of Paul to the Philippians and to Philemon*. Grand Rapids: William B. Eerdmans, 1955.

Murray, John. *The Epistle to the Romans*. Grand Rapids: William B. Eerdmans, 1965.

Neusner, Jacob. *First-Century Judaism in Crisis: Yohanan ben Zakkai and the Renaissance of the Torah*. Nashville: Abingdon Press, 1985.

_____. *From Politics to Piety: The Emergence of Pharisaic Judaism*. New Jersey: Prentice-Hall, Inc., 1973.

Newman, Barclay M. and Eugene A. Nida. *A Translator's Handbook on the Gospel of John*. New York: United Bible Societies, 1980.

Nygren, Anders. *Commentary on Romans*. Philadelphia: Fortress Press, 1949.

Oppenheimer, Aaron. *The "Am ha-aretz: A Study in the Social History of the Jewish People in the Hellenistic-Roman Period*. Trans. I.H. Levine. Leiden: E.J. Brill, 1977.

Price, James L. *The New Testament*. New York: MacMillan, 1987.

Radford, Lewis B. *The Epistle to the Colossians and the Epistle to Philemon*. London: Metheun & Co. Ltd., 1931.

Ramsay, William M. *A Historical Commentary of St. Paul's Epistle to the Galatians*. Grand Rapids: Baker Book House, 1979.

_____. *The Letters to the Seven Churches*. Grand Rapids: Baker, 1979.

Riches, John. *Jesus and the Transformation of Judaism*. London: Darton, Longman & Todd, 1980.

Ridderbos, Herman. *St. Paul's Epistle to the Churches of Galatia*. Grand Rapids: William B. Eerdmans, 1953.

Robs, Alexander. *The Epistle of James and John*. Grand Rapids: Wm. B. Eerdmans, 1954.

Sanders, E.P. *Jesus and Judaism*. London: SCM Press Ltd., 1985.

Schürer, Emil. *The History of the Jewish People in the Age of Jesus Christ (175 BC—AD 135)*. Revised and edited by Geza Vermes, Furgus Miller and Matthew Black. Vol. 2, Edinburgh: T & T Clark, 1979.

Schweizer, Edward. *The Good News According to Luke*. Atlanta: John Knox Press, 1971.

_____. *The Letter to the Colossians*. Minneapolis: Augsburg, 1976.

Sigal, Phillip. *The Emergence of Contemporary Judaism*. Vol. 1, *The Foundations of Judaism from Biblical Origins to the Sixth Century AD*. Part One: From the Origins to the Separation of Christianity. Pittsburgh: The Pickwick Press, 1980.

Simpson, E.K. and F.F. Bruce. *Commentary on the Epistles to the Ephesians and the Colossians*. Grand Rapids: Eerdmans, 1957.

Stibbs, Alan M. *The First Epistle General of Peter.* Grand Rapids: Eerdmans, 1971.

Stott, John R.W. *The Letters of John.* Grand Rapids: Eerdmans, 1988.

Tasker, R.V.G. *The General Epistle of James.* Grand Rapids: Eerdmans, 1971.

_____. *The Gospel According to Matthew.* Grand Rapids: William B. Eerdmans, 1983.

Tenny, Merrill Chapin. *New Testament Survey.* Grand Rapids: Eerdmans, 1961.

Thiessen, Gerd. *The First Followers of Jesus: A Sociological Analysis of the Earliest Christianity.* London: SCM Ltd., 1978.

Westcott, Brooke. *A General Survey of the History of the Canon of the New Testament.* Grand Rapids: Baker Book House, 1980.

Wuest, Kenneth S. *Ephesians and Colossians in the Greek New Testament.* Grand Rapids: William B. Eerdmans, 1953.

Zerwick and Grosvenor. *A Grammatical Analysis of the Greek New Testament.* Rome: Biblical Institute Press, 1981.

ABOUT THE AUTHOR

William A. Simmons
PhD, University of St. Andrews, Scotland
MDiv, Ashland Theological Seminary
MA, Church of God Theological Seminary
BA, Lee College

Professor of New Testament and Greek
at Lee University, Cleveland, Tennessee

Simmons is an outstanding member of Lee's School of Religion faculty. Initially employed in August of 1986, Simmons, also a Lee alumnus, teaches New Testament Studies, including courses such as James, Romans and Galatians, First and Second Corinthians, Prison Epistles, New Testament Greek, Luke-Acts, New Testament Theology and New Testament Survey. He also teaches master's level courses, such as Peoples of First Century Judea, Advanced Pauline Theology as well as several others.

In his doctoral work, Simmons focused on the theological continuity between Jesus and Paul. His area of specialty addresses the historical and cultural background of the New Testament. He is currently researching Pauline anthropology and cosmology.

Simmons received the Lee University Excellence in Research Award in 1994. His published works include *Peoples of the New Testament World: an Illustrated Guide, A Concise Background of the New Testament* (Together with Glossary and Annotated Bibliography*), Paul and Jesus: A Theology of Inclusion, New Testament Survey,* and a commentary on Galatians. Simmons has also published several articles in the "Evangelical Dictionary of New Testament Theology" and the Lexham Project for Logos Bible Software.

Throughout his career at Lee, he has presented papers at the national conferences of the Society of Biblical Literature, the Evangelical Theological Society, and the Society for Pentecostal Studies.

He has also done teaching and mission work at the European Bible Seminary in Rudersburg, Germany. He has taught in other countries such as Romania, Korea, Honduras, the Philippines, Guatemala, Cuba and Peru.

Simmons enjoys contributing to the local church. He and his wife Lenae have two sons, David Andrew and Nathaniel Stewart, and one daughter, Laura Marie. Originally from Metairie, Louisiana, he enjoys reading early American history, doing landscaping and gardening.

Made in the USA
Monee, IL
23 July 2020